# China Studies in the Philippines

As China Studies has grown as a discipline, it has also tended to be dominated by the major international powers, particularly China itself and the United States. It is important to remember, however, that there is a rich and diverse history of China Studies elsewhere, especially in Southeast Asia. The Philippines is one such country. China Studies experts from the Philippines encompass a broad spectrum of individuals, including activists and social workers as well as university experts, think tank analysts, diplomats, and journalists, and thus contribute a valuable new perspective.

This book therefore seeks to provide a deeper understanding of the Philippine approach to China, revealing the unique and complex connections between China Studies, ethnic studies, and policy studies. It highlights that the Philippines, as an epistemological site, complicates China as a category and Sinology as an academic agenda. Thus, the community can embrace nuances in research, as well as in life, to enable the reconsideration and reconciliation of binaries. Furthermore, demonstrating how scholarship is a practice of life, and not merely a neutral process of observation and presentation, it challenges Sinologists elsewhere to see that understanding Sinologists is key to comprehending both their scholarship and China itself. As such, this book will be useful to students and scholars of Southeast Asian Studies and Chinese Studies as well as anthropology and sociology more generally.

**Tina S. Clemente** is an Associate Professor at the Asian Center, University of the Philippines Diliman. She is the former President of the Philippine Association for Chinese Studies (PACS).

**Chih-yu Shih** is Professor of International Relations at National Taiwan University. He is also Co-Editor of the journal *Asian Ethnicity*.

# Routledge Contemporary China Series

**Urbanization, Regional Development and Governance in China**
*Jianfa Shen*

**Midwifery in China**
*Ngai Fen Cheung and Rosemary Mander*

**China's Virtual Monopoly of Rare Earth Elements**
Economic, Technological and Strategic Implications
*Roland Howanietz*

**China's Regions in an Era of Globalization**
*Tim Summers*

**China's Climate-Energy Policy**
Domestic and International Impacts
*Edited by Akihisa Mori*

**Western Bankers in China**
Institutional change and corporate governance
*Jane Nolan*

**Xinjiang in the Twenty-First Century**
Islam, Ethnicity and Resistance
*Michael Dillon*

**China Studies in the Philippines**
Intellectual Paths and the Formation of a Field
*Edited by Tina S. Clemente and Chih-yu Shih*

For more information about this series, please visit: https://www.routledge.com

# China Studies in the Philippines
Intellectual Paths and the Formation
of a Field

Edited by
Tina S. Clemente and Chih-yu Shih

LONDON AND NEW YORK

First published 2019
by Routledge
2 Park Square, Milton Park, Abingdon, Oxon OX14 4RN

and by Routledge
711 Third Avenue, New York, NY 10017

*Routledge is an imprint of the Taylor & Francis Group, an informa business*

© 2019 selection and editorial matter, Tina S. Clemente and Chih-yu Shih; individual chapters, the contributors

The right of Tina S. Clemente and Chih-yu Shih to be identified as the authors of the editorial material, and of the authors for their individual chapters, has been asserted in accordance with sections 77 and 78 of the Copyright, Designs and Patents Act 1988.

All rights reserved. No part of this book may be reprinted or reproduced or utilised in any form or by any electronic, mechanical, or other means, now known or hereafter invented, including photocopying and recording, or in any information storage or retrieval system, without permission in writing from the publishers.

*Trademark notice*: Product or corporate names may be trademarks or registered trademarks, and are used only for identification and explanation without intent to infringe.

*British Library Cataloguing-in-Publication Data*
A catalogue record for this book is available from the British Library

*Library of Congress Cataloging-in-Publication Data*
Names: Clemente, Tina S., editor. | Shi, Zhiyu, 1958– editor.
Title: China studies in the Philippines : intellectual paths and the formation of a field / edited by Tina S. Clemente and Chih-yu Shih.
Description: Abingdon, Oxon ; New York, NY: Routledge, 2019. | Series: Routledge contemporary China series ; 197 | Includes bibliographical references and index.
Identifiers: LCCN 2018025636
Subjects: LCSH: China—Research—Philippines. | Sinologists—Philippines—Attitudes.
Classification: LCC DS734.97.P6 C47 2019 | DDC 951.0072/0599—dc23
LC record available at https://lccn.loc.gov/2018025636

ISBN: 978-1-138-54995-1 (hbk)
ISBN: 978-0-429-50818-9 (ebk)

Typeset in Times New Roman
by codeMantra

# Contents

| | |
|---|---|
| *List of figures* | vii |
| *List of tables* | ix |
| *Notes on contributors* | xi |
| *Preface* | xiii |
| *Acknowledgments* | xv |

| | | |
|---|---|---|
| | **Introduction** | 1 |
| | TINA S. CLEMENTE AND CHIH-YU SHIH | |
| 1 | **Insights on China Studies as a community of practice** | 4 |
| | TINA S. CLEMENTE | |
| 2 | **Social evolution and situational learning in Jose Santiago "Chito" Santa Romana's China Studies** | 23 |
| | ROBIN MICHAEL GARCIA | |
| 3 | **From taboo thinkers to thought leaders: media, Chinese politics, and diplomacy** | 39 |
| | JOSE MARI HALL LANUZA | |
| 4 | **Examining the challenges and possibilities in Tsinoy Studies** | 57 |
| | CARMELEA ANG SEE | |
| 5 | **Narratives and identity: active agency and the formation of counter-narratives** | 81 |
| | YVAN YSMAEL YONAHA | |
| 6 | **China watching and China watchers in the Philippines: an epistemological note** | 107 |
| | CHIH-YU SHIH | |

vi   *Contents*

**Interview Transcripts**                                                131

TERESITA ANG SEE

ERIC BACULINAO

AILEEN BAVIERA

THERESA CARIÑO

RICHARD CHU

JAIME FLORCRUZ

GO BON JUAN

CAROLINE HAU

FLORENCIO MALLARE

CHARLSON ONG

ELLEN PALANCA

JOSE SANTIAGO "CHITO" SANTA ROMANA

*Index*                                                                  225

# List of figures

| | | |
|---|---|---|
| 1.1 | Timeline of Thinkers' Selected Personal Details | 6 |
| 1.2 | Affinity Space | 9 |
| 1.3 | Main Categories of Studies | 11 |
| 6.1 | Two Dimensions of Post-Chineseness | 111 |
| 6.2 | Post-Chinese Evolution in the Long Run | 116 |

# List of tables

| | | |
|---|---|---|
| 1.1 | Thinkers' China Knowledge and Epistemes | 8 |
| 5.1 | A Priori Codes | 86 |

# Notes on contributors

**Tina S. Clemente** is an Associate Professor at the Asian Center, University of the Philippines Diliman. She specializes in China Studies and Philippine Development Studies. Her research interests include various aspects of China's economic development, the intellectual history of China Studies in the Philippines, economics-security nexus in Philippines-China relations, the Chinese in the Philippines, and Philippine development. Dr. Clemente has held associate, senior, and issue editorships in international journals. She served as President of the Philippine Association for Chinese Studies during the book project and continues to be a subject matter expert serving Philippine and international publics.

**Robin Michael Garcia** specializes in the international and comparative political economy of Asian economies and the intersection of social evolution theory, constructivism in international political economy, and the neuroscience of emotions. He obtained his PhD in International Politics with a Dean's Award for Academic Excellence at the School of International Relations and Public Affairs (SIRPA) of Fudan University in Shanghai. He was senior lecturer in politics and international relations at the University of the Philippines and De La Salle University. Currently, he is CEO of Warwick & Roger, a political risk management advisory firm, which he founded.

**Jose Mari Hall Lanuza** teaches political science at the University of the Philippines Manila and the Polytechnic University of the Philippines. He received his master's degree in Philippine Studies with a specialization in Development Studies from the Asian Center, University of the Philippines Diliman. His research interests include Philippine development strategies, elections and democratization, social movements, and media and political communication.

**Carmelea Ang See** is a faculty member of the Educational Leadership and Management Department, Brother Andrew Gonzales College of Education, De La Salle University. She is also currently the Managing Director of Kaisa Heritage Foundation, which houses Bahay Tsinoy, museum of xii *Notes on contributors*

Chinese in Philippine life, Chinben See Memorial Library, and Kaisa Research Center. She was President of Kaisa Para Sa Kaunlaran from 2016 to 2018. The latter is a 30-year-old research-based organization that advocates for the proactive and sustainable participation of the Chinese-Filipino community in local and national development. Her volunteer work includes conducting training for public school teachers on two literacy programs to equip them with the knowledge and skills to teach their students to read.

**Chih-yu Shih** is currently teaching anthropology of knowledge and international relations theory at National Taiwan University. He is the author of many books, including, most recently, *Post-Western International Relations Reconsidered: The Premodern Politics of Gongsun Long* (2015), *Harmonious Intervention: China's Quest for Relational Security* (2014), *Sinicizing International Relations: Self, Civilization and Intellectual Politics in Subaltern East Asia* (2013), and *Civilization, Nation and Modernity in East Asia* (2012). Professor Shih is additionally Co-Editor-in-Chief of the journal *Asian Ethnicity*. He received his MPP from Harvard University and PhD from the University of Denver.

**Yvan Ysmael Yonaha** is currently a member of the faculty in the Department of Social Sciences in the University of the Philippines Los Baños. He obtained his bachelor of arts degree in sociology from the University of the Philippines Diliman and is currently finishing his master of arts degree in Philippine Studies with a specialization in Development Studies from the same university. Some of his research interests include religion, democracy, decentralization, and international studies.

# Preface

This book belongs to a project on the oral histories of selected senior China/Chinese Studies experts in the Philippines. The project is part of an ongoing worldwide initiative on the intellectual history of China Studies, details of which can be accessed on http://www.china-studies.taipei/act02.php. The project team in the Philippines, headed by Dr. Tina S. Clemente, conducted twelve oral history interviews that represented various areas of interest and specializations. These interviews are featured in the book in abridged form (with full transcripts available on the website). Clemente's and Shih's analytical chapters feature aspects of all the oral histories, while the four other essays provide a focused analysis of specific oral histories. Notwithstanding our constraints, we consider the collection a milestone in mapping the intellectual history of a field in the Philippines that many consider difficult to get a handle on. It is the beginning of many meaningful initiatives in enriching the field in the Philippines and elucidating the latter's role in world China Studies.

# Acknowledgments

Taipei Economic and Cultural Office in the Philippines acted as the initial liaison between the Research and Educational Center for Mainland China Studies and Cross-Strait Relations of the Department of Political Science at National Taiwan University and Dr. Tina S. Clemente of the Asian Center, University of the Philippines (UP) Diliman. A collaborative relationship was developed through several small grants from the Ministry of Science and Technology, and the Ministry of Education in Taiwan. We acknowledge the Asian Center, UP Diliman as well as the UP Third World Studies Center for supporting the inception workshop in August 2015. We also acknowledge the Philippine Association for Chinese Studies for facilitating numerous insightful discussions, critical network support, and knowledge sharing. We acknowledge the Ricardo Leong Center for Chinese Studies at the Ateneo de Manila University for organizing an international sinologists workshop where some preliminary results were presented in September 2017. We thank the esteemed senior China/Chinese experts who not only generously allowed the team to interview them but also offered critical feedback: Teresita Ang See, Eric Baculinao, Aileen Baviera, Theresa Cariño, Richard Chu, Jaime FlorCruz, Caroline Hau, Go Bon Juan, Florencio Mallare, Charlson Ong, Ellen Palanca, and Jose Santiago "Chito" Santa Romana (or Sta. Romana). We thank the interviewers: Carmelea Ang See, Robin Michael Garcia, Reynard Hing, Sining Kotah, Lucio Pitlo III, Jose Mari Hall Lanuza, Dorcas Juliette Ramos-Caraig, and Yvan Ysmael Yonaha. To the next-generation contributors, we not only thank you for your work but cheer you on in succeeding scholarly endeavors: Robin Michael Garcia, Jose Mari Lanuza, Carmelea Ang See, and Yvan Ysmael Yonaha. Special thanks go to Pamela G. Combinido for her administrative and research assistance. You have a bright future ahead of you. Finally, we thank Teresita Ang See for her amazing patience and tireless gatekeeping.

# Introduction

*Tina S. Clemente and Chih-yu Shih*

Pressing national issues often invoke the wisdom of thinkers of the pertinent field of study. As a field, China Studies in the Philippines strongly engages with its publics. Especially that Philippines-China relations are challenging, a critical analysis from the field's experts is constantly solicited. For instance, the heightened tensions following the 2012 Scarborough Shoal standoff constituted a conundrum that required expert input in both asking the right questions and seeking the corresponding interventions. It is notable that the tenor in bilateral relations has exhibited infamous shifts, for instance, from the Arroyo administration's (2001–2010) bumper crop of bilateral agreements to the Aquino administration's (2010–2016) recalcitrant position, culminating in taking China to international court, and finally to the Duterte administration's (2016–2022) pivot to China. Despite what China insists as indisputable maritime claims, Philippine concerns on China's growing power, and asymmetry in bilateral economic engagement, it is without a doubt that China remains a major economic partner of the Philippines. Through these periods of engagement and various flash points within them, the need for nuanced insight has always been underscored. China Studies serves as a knowledge base to address the need for such nuanced input and beyond. Hence, we argue further that a textured appreciation of the layered contexts of how expertise on China evolved can be helpful in understanding not only Philippines-China relations but, more importantly, how the narrative of China expertise in the Philippines contributes to China Studies in the world.

Understanding China has become a global agenda with China's ascent being felt everywhere. Not only do China scholars in the world increase quickly in number, but the Chinese authorities also have perceived high stakes in China Studies, which are presumably functional in dissolving the image of a China threat and promoting instead their idea of "community with a shared future for mankind." In their active seeking of contacts among Sinologists all over the world, they realize, to their amazement, that understanding China is an impossible profession in the sense that both the action "understanding" and the category "China" are unlikely to be well defined. There are the notions of (1) critical Sinology that examines

## 2 Tina S. Clemente and Chih-yu Shih

whether China is understood accurately; (2) overseas Sinology that introduces, primarily via translation, how China is being understood in writings; (3) international Sinology that compares the differences and the similarities between China Studies of different counties; (4) global Sinology that attends to emerging global agendas of China Studies; (5) world China Studies that mingle China Studies in China and elsewhere; and (6) subaltern China Studies that re-present those agencies silenced by China Studies, among others.

One can almost see a constant flow of tension between those who insist there is an accurate way of understanding China on whichever agenda and those who are determined to deconstruct such a pursuit of correctness. In between, one could take an eclectic stand by allowing different claims to correctness to parallel one another despite their apparent contradiction because understanding China must reflect purposes of understanding, which are morally relativistic. Once one complicates "understanding China" according to the purposes of understanding, the category "China" must simultaneously be complicated. Complication of these sorts sensitizes the choices and the relations of scholars at two levels: (1) how Sinologists relate to China and their imagined audience via their approaches to understanding China and (2) how those who study Sinologists and their Sinology relate to China as well as Sinologists via reviews of Sinology. One can almost say that all those approaches, which reflect choices of relationships practiced as well as imagined, amount to something one can call relational or post-Sinology.

Embarrassingly, none of the aforementioned kinds of Sinology ever touch on how understanding China is practiced in the Philippines, to our knowledge. The intellectual community working on China in the country peculiarly includes activists and social workers in addition to, as elsewhere, university pundits, think tank analysts, diplomats, journalists, and litterateurs. To that extent, the Philippines as an epistemological site alone complicates China as a category and Sinology as an academic agenda. Epistemologically, the entire community is alerted at oversimplification sometimes seen in the media and certain policy circles. Its members embrace nuances in research as well as in life to enable reconsideration and reconciliation of binaries. China, Chinese, and Chineseness do not always have strict demarcations as subjects, nor do indigenous and Chinese-Filipino scholars on China make two separate communities. For instance, scholarship on Chinese-Filipino history, migration, and identity is also considered within Philippine Studies and not necessarily within China Studies. Nevertheless, such areas of inquiry are accepted in China/Chinese Studies academic programs in Philippine universities, given that the numerous links to understanding China are themselves valuable. Furthermore, scholars are conscious of relations between being who they are and doing research. Philippine Sinology illustrates how relations of various sorts practically constitute research designs, producing the irony of China being ontologically undeniable while epistemologically undefinable.

*Introduction* 3

It challenges Sinologists elsewhere to see that understanding Sinologists is key to understanding both their scholarship and China.

The six chapters in the volume adopt an anthropology of knowledge perspective in analyzing the intellectual history of the field based on the oral history of senior thinkers of China Studies. Tina S. Clemente begins the volume by analyzing China-related expertise as a community of practice in the Philippines. This is followed by Robin Michael Garcia's chapter that embarks on a social evolutionary analysis of the expertise of Jose "Chito" Santa Romana (or Sta. Romana), a foreign relations expert and the Philippine Ambassador to China. The third chapter by Jose Mari Hall Lanuza features Jaime FlorCruz and Eric Baculinao, respected Beijing-based international journalists, and problematizes how their intellectual paths have traversed media, politics, and diplomacy. In the fourth chapter, Carmelea Ang See examines the narratives of historians Go Bon Juan and Richard Chu, drawing insight from their scholarly journeys in elucidating the need for more experts in the field. The fifth chapter by Yvan Ysmael Yonaha focuses on the oral histories of prolific Chinese-Filipino thinkers Caroline Hau, Charlson Ong, and Teresita Ang See in interrogating the role of agency and how ensuing counter-narratives affect thinking about China and Chineseness. The sixth and final chapter by Chih-yu Shih proposes post-Chineseness as an epistemological approach in studying China and the Chinese.

# 1 Insights on China Studies as a community of practice

*Tina S. Clemente*[1]

## Analytical approaches and perspectives

Philippine contentions about Philippines-China relations in recent years have exemplified the need for China expertise. The first knowledge source that is often sought regarding the state's approach to its bilateral issues with China is the pool of experts in foreign relations, security, and economics. Aside from the government sector and business stakeholders, other major producers and consumers of China expertise include think tanks/non-governmental organizations (NGOs), academic units, and media. All these groups seek to exchange knowledge on China in response to a critical issue. While the salience of China knowledge need not be belabored, the evolution of such knowledge as a problematique needs elucidation. Two answers are foremost. First is the relatively expedient and practical usability of inputs when bilateral tension arises. That is, when there is a dearth of analytical response in certain aspects of the complex issue (e.g. integrated security-economic analysis), the nature of the expert knowledge production is queried. This practical use of China knowledge brings about both reactionary (i.e. how do we respond now?) and strategic (i.e. what needs to be done to build such critical knowledge) perspectives. Second is the contextualization of China knowledge as an epistemological reflection. The stance of the Philippines in analyzing and responding to China draws upon its stock of knowledge about it. While such a stance is a product of various social, political, economic, and historical dynamics, we accord keen attention on the knowledge of the thinkers who identify as China experts and the role of community in the generation of knowledge.

On this note, we begin with concepts of agency and context. There is a need to contextualize ideas among the thinkers from which they originate. The chief end of a historical inquiry is to delve into a past occurrence by looking at its external and internal reality in terms of "bodies and movements" and thoughts, respectively, not as mutually exclusive units but as a confluence of two dimensions represented by the agent's actions (Collingwood 1946:213). Said in another vein, sifting through thinkers' narratives, in which embedded meaning is related to individual decisions and internal negotiations, yields valuable insights on society and its oscillations from a broad structural view as well as from a personal view (Kaplan 2014:45, 49).

*Insights on China Studies as a community of practice*   5

The thinkers' intellectual engagement and how they interact with other thinkers captured in various forms of codification becomes important. We focus on oral histories as opposed to textual analysis to underscore the salience of the sociocultural space where values, worldviews, and aspirations are subsumed in the ethos of the thinkers' eras (Cowan 2006:183). We situate the thinkers as actors in an idea-producing habitus faceted with sociopolitical layers and a system of practice—albeit with the attendant issues of subjectivism. We are interested in the phenomenological character of the experts' evolving thinking as an actualization of their internal deliberations and their epistemic interaction with their environment (Boyer 2005:145, 148).

This work, then, problematizes the nature of the China knowledge of senior experts in the Philippines through an analysis of twelve individual narratives. In this chapter, China as a subject casts a wide net as it inclusively pertains to any aspect that relates to China, the Chinese, Chineseness, the overseas Chinese, and other related areas. In this sense, the thinkers who specialize in the Chinese in the Philippines are included in the scope of the China Studies community of practice. The article draws on the multidisciplinary lens of communities of practice, intellectual history, and knowledge management. Aside from the epistemological and ontological significance of constructively unpacking China expertise, the study is an input to understanding how this knowledge, through the community of thinkers that hosts it, affects the Philippines' navigation of its relationship with its dominant regional neighbor.

## Community of mavericks, knowledge, and practice

### *Mavericks as knowers*

> It is entirely fitting for epistemology to be concerned with individual knowers and their minds ... The bulk of an adult's world-view is deeply indebted to her social work. It can largely be traced to social interactions, to influences exerted by other knowers.
>
> (Goldman 1987:109)

Following the semantics of Weisberg and Muldoon (2009:242, 244, 245, 250), we recognize the thinkers in this study as constituting a community of *mavericks*. Mavericks are distinct as they consider past approaches but seek to apply new lens in analyzing issues. Hence, the presence of more thinkers with a high sense of initiative and a strong trailblazing quality "drastically increases the epistemic progress of the community." Since such thinkers push the limit of answering productive inquiries, their intellectual paths also experience substantial "epistemic progress." As movers, mavericks are also able to influence the critical discourse—albeit in various capacities. Ang See, for instance, a pillar in the Chinese-Filipino community through her advocacies, which include integration, anti-violence, and anti-kidnapping efforts, is often invited as a subject matter expert and author for various China-related inquiries. Through these, she insists that she is not an academic. Oftentimes, the most fruitful discussions of China experts can be searched through the efforts of mavericks and their networks, even without formal organizing principles for such activities. In other words, the people are the main drivers. Adapting the framework of Brannen and Nilsen (2011), we present a timeline in Figure 1.1 that structures the thinkers' personal details around the aspects of ethnicity, career trajectory, and leadership positions.

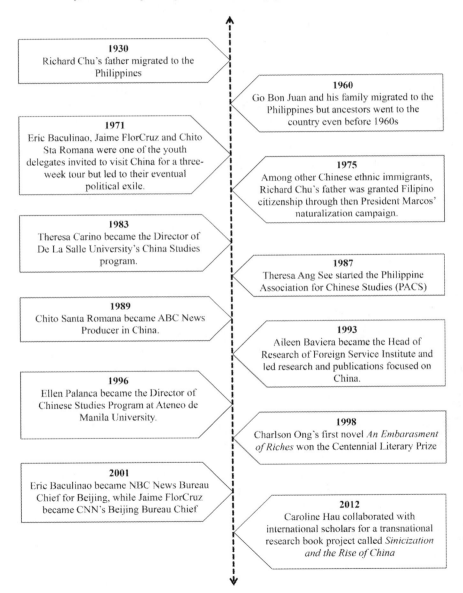

*Figure 1.1* Timeline of Thinkers' Selected Personal Details.

*Insights on China Studies as a community of practice*  7

### Community of knowledge

In contrast to a hierarchy and a market, the organizing principle of the thinkers in this study is that of a community where trust facilitates interaction. The deliberate organizational purview is oriented toward thinkers' inputs rather than behavior/process or outputs. Tasks are contingent on each other, while knowledge and connections are exchanged in unspecific and tacit terms, allowing the stocking of favor for future invocation (Adler 2001; Cardona, Lawrence, and Bentler 2004). The emphasis of interaction is collegial collaboration and partnership within a loose structure, hence, collective networks also span wide local and international spaces. Oftentimes, many of them would insist that even a structure such as the Philippine Association for Chinese Studies (PACS), with which most of the thinkers in this study have been involved, is not an organization but a loose network of China watchers who ask each other for help in approaching a China-related issue. That aside, roles are determined by the contribution of specialized know-how, not authority or position. When one suggests, one gets the idea through by operationalizing it. These thinkers have a strong sense of individualist values but are, at the same time, collectivist (Adler and Heckscher, 2006; Galaskiewicz 1985:639). Table 1.1 shows the thinkers' specialized China knowledge, related bodies of knowledge, and the issues of contemporary and historical significance that they respond to. These issues or more specific problematizations over time intersect with the thinkers' lived experiences (Shoppes 2015:101).

### Spaces of affinity and practice

The space of practice is curiously bound by affinity in interactions. In other words, personal bonds from having gone through similar experiences in history or bonds resulting from sustained interaction take primacy over explicit membership. In this sense, there is no significant need to define group belongingness. Explicit membership has become a formality processed in the most perfunctory manner, without attaching too much meaning. The community is not an imposition of structure but an ongoing experience that is expressed through social interaction. Self-identification as a China watcher facilitates the generation of China knowledge in negotiation with learning and practice. The more one shares knowledge on China as a resource person who engages the discourse, the more one deepens one's China expertise and cultivates possibilities for self-identification as a China watcher. In this sense, self-identification as a China watcher contributes to determining the extent of one's involvement in the community, with the thinkers' agency at play in drawing on his views and beliefs as well as social influences on his/her thinking. On the other hand, the evolution of this self-identification is an outcome of sustained interaction and participation, affected by how the community evolves as well (Brown and Duguid 2001:200, 202; Thompson 2005:151–153).

*Table 1.1* Thinkers' China Knowledge and Epistemes

| | *Related fields/ subfields* | *Specialized knowledge* |
|---|---|---|
| Eric Baculinao | International relations | • China's foreign policy<br>• China's economic strategy |
| Aileen Baviera | Asian Studies<br>International relations<br>Political science | • China-Philippines bilateral relations<br>• Asia-Pacific security, territorial, and maritime disputes<br>• China-Southeast Asia relations<br>• US foreign policy in Asia Pacific<br>• Chinese and Chinese civil society in the Philippines<br>• Political economy of China |
| Theresa Cariño | Development Studies | • Chinese literature in Southeast Asia<br>• China's foreign policy in Southeast Asia<br>• Social development in modern China<br>• Chinese civil society organizations in the Philippines<br>• Integration of Chinese in the Philippines<br>• Status of Chinese women in the Philippines<br>• Religion in China |
| Richard Chu | History | • History and identity (re)construction of Chinese in the Philippines<br>• Chinese diaspora<br>• Asian American Studies |
| Jaime FlorCruz | International relations<br>Journalism | • Philippines-China diplomatic relations |
| Caroline Hau | Literary Studies<br>Cultural Studies<br>Southeast Asian Studies | • Chinese in Philippine history, media, and popular culture<br>• Ethnic Chinese issues in Southeast Asia and the Philippines<br>• Culture and history of modern China |
| Go Bon Juan | History | • History and identity (re)construction of Chinese in the Philippines |
| Florencio Mallare | Law | • History and identity (re)construction of Chinese in the Philippines |
| Charlson Ong | Creative writing<br>Literary work | • Chinese in Philippines history<br>• Chinese in Philippine media and literature |
| Ellen Palanca | Economics | • Philippines-China economic relations<br>• ASEAN-China economic relations<br>• Chinese investments and business in the Philippines<br>• Ethnic Chinese business in the Philippines |
| Chito Santa Romana (or Sta Romana) | International relations | • Philippines-China bilateral relations |
| Teresita Ang See | Political science | • Chinese civil society organizations in the Philippines<br>• Integration of Chinese in the Philippines<br>• History and identity (re)construction of Chinese in the Philippines |

Similar pursuits create the space where new and experienced members participate. While some activities strongly facilitate strong knowledge generation, there are many ways that one can participate and be prominent (e.g. active and respected). Activities are driven by knowledge distribution, and the leaders themselves function as a resource for public intellectualism, the practice of which contributes to the endurance of the community as well as network propagation (Gee 2005:214–215, 225–228). Sustained practice as a facilitator of China knowledge generation becomes significant (Brown and Duguid 2001:198).

Figure 1.2 provides a simple example of a multidimensional community. While we emphasize that this mapping exercise is limited, it nevertheless provides a glimpse of what future network documentation projects can consider. The figure is based on a content analysis of details disclosed in the oral histories, such as long-standing social relations, common or related engagement, shared stories, and shared discourse. In the context of intertwining professional and personal linkages, thinkers also organize apt activities quickly in response to an issue, expressing familiarity with of the knowledge that the others can contribute. In engagements where the thinkers interact, regardless of the level of formality of the organizational structures that host events where knowledge is shared in a free-flowing manner, conversations are "the continuation of ongoing processes" (Wenger 1998:125–126). The figure shows an example of five interaction groupings. The groupings denote the facilitative mechanism of collaboration between the parties. Among the groupings, three are organizations—PACS, Kaisa Para sa Kaunlaran (Kaisa), and

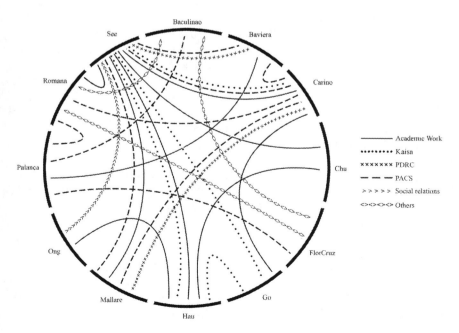

*Figure 1.2* Affinity Space.

10   *Tina S. Clemente*

Philippine-China Development Resource Center (PDRC)—of which the last is now inoperative. The other two groupings pertain to academic work and social relations. Academic work includes publication in journals and attendance in conferences that were not hosted by Kaisa, PDRC, or PACS. The social relations grouping indicates friendly connections as colleagues, co-activists, and so on.

## China watching and issues pursued

The China-related issues that the thinkers confronted are embedded in how they have negotiated their self-identification as a China watcher. This is whether the negotiation was explicitly thought out prior to the confrontation of the issue or practice of expertise, or a "preconceptual," implicit *post hoc* realization. The nexus between such negotiation and how the thinkers made sense of realities that mattered to them draws on a set of knowledge (e.g. feelings, learning, acquired skills) while, in turn, producing knowledge. Knowledge as an employed resource functions as input for reflection and predicates action. As a produced resource, it becomes interactive in a social space; takes on particular forms as utilized by the community; and, to varying extents, can become conventional issue-specific knowledge. While the experts' China watching can be generally categorized into four main categories (Figure 1.3), a more specific inquiry into the parallelisms among the thinkers in examining identity, pursuing issues, and viewing China reveals how much the thinkers shared a space of possibilities for learning from each other, consolidating their knowledge, and complementing each other's expertise. In other words, differences in knowledge pursuits, given the affinity space, motivated, all the more, the need to interact and share know-how, whether this consisted of inside stories or action, such as organizing seminars (Barth 2002:1–2). The thinkers' inception into China watching is interesting due to the diversity in motivations, which broadly cover questions on ethnic identity, ideology, and intellectual fascination.

### *Identity*

Mallare was interested in finding out more about his identity. His work as a journalist brought this out further. He recalls,

> as a journalist, I was very curious about my identity. Who am I? How did I come to be here in the Philippines? What is my role now? As a member of the community, all these questions came out during my eight years, I think, as a journalist.
>
> (Mallare 2015:3)

Mallare saw that it was important to know oneself. He intimates that his passion to know was so strong that he went back to China to look for answers (Mallare 2015:29). While he became a known figure in publishing after he founded *World News*, a daily newspaper in the Philippines in the Chinese language,

*Insights on China Studies as a community of practice* 11

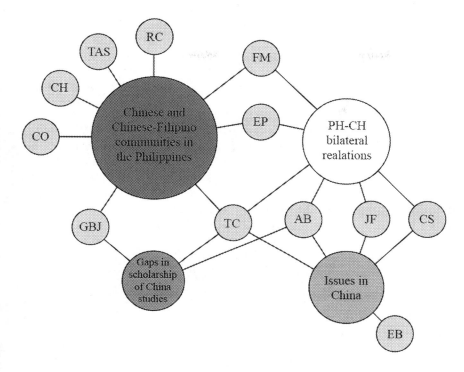

TAS = Teresita Ang See   RC = Richard Chu     FM = Florencio Mallare
EB = Eric Baculinao       JF = Jaime FlorCruz   CO = Charlson Ong
AB = Aileen Baviera       CH = Caroline Hau     EP = Ellen Palanca
TC = Theresa Cariño       GBJ = Go Bon Juan     CSR = Chito Santa Romana

*Figure 1.3* Main Categories of Studies.

Mallare was able to combine his journalistic objectives and his pursuits as a China watcher, but he insists that being a scholar is not his main focus.

Similarly, Chu's journey to China was admittedly a personal quest to find his roots and learn more about his family as well as the larger milieu of China's culture and people. While his motivations later spilled over to professional motivations, his primary push was still his question on identity, drawing from his experience of dual/conflicting identities in having grown up in the Philippines and the semantics that accompanied various conceptualizations of the Chinese, that is,

> how we came up with such a term for the Chinese, and how the Chinese had [equivalent] terms for the Filipino—and why there is an ethnic tension or racial division between the two. I wanted to go into the historical roots of that phenomenon.
>
> (Chu 2016:8)

## 12 Tina S. Clemente

Chu evolved from identifying himself as a scholar of China Studies to one of Chinese diaspora and later of Philippine Studies. He also now considers himself an Asian Americanist, given his interest in Asian American history as well as Chinese in the Philippines and the United States. Transcending considerations on the field of specialization, Chu also emphasizes the need for him to connect the domains of scholarship and public engagement by using historical insight for contemporary application, such as geopolitical concerns (Chu 2016:11, 20).

In Ang See's case, she shares that what ushered her into China Studies was her realization during her university days of a larger society beyond Binondo and the citizenship issue that hounded the Chinese in the Philippines (Ang See 2015:2). She says that she wasn't aware of what being a Chinese citizen meant, except when she had to pay for the alien registration fee in the University of the Philippines. Also, due to her family's not being in business, she has not been conscious of the *othering* faced by Chinese in business. This began her desire to help fight for the rightful place of those born in the Philippines (Ang See 2015:4). Ang See modestly downplays her China watching because her main focus has always remained the Chinese in the Philippines. She says,

> Well, I would still fall short on considering myself a China watcher. I'm still not. In fact, when we went to China, I had to emphasize that the six with me are the China experts; I'm the only one who is not. My study is all on the Chinese in the Philippines. I've never really studied China, but then yes, because again it's by accident, because I became president of PACS.
>
> (Ang See 2015:16)

Despite Ang See's modesty in admitting her China expertise, it must be underscored that the subject of Chinese in the Philippines, while it is a thriving field in itself, has been an emergent avenue to gain insight and study China at a time when China Studies did not exist as a field. Further, it was a strong entry point for scholars into China Studies. There was an advantage in the subject proximity of Chinese in the Philippines and China Studies, and significant overlaps in scholarly and practitioner networks between the two fields.

In a sense, Hau was "born" into being interested in China and the Chinese. Her father used to recount his experiences of growing up in China. While family roots began her burgeoning interest, interactions with nonethnic Chinese also provided an insight into how cultural differences in Philippine society were perceived. Hau recounts that when she spoke Hokkien in public, people would throw a glance at her, and kids would react by uttering "ching chong chang," which pejoratively identifies Chinese speakers as different. Hau did not consider this traumatic, but it did bring

*Insights on China Studies as a community of practice* 13

to light certain differences that were not apparent while she resided in Chinatown (Hau 2015:6–7). She recounts,

> when I was about 11 years old, we moved out of Chinatown and into different places—to Parañaque, to Makati and then later on to Pasig, and we basically lived among Filipino communities. When I went to UP, I was exposed to a wider variety of students from different provinces. It was during conversations with them that I became aware of the kind of similarities and differences I had with my Filipino peers, which sharpened my understanding of who I was, and how I interacted with people. That got me to start asking questions about the history of the Chinese in the Philippines and the current trajectory, as well as changing meanings of Chineseness in the Philippines.
>
> (Hau 2015:7)

Ethnic, identity, and integration issues (including kidnapping issues) that relate to the Chinese in the Philippines are particular interrogations that Hau has pursued in her work as a scholar. Her studies in history, literature, language, and art in university and graduate school gestated interest that traversed a larger regional scope, covering the Philippines, Southeast Asia, and Greater China. In this sense, she concedes that these interests allow her to interrogate China "in a very narrow sense," but she does not count herself as a China scholar (Hau 2015:12).

Similar to Hau, Ong does not consider himself a China scholar (Ong 2016:15). He shares that, since his interests and main work cover narratives related to the integration of Chinese Filipinos in Philippine society, he only touches on China marginally, to the extent that it is where many Filipinos come from and hence forms part of people's narratives (Ong 2016:12–13, 15). Ong's exposure to the China/Chinese issues also occurred early in life. He was aware of the political dynamics between those partial to the Kuomintang as well as those who sided with the Communist Party of China (Ong 2016:10).

Cariño, on the other hand, a Singaporean who married a Filipino, contrasted the Chinese in Singapore, who comprised a majority and whose "identity was never very obvious," with the Chinese in the Philippines, who constituted a minority. She reflects,

> I became aware of some of the prejudices and biases against the Chinese … it really makes a difference once you're part of the minority because you are more conscious of the questions: Who are you? Who am I?
>
> (Cariño 2015:6)

For Go, the experience of being ethnic Chinese and the attendant issues of the Chinese in the Philippines have been a long-standing motivation for

14   *Tina S. Clemente*

his writings and advocacies since the 1960s. He recalls how challenging it was to sustain *Yong Hap (Integration)*, a Kaisa publication that came out every week. He pointedly shares that the publication intended to facilitate a coming to terms on the issue of integration among local Chinese. But Go envisioned something larger, which is the deeper approach. From a macro viewpoint, he saw that the local Chinese needed to "discover and learn about the Philippines." And he recognized that this can only happen if and when the Chinese involve themselves in thoughtfully considering the various dimensions of Philippine society, including the economy, politics, and elections. Interestingly, Go saw that integration as an issue would have been too narrow and would likely be uninteresting if it kept getting discussed without an understanding of the larger and evolving societal dynamic (Go 2015:7).

### Revolutions and transformations

Ideology was also an entry point to China watching. Mallare recalled that when he was young, he unintentionally joined the Wha Chi, an underground leftist Chinese-Filipino guerilla group, which went against the Japanese. Mallare continued his sympathies for the left during the anti-Marcos days. Santa Romana, on the other hand, began his interest in China as a student activist during Marcos's martial law. Santa Romana says that the student activists during those days were "influenced by China's Cultural Revolution, which we thought demonstrated student power" (2016:1). Santa Romana started perusing material on China and Maoism in aid of getting a picture of developments in China and drawing insights that the Philippines can learn from. He was interested in how China grappled with global developments (e.g. Sino-US rapprochement, Union of Soviet Socialist Republics, and Soviet revisionism). As a China-based China watcher, he took advantage of both insider and outsider perspectives as well as worked for an international news outlet, enriching his experience as a journalist. Looking back at the many years of being a journalist, he reflects on the evolution of his thinking. He began with a measure of fixation on the China model and how it can be adapted to the Philippine case. Now, he recognizes how his views have matured and how immensely important it is to still deepen understanding of China. However, it was important to contextualize lessons that the Philippines can draw, considering the Philippines' own narratives and nuances in development (Santa Romana 2016:2, 12, 15).

For Cariño, her interest in anything related to the Cultural Revolution began as vicarious when she met her husband:

> I think the turning point for me was when I met my husband, a Filipino who was then working at the Presbyterian Church in New York. He was particularly interested in China and was very much aware of the Cold

*Insights on China Studies as a community of practice* 15

War. It was then the height of the Cultural Revolution, and the church where he was working had a project to study it. They wanted to understand what it was about, how it would affect China's future, and what its implications were for the rest of the world.

(Cariño 2015:2)

For Baviera, her

interest was less ideological and dogmatic, and rather more of a fascination about the human experience and social transformation going on in China then. China also comes from a different kind of social system and there was great interest in that as well.

(Baviera 2016:1)

She recalls that she "first became aware of China's history, its twists and turns," in her history class during university days (Baviera 2016:1). This interest bore into her as she became a well-respected international relations and foreign relations public intellectual, often invited by critical stakeholders in the Philippines and abroad to give significant input.

While Florcuz and Baculinao were also anti-martial law student activists and were likewise exiled in China together with Santa Romana, it is interesting to point out their respective beginning and continuing intellectual fascination with China. Florcruz says that he was very interested in China, even as early as high school. He read up on the basic history of China. The stories he got from his sister, who visited Hong Kong and Macau, also piqued his interest about China as a mystical place. When he was much older, Florcruz's interest was further piqued when he heard the stories of Orly Mercado and Charito Planas in a forum at the University of the Philippines (FlorCruz 2015:1). This fascination toward China matured into insider-outsider China watching in his capacity as a journalist. He made sense of China-related goings-on by being both immersed and detached (FlorCruz 2015:8).

Even so, my main source of contributions in sharing my experiences is by being a journalist. I have been invited to speak in journalism schools in my alma mater, Peking University, and in Tsinghua University. I never miss an appropriate chance to say that I am a Filipino who happened to be working in an American company in China. They like the fact that I am a third-country observer. In other words, for them, I am neither a Chinese nor an American. Even though I work for an American media outfit, I think they appreciate the fact that not being an American, I look at them from a unique and different perspective ... I compare China now and China thirty years earlier because I have seen what China was like thirty to forty years ago. I can appreciate the changes—big and small—whenever I compare China now and China

## 16 Tina S. Clemente

then. I will say that the situation is a glass half-full, not half-empty, because I have seen it empty. I think Chinese appreciate it whenever I say that.

(FlorCruz 2015:8)

Baculinao pointed out that his interest in China deepened, and it prompted him to stay in China, even when he could have gone home to the Philippines in 1986. He says,

> I started working in media and China was becoming **interesting intellectually**, with all the reforms being launched by Deng. By 1986, the Marcos regime was toppled and I could go home, since I got my passport back. However, **China was changing, and that kept me going**. I wanted to know what would happen to the so-called opening up of China, and before I knew it, forty-four years had gone by.
>
> (Baculinao 2015:1–2, emphasis added)

Baculinao sees himself as a generalist, as opposed to a specialist, who is most concerned with Chinese foreign policy and Chinese economic strategy as his primary interrogations. The formal mechanism through which he proceeds as a watcher is his profession as a journalist. Hence, he maintains an objective stance in his reports. However, in an informal capacity, he gives his opinions freely when opportunities arise, such as forums where he is invited to speak or meetings with other watchers where inputs on issues are privately shared. Such inputs may involve "international security or how to find better ways of realizing peace, especially between Philippines and China" for the sake of contributing to peace, development, and security (Baculinao 2015:13).

While Santa Romana, Florcruz, and Baculinao were able to learn about China by being there as exiles at first, then as journalists later, Ellen found herself on the other side, as a consumer of news on China's opening up in the 1980s. She recalls being surprised at what *Time* and *Asiaweek* reported, and she became extremely interested in the succeeding events. Since she wanted to have a chance of witnessing China's transition into a market economy, she decided to go to China, notwithstanding that her son was still in his formative years. Palanca pursued scholarly work on economic relations among the Philippines, countries in the Association of Southeast Asian Nations (ASEAN), and China (Palanca 2016:2). In parallel fashion, she also pursued issues on ethnic Chinese business in the Philippines, which were also evolving (Palanca 2016:4).

Cariño's interest in China's development arose from her work as an NGO practitioner and government consultant. Her work with Amity in the 1990s, which was involved with many initiatives to develop China's rural sector, allowed her to appreciate that much work still had to be done to alleviate poverty in China, which was very poor then (Cariño 2015:13).

## China watching and China Studies

### Enriching the discourse

China watching in the Philippines began early, albeit indirectly, motivated by historical studies concerning Chinese migration, Chinese commerce, and identity politics. In terms of studies focusing on contemporary China Studies, Philippine interest began in China's economic shift and the ties (intellectual, aspirational, or political) in China that the Philippines left maintained. Cariño perceives that there was an early strategic interest in wanting to know what was transpiring in China and what could be learned from it (Cariño 2015:15). However, what Cariño prescribes, that there should be a critical understanding between the Philippines and China, has not fully taken form and leaves much room for growth (Cariño 2015:15–17). For instance, Baculinao argues for more critical discussion and written work in the Philippines about China, both focusing on an impassioned understanding of China's strategy and underpinning sociopolitical contexts. However, he points out that the dynamics of nationalist views arising from maritime issues may impede such a balanced understanding. Baculinao suggests that Philippine scholars not only relate more with Chinese scholars but should also access European and American scholarship on China. These strands of scholarship are vital because of the differences in the geopolitical rivalry that Europe and the United States have with China (Baculinao 2015:9). Ideological baggage is de-emphasized in the former, viz., the latter. Also, the latter provides valuable insights into power relations whose dynamics are strongly felt in Asia. It is also extremely incisive of Baculinao to delink "advanced studies about China" and geopolitical perspectives (Baculinao 2015:9). The dangers in conflating the two are implicit in Cariño's emphasis on having a "multi-sourced, independent perspective on China" that is "less reliant on Western sources of scholarship," in spite, she posits, of some of the latter being of quality and critical utility (Cariño 2015:15). She argues that "the interaction with other ASEAN scholars is just as important as frequent interaction with Chinese academics. The more dialogue and exchange there is, the better off we will be" (Cariño 2015:16). Hau, on the other hand, takes the perspective that Asian studies need to be cultivated. This recognizes that China Studies should be in cognizance of Japanese Studies and Southeast Asian Studies, especially that neighbor relations and increasing regional economic integration cannot be ignored (Hau 2015:9).

Interestingly, Hau admonishes that there should be "more China experts working in Philippine academia who can explain in a more nuanced way some of the pressing issues that affect our economy, our politics, and geopolitics at regional and local levels" (Hau 2015:9–10). Parallel to this, Florcruz wants to see more public intellectuals, those who are focused on not just deepening knowledge of China but also sharing this to the public and policymakers specifically. China experts admit that more dimensions—not

18 *Tina S. Clemente*

just foreign relations—are needed in an integrated study of China and Philippines-China relations. Interestingly, it is often the case that China experts in the Philippines are practitioners outside the academe. They watch China as journalists, analysts in think tanks or government agencies, and so on. Hau's comment implies the enrichment of the field by anchoring China expertise in the academe, thereby cultivating a better symbiosis between scholarship and public service. Continuing studies of Chinese migration and integration in the Philippines in all aspects are needed (Go 2015:5). Further, a fresh pair of lenses can be applied to the study of new Chinese migrants and how better integration of later generations of Chinese Filipinos affects mindsets (Chu 2016:19).

### *The need for institutionalization*

Baviera astutely raises the lack of institutionalization of China Studies as a concern, notwithstanding the rising recognition of China's importance to the Philippines in the academe, government, and general public. With an increasing stake for the Philippines to study China, she observes that there would have been a corresponding rise of regular programs in the Philippines that promote cross-pollination with similar programs in China, Southeast Asia, Japan, and the West. Organizations like PACS "remained as informal as when they started" (Baviera 2016:7). Baviera's critique draws from her long experience as a national and international public intellectual, an organizational head, and head of various academic programs. Ang See makes the case for groups such as PACS as it has a role in promoting more understanding by facilitating "people-to-people exchanges, dialogues, research" (Ang See 2015:20). As she observed, diplomatic relations were so strained during the Aquino administration, to the point that any "research or policy paper" would not de-escalate the situation (Ang See 2015:20). This chapter argues that institutionalization becomes all the more valuable, given that it can have mechanisms in place even before volatility breaks out. While the strong personality of a president runs the risk of overturning policies, a stronger institutionalization of China Studies opens more opportunities for interactions that lead to more understanding. Florcruz has encouraged immersion in China to be able to have ground knowledge of the country. His own insights on how China has changed indeed reflect how his China expertise has drawn from his lived experience:

> China in 1971 and China now are as different as night and day. There is a huge billboard in a Beijing intersection which advertises Nokia phones or some commercial product. When I first saw that signboard over forty years ago, it carried the slogan "NEVER FORGET CLASS STRUGGLE." That shows how much China has changed over the years. When I first saw China, it was poor, backward, and dull. It was in the throes of the tumultuous Cultural Revolution. After years of chaos and isolation, China is now firmly locked into the global community through diplomacy, tourism

*Insights on China Studies as a community of practice*   19

and trade and, yes, through the news media and the Internet. After years of stagnation, China now is now bursting at the seams with explosive energy along the road to modernization. Having seen what China was like in 1971 makes me appreciate even the most incremental changes. Just about any change has been an improvement from where I started.

(Florcruz 2015:12)

Today, I see an enormously complex China. Great achievements stand alongside daunting challenges. The country's economic growth the past twenty years has been phenomenal, but it has also triggered inevitable and often unintended consequences: rising unemployment, yawning income gaps, regionalism, rampant corruption, rising criminality, and social malaise. Millions of Chinese still live on $1 a day, and large income disparities persist. Yet the Chinese cannot be blamed too much for optimism after decades of rapid socioeconomic transformation on the back of a historical calamity. Compared with the past, the future for them beckons not as an inevitable crisis but as an extraordinary opportunity. For better or worse, the changes taking place here are simply breathtaking. More changes can be expected now that China is closely linked with the global ecosystem.

(FlorCruz 2015:12)

### *Bridging greater understanding*

Ong pointedly commented that there is a need for more strategic thinking regarding the Philippines' relations with China in reference to what transpired during the height of tension (Ong 2016:17). Incidentally, there have been a number of China Studies experts undertaking various efforts in setting up programs in aid of strategic studies beyond China Studies. On another note, Mallare points out the lack of sufficient familiarity about the Philippines in China. He points out that regardless of the funds that are available, there is a dearth of researchers there on the Philippines. And so, he suggests that scholars from the Philippines collaborate with counterparts in China. While collaborations through dialogues, visits, and study tours are not new, structured study programs on the Philippines in China are still too few (Mallare 2015:17). This provides an opportunity for China experts who are already engaged with Chinese colleagues in the academe to help facilitate such programs that focus on Philippine history, society, culture, and political economy.

### Closing reflections

As a framework for analyzing twelve oral history transcripts, this study drew upon the multidisciplinary perspectives on communities of practice, intellectual history, and knowledge management. The research began with the objective of critically characterizing the nature of China Studies in the

20  *Tina S. Clemente*

Philippines by interrogating the intellectual paths of thinkers. We find that the field has been issues-driven—and practice-driven—regardless of the academic engagement of the thinkers or the existence of programs. Further, the evolution of the community is based on multiple factors and is highly contextual. It is determined by intertwining intellectual histories across individuals, communities, fields, and historical events. From the sense of disciplinal boundaries and parameters, the field has had limited advancement. But from an issues-based community of practice, the intellectual advocacy is thriving and presents itself as a dynamic area of study going forward. This calls for a reorientation in the practice of mapping communities as an insight into how strategic input can be gleaned and cultivated. The study emphasized how a dynamic community that emphasizes practice beyond the confines of organizational structure can contribute in facilitating the generation of China expertise. Nevertheless, taking off from Thompson (2005:151–152), we recognize that there is also something to be learned from structure. The latter can be harnessed as an efficient instrument in cultivating the community. While this chapter underscores context, it also implies that changing social context will mean changing community configuration to address generational transition in experts, emerging issues requiring a new pool of competencies, and new modes of interaction.

## Note

1  The research conducted for this article was made possible by the University of the Philippines (UP) Asian Center Research Grant. The research also benefitted from the Research Dissemination Grant from UP Diliman and the UP Office of the Vice President for Academic Affairs. The author thanks Pamela G. Combinido for her research assistance.

## References

Adler, Paul S. 2001. "Market, Hierarchy and Trust: The Knowledge Economy and the Future of Capitalism." *Organization Science* 12(2):215–234.

Adler, Paul S. and Charles Heckscher. 2006. "Toward Collaborative Community." In *The Firm as a Collaborative Community: Reconstructing Trust in the Knowledge Economy*, edited by Charles Heckscher and Paul Adler. Oxford: Oxford University Press, 11–105.

Ang See, Teresita. 2015. "Interview by Reynard Hing." *Department of Political Science, National Taiwan University: For China Studies and Cross Taiwan Strait Relations*, 6 November. Retrieved 23 February 2018 (http://www.china-studies.taipei/act02.php).

Baculinao, Eric. 2015. "Interview by Jose Mari Hall Lanuza." *Department of Political Science, National Taiwan University: For China Studies and Cross Taiwan Strait Relations*, 3 November. Retrieved 1 March 2018 (http://www.china-studies.taipei/act02.php).

Barth, Fredrik. 2002. "An Anthropology of Knowledge." *Current Anthropology* 43(1):1–18.

Baviera, Aileen. 2016. "Interview by Lucio Pitlo III." *Department of Political Science, National Taiwan University: For China Studies and Cross Taiwan Strait Relations*, 29 February. Retrieved 23 February 2018 (http://www.china-studies.taipei/act02.php).

Boyer, Dominic. 2005. "Visiting Knowledge in Anthropology: An Introduction." *Ethnos* 70(2):141–148.

Brannen, Julia and Ann Nilsen. 2011. "Comparative Biographies in Case-Based Cross-National Research: Methodological Considerations." *Sociology* 45(4):603–618.

Brown, John and Paul Duguid. 2001. "Knowledge and Organization: A Social Practice Perspective." *Organization Science* 12(2):198–213.

Cardona, P., Lawrence B.S., and Bentler P.M. 2004. "The Influence of Social and Work Exchange Relationships on Organizational Citizenship Behavior." *Group Organ Management* 29(2):219–247.

Cariño, Theresa. 2015. "Interview by Dorcas Juliette Ramos-Caraig." *Department of Political Science, National Taiwan University: For China Studies and Cross Taiwan Strait Relations*, 7 December. Retrieved 23 February 2018 (http://www.china-studies.taipei/act02.php).

Chu, Richard. 2016. "Interview by Carmelea Ang See." *Department of Political Science, National Taiwan University: For China Studies and Cross Taiwan Strait Relations*, 14 January. Retrieved 23 February 2018 (http://www.china-studies.taipei/act02.php).

Collingwood, R.G. 1946. *The Idea of History*. Oxford: Oxford University Press.

Cowan, Brian. 2006. "Intellectual, Social and Cultural History: Ideas in Context." In *Palgrave Advances in Intellectual History*, edited by Richard Whatmore and Brian Young. New York: Palgrave Macmillan, 171–188.

FlorCruz, Jaime. 2015. "Interview by Robin Michael Garcia." *Department of Political Science, National Taiwan University: For China Studies and Cross Taiwan Strait Relations*, 8 October. Retrieved 23 February 2018 (http://www.china-studies.taipei/act02.php).

Galaskiewicz, Joseph. 1985. "Professional Networks and the Institutionalization of a Single Mind Set." *American Sociological Review* 50(5):639–658.

Gee, James Paul. 2005. "Semiotic Social Spaces and Affinity Spaces: From the *Age of Mythology* to Today's Schools." In *Beyond Communities of Practice: Language, Power and Social Context*, edited by David Barton and Karen Tusting. Cambridge: Cambridge University Press, 214–232.

Go, Bon Juan. 2015. "Interview by Carmelea Ang See." *Department of Political Science, National Taiwan University: For China Studies and Cross Taiwan Strait Relations*, 18 November. Retrieved 23 February 2018 (http://www.china-studies.taipei/act02.php).

Goldman, Alvin. 1987. "Foundations of Social Epistemics." *Synthese* 73(1):109–144.

Hau, Caroline. 2015. "Interview by Jose Mari Hall Lanuza." *Department of Political Science, National Taiwan University: For China Studies and Cross Taiwan Strait Relations*, 5 November. Retrieved 23 February 2018 (http://www.china-studies.taipei/act02.php).

Kaplan, Lauren. 2014. "Biographical Analysis Using Narrative and Topical Interviews." *People Living with HIV in the USA and Germany*, 45–60.

Mallare, Florencio. 2015. "Interview by Sining Kotah." *Department of Political Science, National Taiwan University: For China Studies and Cross Taiwan Strait*

## 22    *Tina S. Clemente*

*Relations*, 25 November. Retrieved 23 February 2018 (http://www.china-studies.taipei/act02.php).

Ong, Charlson. 2016. "Interview by Yvan Ysmael Yonaha." *Department of Political Science, National Taiwan University: For China Studies and Cross Taiwan Strait Relations*, 18 January. Retrieved 23 February 2018 (http://www.china-studies.taipei/act02.php).

Palanca, Ellen. 2016. "Interview by Dorcas Juliette Ramos-Caraig." *Department of Political Science, National Taiwan University: For China Studies and Cross Taiwan Strait Relations*, 27 January. Retrieved 23 February 2018 (http://www.china-studies.taipei/act02.php).

Santa Romana, Jose Santiago "Chito." 2016. "Interview by Lucio Pitlo III." *Department of Political Science, National Taiwan University: For China Studies and Cross Taiwan Strait Relations*, 14 April. Retrieved 29 March 2018 (http://www.china-studies.taipei/act02.php).

Shoppes, Linda. 2015. "Community Oral History: Where We Have Been, Where We Are Going." *Oral History* 43(1):97–106.

Thompson, Mark. 2005. "Structural and Epistemic Parameters in Communities of Practice." *Organization Science* 16(2):151–164.

Weisberg, Michael and Ryan Muldoon. 2009. "Epistemic Landscapes and the Division of Cognitive Labor." *Philosophy of Science* 76(2, April 2009): 225-252.

Wenger, Etienne. 1998. *Communities of Practice: Learning, Meaning, and Identity.* New York: Cambridge University Press.

# 2 Social evolution and situational learning in Jose Santiago "Chito" Santa Romana's China Studies[1]

*Robin Michael Garcia*

## Introduction

This chapter is inspired by the premise that the people who observe China have different lenses, and these lenses are determined by their unique peculiarities and experiences. The vast differences among those who look at China and the notions that they develop must be acknowledged through an admission that these notions are premised differently (Shih 2013). The purpose of this article is to disaggregate and make explicit the causal pathways, mechanisms, and social contexts that had influenced the ideas of Santa Romana—an important figure in the epistemic practice of China Studies in the Philippines—about China and about China Studies in the Philippines.

This article argues that the evolution of Santa Romana's epistemic orientations about China and China Studies can be derived from his unique participation in the left-leaning youth movement in the Philippines and his long-distinguished career in China as a journalist. More specifically, his ideas about China were imbibed from his participation in the progressive bloc of the National Union of Students of the Philippines (NUSP). He headed the student council at De La Salle University, which was a member of the NUSP. The NUSP at that time had a progressive wing that was influenced by youth organizations with ties to the Maoist-inspired Communist Party of the Philippines (CPP) who fought fiercely against the Marcos dictatorship. Santa Romana led the Philippine Youth Delegation to China to various Chinese provinces including Beijing and Shanghai in August 1971. Composed of around fifteen youth-leaders from different Philippine universities, the delegation journeyed to learn and understand China's politics, society, and culture for 3 weeks. However, there were some members of the delegation who were blacklisted by the Marcos dictatorship from coming back to Manila, while some members were able to come home. Santa Romana was among those who were not able to go home. Deciding to stay on in China for political exile, the experience subsequently launched a successful career as journalist and China watcher culminating as the Beijing Bureau Chief of ABC News or the American Broadcasting Company. As such, his days as a student leader, which eventually led him

24  *Robin Michael Garcia*

to China, and his journalism career in China where he eventually held a coveted position, are two of the essential contexts where he formed his ideas about China.

Later in his career, Santa Romana became part of an important "epistemic community" after he retired from a long illustrious career as a China observer in Beijing. This epistemic community in the Philippines advocated for a deeper understanding of China and thus welcomed Santa Romana's ideas. Appointed by President Rodrigo Duterte as the Philippine Ambassador to China, his view of China and his epistemic influence and stature as a "norm entrepreneur" for a deeper understanding of China is strengthened by being inside government—ironically because he spent most of his career outside of the ambit of government.

The arguments presented here rely on the theoretical bridge I build between both the Social Evolution Paradigm of Tang and situational learning theory associated with Vygotsky, Lave, and Wenger. Briefly, the fundamental idea that this chapter postulates is that how and what China watchers learn is influenced by their participation in specific social practices and interaction which is then determined by the sociohistorical contexts in which these practices and interactions are located. This argument is premised on the idea that learning is not only a biological process but also a socially constructed one. The two processes work hand to produce important social outcomes at the individual cognitive level.

The next section features the theoretical discussion of Tang's Social Evolution Paradigm and the Situated Learning Theory of Vygotsky, Lave, and Wenger. We lay down their basic premises and attempt to bridge the two by highlighting their similarities. The third section is a discussion of Santa Romana's ideas on China in the aspects of development, institutionalism, and social change, while the fourth section focuses on the evolution and context in which Santa Romana developed his ideas disaggregating particularly the meaning of de-Marcosification and how China might be part of this narrative. Here we also discuss how he had developed the ideas he did by focusing on his participation in this youth movement and his long stay in China. This is followed by a conclusion.

## Insights from the social evolution paradigm and situated learning theory

What theoretical lens can broadly inform how and why Santa Romana developed his ideas on China and how it should be studied? I argue that this question can be answered by referring to the Social Evolution Paradigm and Situated Learning Theory.

The Social Evolution Paradigm (SEP) developed by Shiping Tang (2011, 2012, 2013) attempts to explain how and why certain social outcomes, such as institutional change or the evolution of the international system, transpired in specific forms and not other forms and how they have transformed

*Social evolution and situational learning*   25

over time. This is inspired by, but dissimilar to, the other evolutionary theories in the social sciences (see Campbell 1960, Hodgson and Knudsen 2006)

On the other hand, Situated Learning Theory fits nicely as an auxiliary theory to the Social Evolution Paradigm because it proposes a "selection mechanism" with which certain ideas are taken up instead of an array of other competing ideas: a fundamental theoretical question that the SEP seeks to answer. In our current context, we want to theoretically understand why an agent—Santa Romana—developed the ideas that he has about China, which he diffused to an epistemic community of China specialists and then used, and continues to use, in his high-level diplomatic work as Philippine ambassador to China.

More specifically, the Social Evolution Paradigm has three fundamental themes which distinguishes it from other evolutionary theories that aim to explain the social world. First, the analysis must be cognizant of the following ontological forces: ideationalism and materialism, individualism and collectivism, socialization, anti-socialization and biological evolution, and conflict and harmony. Second, the theory underscores the value of interactions and transformation, creating social outcomes while allowing diversity because of the different ways in which such ontological forces interact with each other. The third theme argues that social outcomes go through time and transform according to varied ideas being produced, the selection of an idea over others, and the retention and diffusion of the idea.

Situational Learning Theory propounds that human learning is dynamic, embedded in various situations, contexts, and social settings (Dryfus 1972), and goes through different stages over time. We also consider Lev Vygotsky's sociohistorical approach to cognitive development in that mental development and learning cannot be reduced to biological factors alone but must also take into account the social dimensions of mental development, which go through stages through time instead of simply being a fixed or static characteristic that uniformly informs human cognition (Holland et al. 1998). The central argument is a person's mental affairs are shaped by the activities he participates in. In other words, the social contexts in which people are embedded determine how and what is being learned. The learner learns with the concept of social practice where he acquires new knowledge not just through communicative interactions with people but through the participation in communities of practice, a group of like-minded individuals who share certain ideas and activities. Hence, scholars and observers, such as Santa Romana, are embedded in the contexts they observe (Bredo 1989; Bruner 1962; Lave 1991; Lave and Wenger 1991; Wenger 1998; Wertsch 1985).

Situated Learning Theory in the context of the Social Evolution Paradigm, therefore, provides a theoretical mechanism in understanding the evolution of Santa Romana's ideas, the ideational and learning process, and the social contexts in which Santa Romana as a China watcher was embedded.

## 26  *Robin Michael Garcia*

### Exploring Santa Romana's China Studies: developmental exceptionalism, sociological-historical institutionalism, and radical social change

Santa Romana's China Studies transcend the descriptive enterprise of most academic endeavors. His epistemic activities are decidedly prescriptive: the ideas about China and how China should be observed were shared with the goal of influencing actual political practice in the Philippines and, perhaps, elsewhere. However, all prescriptive ideas have descriptive underpinnings that premise them. As such, Santa Romana's practical impetus for studying China does not preclude its potential application for scholarly purposes. Indeed, two of his most notable ideas—one substantive idea or what China is and one theoretical or how China must be understood—should have profound implications for the ontological and epistemological evolution and maturation of China Studies in the Philippines, a budding area of scholarship.

I argue that two ideas are notable from Santa Romana's thinking: developmental exceptionalism or the belief that China's development is unique. Another is his idea of how China should be studied. In this latter question, he advocates for what can be understood as sociological-historical institutionalism. We shall turn to each one of these ideas and how it relates to broader epistemic projects in China Studies as a discipline within area studies and the social sciences in general. In addition, I draw some possible implications of these ideas to several research projects in the social sciences particularly.

### *Developmental exceptionalism: neoliberalism, East Asian developmental state, or Beijing consensus?*

Perhaps the most notable of Santa Romana's ideas is his reflection on China's development, which he had observed from the time of Mao until a little before the leadership of Xi Jinping. This time frame undeniably saw China's tremendous and remarkable political, economic, and cultural transformation amid continuity. So, his argument that China's development should be seen as unique or exceptional can be taken as a challenge to scholars and observers who hypothesize that China's development had been because it had replicated either the neoliberal ideology or liberalization in all aspects of economic life, or the "developmental state" of its East Asian neighbors where a strong bureaucracy and interventionist state manages an export-oriented development paradigm.

Surely, there is some merit to the contention that some western-inspired neoliberal norms, policies, and institutions had been diffused especially during the liberal capitalist turn in China's economic development paradigm during Deng Xiaoping in 1978: around the time, the neoliberal orthodoxy came into prominence the world over (see Harvey 2005). Still, a healthy level of credence should be given to the argument that some form of

*Social evolution and situational learning*   27

diffusion had also come from the East Asian or more specifically the Japanese developmental state model which had been the inspiration of Hong Kong, Singapore, Taiwan, or the "little dragons." Inasmuch as Southeast Asian industrializing states had learned from Japan and others (Jomo 2001), China had also been argued to learn from Singapore especially in light of the numerous conversations between Deng Xiaoping and Lee Kuan Yew on the "Singapore Model" (see e.g. Ortmann and Thompson 2016). Of course, the debate is not a dichotomy between the two ideal types described above on how to describe Chinese development. Instead, there is a healthy discussion of gray areas and gradients where China's development model falls under.

However, another perspective on what *the* China Model *is* transcends these discussions toward the concession that the model should not be seen to fit these titles and labels but that China should be a special unique case and possibly non-replicable model or a case of what can be called "developmental exceptionalism." Like the developmental state model of East Asian which had been the craze of comparative and international political economy for some time, this idea challenges the postulate that political and economic development must go through the hegemonic Western belief in political and economic liberalization guised as "modernization" should. It defers from the developmental state hypothesis, however, in its insistence that China's development model, while similar to it, should not be seen as the same. Some had called this idea the "Beijing Consensus" (Ramo 2004) echoing the catchy "Washington Consensus" which had catapulted economic liberalism in the United States. But perhaps the most important premise in this idea of exceptionalism is that countries should cultivate its own path to development and should not copy or listen to those who impose what had been done elsewhere. This idea is very clear in Santa Romana's thinking, a reflection he had perhaps made even before the popular debates on the China model. Asked on about China's development experience and how developing countries could learn from it, he shares:

> At that point, we had not decided yet. We only did so only after years of experience. China's position shifted away from Mao's model to Deng's. Deng maintained that each country should tread its own path according to its own conditions. Actually, even under Mao, this approach was already surfacing. You should develop a model to suit your own conditions. So eventually, the Chinese went their own way.
>
> (Santa Romana 2016:11)

When asked if China is a model to be replicated, he argues "overall, no." (Santa Romana 2016:9). Instead, he argues that you should follow your own path admitting that "there are lessons that can be looked into, but you cannot take them as a whole." It is "how you apply and practice" the lessons and "adjust as you go along based on the results." Further, he argues that "you

## 28 *Robin Michael Garcia*

really have to cross the river by feeling the stones. And feeling the stones is always interesting" (Santa Romana 2016:15). A crucial theme in Santa Romana's thinking is that he understood that the supposedly grand shift in China's development paradigm is actually some form of continuity: a continuation of the unique development path that China had been taking ever since.

The choice of going to China had been partly for ideological reasons particularly that of learning from Mao's youth-led Red Guards. While the reconceptualization of a distinct version of communism through Mao Zedong already demonstrates China's belief in establishing its own path, this had been clearer and explicit in Deng Xiaoping. Thus, he remarks,

> The point here is that I think there are certain things in Philippine society and culture that need to be factored in when coming up with our own model. That model should be our own and reflect our conditions and integrate the positive aspects of our culture that suit developmental requirements. Filipinos are a little more spontaneous and freewheeling. The Chinese, on the other hand, are ritualistic and Confucian values are very strong. Of course, I did not know then China's culture was Confucian. I thought it was just being Chinese. Certain aspects of Filipinos' religion, culture, and politics, which make it difficult for authoritarianism to take root, although there seems to be a recent surge and inclination towards a strongman leader. The appeal of a strongman is becoming more popular.
> (Santa Romana 2016:11)

It is thus clear Santa Romana adopted a more "Dengist" narrative in advancing developmental exceptionalism as a model. He shares "I would not call myself a Maoist. I was interested to learn. And I lived, learned and experienced China, particularly during the Cultural Revolution" (Santa Romana 2016:15).

### Culture and history matter: institutions and how China can be understood

Another notable idea in Santa Romana's thinking on China is how China should be studied. Undeniably, this should have epistemological implications or how to conduct research on China. Based also on his empirical observations from Mao Zedong to the current leadership of Xi Jinping, he argues that most of what can be seen in China in the past and in the future should be understood and studied according to two separate but intimately intertwined ideas: political history and culture and how these jointly affect the actions of individuals in Chinese society including its leaders. This idea is explicit when asked about the project of understanding China:

> You cannot judge from the surface. Instead, you have to view it in the context of their history. The Chinese people have a very strong culture

*Social evolution and situational learning* 29

heavily influenced by Confucianism. And there is a Marxist veneer, as well as Maoist and Dengist veneers too. You have to see the situation from there; and the bottom line is that you have to understand that human beings are influenced by all these cultural and historical forces.

(Santa Romana 2016:15)

This idea can be located in the broader research interest on the "institutional turn" or new institutionalism that had been a very important topic for political scientists, sociologists, anthropologists, institutional economists, or basically the broader social sciences in recent decades (see e.g. Campbell and Pedersen 2001). I follow one of the most popular definitions of an institution in that they "are the humanly devised constraints that shape human interaction" (North 1990), but like Tang (2011:3), who follows Giddens (1993:169), I include in the definition an idea that institutions both constrain and enable agents' actions. Institutions can have informal or formal rules that define the actions of individual agents and include culture, laws, social rules, and history, among others. Thus, Santa Romana's ascription of China's past and future actions to its history and culture which he argues influence human action can be seen in light of the institutional term in the social sciences.

For a couple of decades, the social sciences were mired in "methodological individualism" or the assumption that society and social change should be understood only through the unconstrained action of individuals which is said to be inspired only by the expected material utility. The implication is that these themes presented are ahistorical, noncultural, and devoid of power and political considerations. Prevalent in much of the neoclassical economic theory which spread across the social sciences, including realist and neoliberal theory in international relations (Tang 2013), historically and culturally inspired perspectives prevalent in sociology, anthropology, and political science tended to be ignored and considered subpar. The institutional turn in the social sciences largely replaced this conceptualization to appreciate that institutions, and not simply material utility functions, actually influence agential behavior and drive history. While China Studies as area studies in the Philippines had inevitably been involved in historical and cultural research traditions, it had remained nonsocial scientific. Santa Romana's insistence on the explanation of China's society seems to call for a social scientific perspective particularly that of institutionalism.

The literature had already expanded to four perspectives: historical institutionalism, sociological institutionalism, rational choice institutionalism, and discursive institutionalism. The call for "cross-fertilization" among these perspectives is also being discussed. It is not the intention of this research to expand on the discussion on each of these perspectives on institutionalism but suffice it to say, the sociological and historical variants are reflected in Santa Romana's thinking. Briefly, historical institutionalism

# 30 *Robin Michael Garcia*

(HI) argues for the "logic of path-dependence" or the notion that future actions can be understood as the product of past historical choices which are solidified and made into institutions which then constrain or enable subsequent actions. Meanwhile, sociological institutionalism argues for the "logic of appropriateness" or the perspective that agential actions are made in the context of cultural and social rules. A cross-fertilization of the two perspectives would suggest that past political and cultural actions constrain or enable agents' actions (for a good review, see Campbell and Pedersen 2001; Mahoney and Thelen 2009; Schmidt 2010; Streeck and Thelen 2005; Tang 2013).

With this backdrop, Santa Romana's suggestions that "you cannot judge from the surface" and "you have to view it in the context of their history" (Santa Romana 2016:15) call for a deeper appreciation of the historical, cultural, and the institutional influences of China's behavior. He argues further that that "was lesson 101. Bu qingchu (not clear) compared to bu zhidao (not knowing). It's like something is out there but it is not clear" (13).

## Explaining the origins of Santa Romana's ideas: the pursuit for de-Marcosification

The 20-year Marcos Dictatorship in the Philippines, running from 1965 and culminating in the Epifanio Delos Santos Avenue (EDSA) People Power Revolution (EDSA is a national road) that toppled it in 1986, proved to be the fundamental context, which had been the driving force in how Santa Romana developed his ideas about China and how to study it. To the extent that his ideas were forged under this context, I argue that it was particularly that of what Velasco (1997) called "de-Marcosification," a description of how the "People Power Movement" should be appreciated, which had served as the selection mechanism.

Most particularly, a crucial sector in society that had fought against the dictatorship was the youth. The most prominent series of social movement activity where the youth played a big important part was what came to be known as the First Quarter Storm (FQS), a series of demonstrations which ran from January to March of the year 1970, 2 years before the imposition of the martial law in 1972. Santa Romana was an important part of this movement, along with the late Edgar Jopson who died in the hands of the military. Santa Romana, in fact, was one of those who lead the youth in the first demonstration in front of the Congress of the Philippines during the State of the Nation Address (SONA) of Marcos.

During the dictatorship, many people were ruthlessly murdered, and public coffers were stolen from. Marcos cronies have taken hold of major protected industries leading to severe economic crisis, and the United States participated in the perpetuation of the Regime. All these culminated in the assassination of Benigno Aquino, the leading opposition figure and husband of Corazon Aquino, as he deplaned at the Manila airport following his long exile in the United States in 1983.

*Social evolution and situational learning* 31

This is the context within which Santa Romana decided to go to China. As he reflects:

> In a sense, it was actually accidental. My interest in China basically came as a result of my involvement in the student activist movement during Martial Law. I was then a young student leader in De La Salle University, where there was hardly any activism. My batch was in fact among those who pioneered it. I was part of the Council and the student organ, and I was exposed to the movement through contacts with colleagues from UP and other universities, from the National Union of Students of the Philippines (NUSP), and from the College Editors Guild of the Philippines (CEGP). I was very active as head of NUSP-Manila. This experience really led me to the student movement. I graduated in 1970, right after the First Quarter Storm. And I knew renowned student leaders like Edgar Jopson, who was then the Head of Ateneo's Student Council, while I headed that of La Salle. As contemporaries, we were together during the first demonstration in Congress during former President Marcos' State of the Nation Address. NUSP organized it, and we marched to Congress together with other protesters.
>
> (Santa Romana 2016:1)

### *The martial law atrocities: human rights violations under the specter of a dictatorship*

First and foremost, martial law was imposed on September 21, 1972, in the second term of the Marcos administration. When the martial law was implemented, many atrocities were committed, and these years saw the imprisonment of around 30,000, as of 1975, mostly real or perceived political opponents. It was also during this time when many oppositionists would be murdered and tortured by the military including young students (Quimpo and Quimpo 2012). Moreover, during this time, the Armed Forces of the Philippines (AFP) received one of the biggest allocations of the national budget particularly rising to four billion Philippine pesos from just 880 million aside from the expansion of its forces, which include adding the Philippine Constabulary and municipal police forces (Abinales and Amoroso 2005).

The 21-year Marcos rule did not begin as bad when it began in 1965. There were already seeds of discontent that begun in his first term particularly because of economic distress. Marcos, however, was re-elected for the second term, the first-ever president to have been. His re-election, however, is questionable and mired in corruption. He used about 50 million US dollars, most of it from the public coffers, to secure his win, aside from other noteworthy tactics. The defeated candidate Sergio Osmeña Jr. remarked in a case he filed at the Presidential Electoral Tribunal (PET), "maximum use by Marcos of the power of his office through organized terrorism, massive vote-buying,

## 32  *Robin Michael Garcia*

and rampant fraud." His second term was mired with more economic devastation and more social movements began to stage oppositionist protest. Most notably was the Partido Komunista ng Pilipinas or PKP (Party of Philippine Communists) that had one of its arms, the Kabataang Makabayan (Nationalist Youth), headed by Jose Sison, the founder of the 1968 break-off group called CPP, specifically invoking Mao Zedong's militant ideas. Many students and young people were recruited here and served, and after a year, in 1969, the CPP had formed the New People's Army, (NPA) the militant arm of the CPP. Oppositionist senators announced their sympathy to the cause after four students were killed. Ranks swelled as the cause became more popular, and more demonstrations were staged, which eventually made Marcos declare martial law, which included the jailing, torture, and murder of many of his opponents with the use of the AFP. He also closed down media outlets and put his cronies in national companies (Abinales and Amoroso 2005:198–202).

Marcos would justify the imposition of the martial law in the following terms, an excerpt of his speech when he announced it provides a good view of his reasons:

> Whereas, on the basis of carefully evaluated and verified information, it is definitely established that lawless elements who are moved by a common or similar ideological conviction, strategy and goal and enjoying the active moral and material support of a foreign power and being guided and directed by intensely devoted, well trained, deter- mined and ruthless groups of men and seeking refuge under the protection of our constitutional liberties to promote and attain their ends, have entered into a conspiracy and have in fact joined and banded their resources and forces together for the prime purpose of, and in fact they have been and are actually staging, undertaking and waging an armed insurrection and rebellion against the Government of the Republic of the Philippines in order to forcibly seize political and state power in this country, overthrow the duly constituted government, and supplant our existing political, social, economic and legal order with an entirely new one whose form of government, whose system of laws, whose conception of God and religion, whose notion of individual rights and family relations, and whose political, social, economic, legal and moral precepts are based on the Marxist-Leninist-Maoist teaching and beliefs.
>
> (Abinales and Amoroso 2005:206)

Nick Joaquin (1990:329–334),[2] a prominent Filipino essayist and critic penned,

> What Filipinos never thought to see in their lifetime, they say this year: street fighting at barricades. Almost no month in Manila when no streets emptied, no stores closed in a hurry, and no pavement became

*Social evolution and situational learning* 33

a battleground between the youth marching with red flags and placard and helmeted troops with truncheon and wicker shield ... [T]he man on the street came to learn what tear gas smells like.

After a new justification for the martial law in what he calls the "New Society," a staged process of revising the Philippine Constitution, economic devastation, the assassination of the eloquent opposition leader Benigno Aquino, and a staged election, a popular uprising, starting with the deflection of important segments in the military—General Ramos Chief of the AFP and Secretary Enrile, National Defense Chief—and eventually most other sectors in Philippine society, flocked to the EDSA and overthrew Marcos in a bloodless revolution known as the "EDSA People Power," which installed Cory Aquino to presidential office. What particularly sparked this was the assassination of Benigno Aquino because "for the first time, the Manila upper and middle class felt physically threatened by the Marcos government" (Dohner and Intal 1989:560).

As the political scientist, Belinda Aquino provides,

EDSA was the ultimate expression of the people's anger that had been building up for years against the Marcos dictatorship. It was the final explosion of the outrage that escalated with the assassination of Aquino and the near collapse of the economy as a result of the regime's corruption. EDSA was the final test of people's courage as they determinedly face the tanks with "Walang aalis, huwag matakot" (Don't leave, don't be afraid).

(Aquino 1988:715)

Around the same time, China was seen as a model for youth power under the Cultural Revolution and Santa Romana, as well as many other groups, had seen this to be a model and inspiration for their participation in the broader anti-Marcos dictatorship movement. Hence, he reflects:

China was under the Cultural Revolution, where students and the youth played prominent roles. Student power was very popular the world over. Like other students then, I saw a lot of ills in society, the disenchantment against Marcos' rule, and his rigging of the elections to stay in power.

Like many student activists at that time, we were influenced by China's Cultural Revolution, which we thought demonstrated student power.

In order to better channel and harness this protest, people had to be politicized and mobilized. And it was on the question of how to do it that the Chinese model came into prominence.

Back then, our impression was that the Red Guards were part of student power and youth rebellion. We did not know that they eventually went out of control. The Cultural Revolution was a model at that point,

34 *Robin Michael Garcia*

and the young Red Guards conveyed the sense that rebellion was jus-
tified. What they did and what really transpired during that time only
came to light after, with the benefit of hindsight.

(Santa Romana 2016:1)

Undeniably, the search for social movement models under the backdrop of
youth involvement in the pursuit for and under the prevailing social narrative of de-Marcosification was the fundamental reason for Santa Romana's
decision to decide to observe China. This initial decision was a crucial factor in subsequent beliefs he had formed. He had not been able to observe
China as closely as possible if he did not have the wherewithal to actually
observe up close. However, and more importantly, the search for an alternative model to the current social architecture because of dissatisfaction with
the current system led him to look closely and understand China's development paradigm.

Before his journalism career, Santa Romana and the others who were part
of the delegation actually experienced farm-life. Why China is not a model
and why developmental exceptionalism should be pursued was further reinforced in this experience:

When we saw first what happened, there were positive and negative
sides. What we experienced in the Hunan farm (although we had never
been to a farm in the Philippines, and most of us are from the landed
class, not the peasant class) seemed similar to most rural areas in the
Philippines. If you looked at their living conditions, they were not very
dissimilar from the Philippines, except perhaps that they were more
egalitarian and there was no pronounced social disparity. But having
gone through all that happened in China, you would want economic
growth to improve, as it did during the time of Deng. But the political
system would probably not work in the Philippines.

(Santa Romana 2016:9)

A second important part of the de-Marcosification rhetoric was opposing the United States because of its support for the dictatorship. The close
relationship between the dictatorship and the United States can be aptly
illustrated when then United States President George Bush went to the
Philippines to attend the inauguration of Marcos as President in 1981 and
Marcos visited the United States in 1982 and spoke with Ronald Reagan
(Abinales and Amoroso 2005; Dohner and Intal 1989:560). This is particularly important because these years saw the swelling of the opposition as
Benigno Aquino, the most prominent opposition leader, was executed. This
act would be attributed to Marcos. The support of the United States to the
Philippines was particularly set in the context of the Cold War where the
military alliance. The interest of the United States was specifically the two
military bases in the Philippines—Subic Bay Naval Base and the Clark Air

*Social evolution and situational learning* 35

Base. US support in terms of military assistance saw a 100 percent increase in 1972 to 1973, from 18.5 million US dollars to 45 million US dollars, aside from nonmonetary aid, such as material and training assistance (Abinales and Amoroso 2005:209). This is all set in the context of the increasing suppression because of the martial law.

Moreover, government borrowings had been significant, reaching around 25 billion US dollars by 1983, making the Philippines one of the most indebted countries in a list of developing countries (Abinales and Amoroso 2005:213). Filipinos and opposition elites would thus attribute the perpetuation of the martial law and its attendant atrocities to the support of the United States to the Philippines.

It is in this context that the Aquino administration was beset with the conundrum of asserting its sovereignty vis-à-vis the International Monetary Fund's economic stabilization program which required the Philippines to pay the debts that it inherited from the loans of the Marcos dictatorship. The proponents of debt repudiation asked: why should the Philippine citizens pay back the loans that the dictatorship borrowed to sustain its anti-people regime? The Aquino administration's technocrats had to justify: why it had to continue to honor these debts considering that it could be a breach of the administration's legitimacy which is based on serving the people and not foreign institutions which had been a policy that Marcos adopted. In this particular issue though, Aquino followed the advice of a "conservative" group of business people whom Aquino appointed, who argued that the Philippines had to pay the debts, a move toward a more "friendly" rather than a "confrontational" policy toward international financial institutions. Despite what many saw as a setback, particularly the National Economic and Development Authority under Monsod (Jayasuriya 1992:57; Lindsey 1992:87–89), many areas of economic policy particularly in trade had to be put in the context of a subtle anti-Western hue. The efforts of finance secretary Jesus Estanislao to ensure that the public saw liberalization efforts as a Filipinized effort and to justify the proposal to Aquino herself is an important testament to this. Trade policy aside from the debt repayment issue is the most contentious economic policy issue that was fought.

This context is important for the simple reason that Santa Romana actually also went to the United States to study youth movements. He shares,

> Student activism was becoming a model for effecting change. While I was in my junior year at La Salle, I got a grant through the university and the US Embassy to travel in the U.S. for three (3) months. Traveling to different universities like University of California Berkeley and Columbia University, among others, exposed me further to the student movement, which was very popular in the U.S. Student activists strongly opposed the Vietnam War. This experience impressed on me the value of student power as a source of inspiration and as a model.
>
> (Santa Romana 2016:1)

## 36 *Robin Michael Garcia*

Why then was China a model for youth power and mobilization and not the United States? The reason based on the previous discussion is because of how the United States actually helped perpetuate the Marcos dictatorship. The idea of fighting the dictatorship would be null if it drew lessons from it.

## Conclusion

The discussion sought to identify the reasons and explanations for the origins of Chito Santa Romana's ideas about China. The movement to remove a dictator led him to observe China more closely inspired first by the model of youth empowerment in social change. In the search for alternative models or to "de-Marcosify" and the opportunity to stay in China and actually experience its transition from Mao to Deng proved to be the important variable in his ideas about developmental exceptionalism and an analytical bias for institutionalism particularly the historical and sociological variant.

At the onset of this chapter, we underlined that the goal was to explain how and why these ideas were developed. Since the issue was the development of ideas, an evolutionary perspective was the apt framework that could shed light on the topic. However, the Social Evolution Paradigm demands specific mechanisms for specific cases. We employed Situational Learning Theory or the theory which argues that cognitive influences at any given time are not limited to simple biological factors. Instead, we highlighted the power of the ideational context within which agents find themselves in and thus define how they will act and the ideas that they harbor.

Finally, China Studies in the Philippines could benefit from the ideas of Chito Santa Romana that we made explicit here. Specifically, it reinforces the need to understand China in its own terms that its development is unique and special and should not simplistically be understood as an outcome of the diffusion of international norms such as that of neoliberalism and the East Asian developmental state. For students of comparative political economy, this is an important notion. In any case, analyzing China whether for its political economy or for its foreign policy can be understood in light of institutionalism. Employing the institutional turn may be instructive.

## Notes

1 In this book, we use Santa Romana to denote the official surname "Sta. Romana" and indicate the pronunciation of the same.
2 Cited in Abinales and Amoroso 2005, 203 Box 8.2.

## References

Abinales, Patricio N. and Donna J. Amoroso. 2005. *State and Society in the Philippines*. Lanham, MD: Rowman and Littlefield.
Aquino, Belinda. 1988. "Review of the Philippines under Aquino: Papers Presented at a Conference Held in Sydney, November 1986 and Organized by the Development

*Social evolution and situational learning* 37

Studies Colloquium, Sydney and the Australian Development Studies Network, by Peter Krinks; Regime Change in the Philippines: The Legitimation of the Aquino Government, by Mark Turner; President Marcos and the Philippine Political Culture, by Lewis E. Gleeck." *Pacific Affairs* 4(1):714–716.

Bredo, Eric. 1989. "Bateson's Hierarchical Theory of Learning and Communication." *Education Theory* 1(39):27–38.

Bruner, Jerome. 1962. *On Knowing.* Cambridge: Belknap Press.

Campbell, Donald. 1960. "Blind Variation and Selective Retention in Creative Thought as in Other Knowledge Processes." *Psychological Review* 67(6):380–400.

Campbell, John and Ove Pedersen. 2001. *The Rise of Neoliberalism and Institutional Analysis.* Princeton, NJ: Princeton University Press. Dohner, Richard and Ponciano Intal. 1989. "The Aquino Government and Prospects for the Economy." In *Developing Country Debt and Economic Performance* Volume 3, edited by Jeffrey Sachs and Susan M. Collins. Chicago, IL: Chicago University Press.

Dreyfus, Hubert. 1972. *What Computers Can't Do.* New York: Harper & Row.

Giddens, Anthony. 1993. *New Rules of Sociological Metho.* Cambridge: Polity Press.

Harvey, David. 2005. *A Brief History of Neoliberalism.* Oxford, New York: Oxford University Press.

Hodgson, Geoffrey and Thobjorn Knudsen. 2006. "Why We Need a Generalized Darwinism, and Why Generalized Darwinism is Not Enough." *Journal of Economic Behavior and Organization* 61(1):1–19.

Holland, Dorothy, William Lachoite, Debra Skinner, and Carole Cain. 1998. *Identity and Agency in Cultural Worlds.* Cambridge, MA: Harvard University Press.

Jayasuriya, Sisira. 1992. "Structural Adjustment and Economic Performance in the Philippines." In *The Dynamics of Economic Policy Reform in South-East Asia and the South-West Pacific*, edited by Andrew MacIntyre and Kanishka Jayasuriya. Singapore: Oxford University Press.

Joaquin, Nick. 1999. *Manila, My Manila: A History for the Young.* Manila: Bookmark.

Jomo, Kwame Sundaram, eds. 2001. *Southeast Asia's Industrialization: Industrial Policy, Capabilities and Sustainability.* London: Palgrave Macmillan.

Lave, Jean. 1991. "Socially Shared Cognition." In *Perspectives on Socially Shared Cognition*, edited by Lauren B. Resnick, John M. Levine, and Stephanie D. Teasley. Washington, DC: American Psychological Association, 63–82.

Lave, Jean and Etienne Wenger. 1991. *Situated Learning: Legitimate Peripheral Participation.* Cambridge: Cambridge University Press.

Lindsey, Charles. 1992. "The Political Economy of International Economic Policy Reform in the Philippines: Continuity and Restoration." In *The Dynamic of Economic Policy Reform in South-East Asia and the South-West Pacific*, edited by Andrew MacIntyre and Kanishka Jayasuriya. Singapore: Oxford University Press.

Mahoney, James and Kathleen Thelen. 2009. *Explaining Institutional Change: Ambiguity, Agency and Power.* Cambridge: Cambridge University Press.

North, Douglas. 1990. *Institutions, Institutional Change and Economic Performance.* Cambridge: Cambridge University Press.

Ortmann, Stephan and Mark Thompson. 2016. "China and the 'Singapore Model'." *Journal of Democracy* 1(27):39–48.

Quimpo, Susan and Nathan Gilbert Quimpo. 2012. *Subversive Lives: A Family Memoir of the Marcos Years.* Ohio: Ohio University Press.

## 38   *Robin Michael Garcia*

Ramo, Joshua Copoper. 2004. *The Beijing Consensus.* London: Foreign Policy Center.

Santa Romana, Jose Santiago "Chito." 2016. "Interview by Lucio Pitlo III." *Department of Political Science, National Taiwan University: For China Studies and Cross Taiwan Strait Relations*, 14 April. Retrieved 29 March 2018 (http://www.china-studies.taipei/act02.php).

Schmidt, Vivien. 2010. "Taking Ideas and Discourse Seriously: Explaining Change Through Discursive Institutionalism as the 'Fourth' New Institutionalism." *European Political Science Review* 2(1):1–25.

Shih, Chih-Yu. 2013. *Sinicizing International Relations: Self, Civilization, and Intellectual Politics in Subaltern East Asia.* New York: Palgrave Macmillan.

Streeck, Wolfgang and Kathleen Thelen, eds. 2005. *Beyond Continuity: Institutional Change in Advanced Political Economies.* Oxford: Oxford University Press.

Tang, Shiping. 2011. "Foundational Paradigms of Social Sciences." *Philosophy of the Social Sciences* 41(2):211–249.

Tang, Shiping. 2012. *A General Theory of Institutional Change.* London: Routledge.

Tang, Shiping. 2013. *The Social Evolution of International Politics.* New York: Oxford University Press.

Thelen, Kathleen and James Mahoney, eds. 2009. *Explaining Institutional Change: Ambiguity, Agency and Power.* London: Cambridge University Press.

Velasco, Renato. 1997. "Philippine Democracy: Promise and Performance." In *Democratization in Southeast and East Asia*, edited by Anek Laothamatas. New York: St. Martin's Press.

Wenger, Etienne. 1998. *Communities of Practice: Learning, Meaning and Identity.* Cambridge: Cambridge University Press.

Wertsch, James. 1985. *Vygotsky and the Social Formation of the Mind.* Cambridge, MA: Harvard University Press.

# 3 From taboo thinkers to thought leaders

## Media, Chinese politics, and diplomacy

*Jose Mari Hall Lanuza*

### Introduction

The intellectual histories of Jaime FlorCruz and Eric Baculinao, former exiled students-turned-Filipino journalists working for foreign media outlets in Beijing, provide a rich context alongside a historicization of China's paradigms of interaction with mass media, allowing a view of how China's changing approach to political communication affects its domestic and foreign policy.

China's interesting position in the world as an emerging hegemon comes with challenges in peacefully maneuvering the spaces in domestic, regional, and international politics (He 2016). These challenges are further complicated by China's Party-state political setup, where virtually all facets of political, economic, social, and cultural life are determined by the Chinese Communist Party (Guo 2013). While China seeks to remain in control, it projects itself as a state that allows some democratic space for political participation in aid of increasing its political values capital (Li and Worm 2011). This exercise can be seen as an exhibition of soft power, which China can use to consolidate regional influence. Soft power has been conceptualized to come from three different sources: culture, political values, and foreign policy (Nye 2006). In addition, other scholars have added economic model, international image, and economic temptation as other possible sources (Li and Worm 2011).

For China, the portrayal of a partially democratic image means allowing a certain degree of openness to mass media without necessarily compromising party influence in state operations. Tight or lax control over media is contingent on whether media outlets are "inside" or "outside" (Yamada 2011). The evolution of state policy on Party-state relationship with the media has a lot to do with the evolution of the Party's ideology more than anything else.

The media is a factor in Chinese policy making, albeit one with a difficult role to analyze, given China's nondemocratic setup (Wang and Wang 2014). This role, which will be expounded on later in the text, has carefully expanded over the years thanks to the opening up of Chinese policy on media (Chinascope 2011; Stockmann 2013; Tibetan Review 2009; Zhang 2016), but

## 40  *Jose Mari Hall Lanuza*

the state of press freedom in China remains very poor to this day (Freedom House 2016; He 2008; Shirk 2011) and censorship is still the norm. This dynamic of Party control and influence together with market-adapting behavior has defined mass media in China (Scotton and Hachten 2010).

### Mass media during Mao's China

When the Communist Party came into power in 1949, there was a reorganization of all state institutions and policies. During this period, media was viewed and characterized as an ideological state apparatus that served to echo the regime's ideological leanings and views (Chang 1989; Zhang 2016; Zhao 1998), which was referred to as thought work (Kalathil 2003). The Party quickly capitalized on the political potential of mass media and developed newspapers and periodicals. This was done to promote Marxist propaganda and prepare the people for a new ideological status quo in China (Chang 1989; Zhang 2016).

During the early 1950s, the Party had already controlled virtually all mass media outlets, from printing presses to radio stations (He 2008). By this period, the Party-led government had incorporated the entire media structure into their own operations. More than promote Marxist ideology, mass media was now being used as a Party organ for dissemination of information, values, and other traits and characteristics (Zhang 2016) beneficial in maintaining the influence of the Party.

In 1957, Mao Zedong delivered a speech on propaganda work, where he said the now-famous quote "let a hundred flowers bloom and a hundred schools of thought contend." Essentially, Mao called not for restriction but for the open encouragement of opposing views in information dissemination in the public sphere (Mao 1957). However, this was difficult to realize since the Party owned nearly all media organs and used them to saturate the public with content that helped establish the Party and its ideology. Journalism was equated with state propaganda before the reforms, and media outlets were used to control popular opinion (Shirk 2011). This period was also the time of the Great Leap Forward, where exaggerated figures of production were reported in the press (Zhang 2016).

Another important use of the media for China is to create an alternative image internationally (Rawnsley 2015; Romashkan 2013), which had already been used for that purpose during Mao's time, regardless of whether the created image then was accurate (He 2008). Even the foreign language presses were already co-opted into this purpose during that time (Alvaro 2015). By using the media as such, the Party was able to co-opt mass media into the state's political machinery. This allowed the Party-state to produce a strong ideological narrative that was able to form a collective identity which adhered to the Party-state's teachings.

The late early 1970s was a period where opening up to the West and the rest of the world was being contemplated. In fact, the Party-state allowed

*From taboo thinkers to thought leaders*  41

many tourists (including Americans and Canadians), who came in their private capacity, for brief stays in mainland China. These trips were part of a plan to build diplomatic relations with foreign countries. Such exchanges helped China in many aspects of development and modernization, such as science and industry (Wang 1999), athletics (Hong and Sun 2010), and foreign relations. These stays targeted people of different backgrounds—journalists, activists, educators, among others—and were usually invited by the government through "quasi-government agencies" (FlorCruz 2015; Lin 2016). Non-governmental organizations such as the China Travel Service and the Chinese People's Association for Friendship with Foreign Countries arranged (highly controlled) tourism appointments through the National Committee on US-China Relations (Lin 2016). In the experience of Baculinao and FlorCruz, it was the government who invited them and other progressive student leaders through the China Friendship Association (FlorCruz 2015).

Baculinao and FlorCruz were students in the Philippines at the time of the Cultural Revolution. Baculinao was a law student from the University of the Philippines, an institution known for being highly progressive and anti-imperialist. He was also the student regent in 1970–1971, a seat for student representation in the university's highest policy-making body. FlorCruz was a campus journalist from the Polytechnic University of the Philippines and a member of nationalist organizations. FlorCruz explained how he became sympathetic with the left movement:

> There was the influence of Mao Zedong's ideas among student groups like ours; we were looking for alternative models in terms of how we could change the country. We were influenced by Mao's ideas on land reform; we opposed the Vietnam War and called for freedom of expression and assembly. For that, some people branded us Maoists. But apparently, I hardly understood what Mao said. Before I went to Peking, I was attending PUP, where I was editor in chief of our college paper. And I was concurrently the President of the League of Editors for a Democratic Society, which was one of the national college editors associations. I was also active in a nationalist theatre group.
>
> (FlorCruz 2015:2)

This sympathy with the left produced opportunities. Both of them had interests in China and was invited by the Chinese government for a short trip to China. Seen as nationalist and anti-imperialist youth, they were offered a chance to come to China in 1971. Baculinao explains how this chance turned into a 15-year stay in China:

> [I began as a China watcher] in exile. It was by accident, a political accident. We came to China in 1971 together with a youth delegation, planning to visit China for 3 weeks, but a few days after we arrived in

42  *Jose Mari Hall Lanuza*

Beijing, there were bombings in Manila, and the writ of habeas corpus was suspended. Marcos was arresting lots of students and anyone in opposition, and then one year later, it went on to full Martial Law. I thought I would wait for two months, or a year or so; but in fact, we ended up waiting for 15 years, because had we gone home, we would have been arrested ... At that point, I had already finished studying Chinese and I mentally became prepared for a long stay in China. I started working in media and China was becoming interesting intellectually, with all the reforms being launched by Deng. By 1986, the Marcos regime was toppled and I could go home, since I got my passport back. However, China was changing, and that kept me going. I wanted to know what would happen to the so-called opening up of China, and before I knew it, forty-four years had gone by.

(Baculinao 2015:1–2)

The day they left for China was the day of the Plaza Miranda bombing, which was followed by a series of other bombing incidents in Manila. Soon after, the writ of habeas corpus was suspended and the students thought that it would be best to stay since they may be arrested and detained indefinitely the moment they step on Philippine soil. Eventually, other members of the group were able to return, but Baculinao and FlorCruz were blacklisted with some other members of the group and were not able to return. Thus, they lived like the Chinese during the Cultural Revolution:

The trend at that time was to go the farms. So we worked on a farm in Hunan province for about seven months. We woke up early at five in the morning. But we were not required to work the whole day. The initial deal was to work in the mornings through noon or until early in the afternoon. After working, we studied to learn Chinese—elementary Chinese—from an interpreter who went with us. He doubled as our Mandarin teacher. And we did that for, like, 3 months, until we were conversant in Chinese. After the interpreter went back to Beijing, we began working almost the whole day. It was very difficult because we had not done any farming in our lives. It was very romantic in the beginning. We were not really paid; we got a monthly stipend, 40 yuans, which was a lot of money at that time. We also had free board and lodging at the farm.

(FlorCruz 2015:3)

When martial law was declared, they realized that they would be staying longer, and so they asked to work again to be able to live. They learned more about China through reading and talking with their guides or friends that they worked with. Later on, they were also able to study in universities and learn more about China formally and informally, through engaged discussions with peers.

## Mass media in the post-Mao era

China's economic reforms after Mao died in 1976 also resulted in paradigm shifts with the mass media. Baculinao (2015) reflects that before the reforms, there were limited materials accessible to the people, other than *People's Daily*, *Red Flag*, and other theoretical publications. For foreigners in China then, learning about China had to be a personal endeavor about learning Mandarin to understand the government programs:

> There were very limited publications in China at that point in time, but by studying the language, we learned what political programs of the Communist Party of China [were there that] would help us understand where China was going, and what direction it was taking at that point in time ... I went to school in China to study language, and all the rest about learning and understanding China was on my own, with my acquired language facility. I learned to read all possible books about China that were available in Beijing. There weren't that many in the 1970s, early 80s; not that many publications. Now of course, there are many books about China—but in those days, very limited.
>
> (Baculinao 2015:2)

After Mao died, China opened up: the economy to external markets, the society to other reforms. At the same time, mass media was allowed to be self-sustaining through market competition and advertisements (Shirk 2011). The reforms allowed China's economy to grow, which also allowed for the proliferation and diversification of mass media (Zhang 2016). China's opening up also led to a relatively less centrally controlled news reporting (Guan, Xia, and Cheng 2016), a sentiment that also resonated with Baculinao (2015:2):

> China's open door policy meant that its media policies had to be reformed over time. Indeed, that Beijing now boasts of what probably is the biggest foreign press corps in Asia attests to the advances made, especially after the Beijing Olympics, although strict controls do remain.

Aside from media expansion, media marketization from the late 1970s also led to a few other things: the import of cultural and media content from foreign media companies, the build-up of Chinese international networks for image-formation internationally, and the advancement of media technology (Zhang 2016). The growth of Chinese media has also allowed it to be a big part of the economy (Hong 2010), thus becoming a great asset to the state. All of these contribute to China's reconfiguration of its media policies following the reforms. Instead of being reactive, China retained the lessons it got from its Leninist influence of treating the media as a powerful tool for consolidation and proactively used the old and new forms and structures of mass media for its own benefit.

44   *Jose Mari Hall Lanuza*

It did this through a policy referred to as the need to provide correct guidance to public opinion, especially after the Tiananmen Square Incident in 1989 (Chan 2007). It is important to notice the difference in the Party's approach to public opinion formation. Whereas, in the past, they resorted to censorship and outright suppression of public opinion unrepresentative of Party teachings, the changing times led them to instead guide or direct the flow of public opinion. More than limiting what people can think about, the Party-state now decided to use the media to change what people can think of *instead* (Chan 2007) and what people can ignore. This was also a period where people were not discouraged from debating and discussing what happened during the Cultural Revolution, and what was next for China, according to FlorCruz (2015):

> But it was also a time of reflection – a time when students and teachers were debating about what happened in the Cultural Revolution; where China should go; and what it meant to reform China. It was just the beginning of that period. There was this intellectual ferment and they called it, "the liberation of the mind" – wherein people were really starting to break away from the dogmas of the recent eras, and to think out of the box and just debate about where we should go from here.
>
> (FlorCruz 2015:5–6)

These were changing times for China, and Baculinao and FlorCruz were able to experience them firsthand as people who lived through the experiences, and as journalists who covered them as well thanks to the entry of foreign media in China. Without making the false assumption that China exhibits absolute press freedom, it is important to note that gradually China has eased a certain level of control over media—not to the extent that it can create and influence effective dissent against the state but enough to create spaces of discourse that differ from the officially sanctioned views and directives propagated by the state. Surely, China has had changes in the overall sense of public communication allowed. FlorCruz (2015) provides an example of the interconnected changes to China's economy and mass media:

> China in 1971 and China now are as different as night and day. There is a huge billboard in a Beijing intersection which advertises Nokia phones or some commercial product. When I first saw that signboard over forty years ago, it carried the slogan "NEVER FORGET CLASS STRUGGLE." That shows how much China has changed over the years.
>
> (FlorCruz 2015:12)

This change reflects not only the ideological shift in media and public communication but also in economy and society, with a more globalized and commercialized mass media changing its messages according to

*From taboo thinkers to thought leaders* 45

demand—whether from domestic commercial and ideological demands or from international moral and ethical requirements.

In another instance, in 2001, despite being more ideologically open compared to decades before, the Party-state exercised a sort of mass media cleansing, where closure of publications was enforced, and journalists were taken in for political training in Beijing (Kalathil 2003). At the same time, the opening up has led the mass media to pursue topics that would have previously been considered as either taboo or contrary to the values and ideals being promulgated by the Party.

Eventually, both Baculinao and FlorCruz were able to get jobs in journalism: with Baculinao starting as a translator and researcher for media companies and a columnist for a Hong Kong paper, and FlorCruz starting as a stringer for Newsweek's newly opened Beijing Bureau in 1981 and Time Magazine in 1982. Baculinao eventually settled at NBC's Beijing bureau, where he later on became bureau chief. FlorCruz became Time's Beijing bureau chief from 1990 to 2000, which then led him to take a fellowship in New York from the Council of Foreign Relations (CFR). After his fellowship, he was offered a position in China as a CNN correspondent and bureau chief.

As foreign journalists in the media, they are "hosted by the Chinese foreign ministry. That is the official relationship, a professional relationship whereby we are able to do our work, do interviews ... but we have to follow the rules of China. It's a very professional relationship" (Baculinao 2015:14). Therefore, their engagements with the Chinese government are purely professional, and their journalism is also bound by what the government deems within the acceptable range, further proving that while there are attempts at loosening up, press freedom is still farfetched.

## Contemporary Chinese mass media

These shared and similar track of experiences have produced similar interpretations of Chinese foreign policy and state relations. The views of Baculinao and FlorCruz' on how to resolve the disputes between China and the Philippines, which are spread throughout their networks in the Philippines and other countries through talks, fora, and literature, are discussed in this chapter as a product of their lived experiences both as exiled youth and student leaders, and as members of the media who get to interact with both the Chinese government and Chinese academic societies.

For instance, the need for greater understanding of China on the side of Philippine policy makers and citizens alike is recognized. Baculinao even goes so far as to say that there is a strong, passionate appeal to national interest that—albeit positive—also restricts and hinders Philippine creativity in imagining other possible peacebuilding scenarios with China (2015). In this light, the call for more agents of Chinese understanding is recognized and advocated for by both Baculinao and FlorCruz, especially in Track 2 diplomacy engagements.

46  *Jose Mari Hall Lanuza*

The explicit call for the creation of mutual understanding and greater development of knowledge of China in the Philippines works positively for both countries. For the Philippines, such calls by thought leaders offer a more prudent alternative to Philippines-China relations, which aims to maximize Philippine gains without jeopardizing domestic interests. China, on the other hand, gains non-Chinese allies which can see both sides and offer analyses and insights that are more understanding than abrasive to China in general. That these outcomes exist from a China that is more open to foreign media shows how foreign media can affect Chinese foreign policy.

Socially, aside from limited approval to tackle once-taboo topics, the reforms have led the Party-state to accord certain rights to foreign mass media. The Foreign Correspondents' Club of China—which Baculinao is affiliated with—is allowed to exist and operate, and foreign press corps are free to join. Furthermore, it acts as a mediator between foreign press corps and the Party-state in terms of protection and representation. Foreign media members are also allowed to participate in international endeavors of a journalistic nature, such as fellowships hosted by foreign institutions like the CFR (FlorCruz 2015). They are also allowed to interact (although not extensively) with academic institutions as *scholars* and not just as journalists (Baculinao 2015).

However, it is wrong to equate China's market liberalization with media liberalization (He 2008); in fact, China has continuously re-instituted and re-removed oppressive policies on mass media in China in the 2000s, depending on its situation. FlorCruz illustrates the difficulties of gathering data in China:

> only three decades ago, weather forecast in China was virtually considered a state secret. Phone numbers of officials and government agencies were also difficult, often impossible, to obtain. Twenty-five years ago, reporters were permitted nothing more than carefully guided visits and predictable interviews. Until 2007, on the eve of the 2008 Olympics hosted by Beijing, foreign reporters in China were not allowed to travel and conduct interviews outside Beijing unless they secured permission from local foreign affairs offices 10 days in advance. Of course, we had to defy that rule to do our usual job as reporters. That "10 day rule", ridiculous as it was, was not rescinded until 2007. Now, as China evolves into a freer, more pluralistic society, getting timely information, conducting interviews, and going on reporting trips have become relatively easier.
>
> (FlorCruz 2015:10)

The evolution of China's relationship with the media post-reforms has resembled a very limited granting of autonomy. China's responsive or adaptive authoritarianism (Han 2015; Stockmann 2013) has allowed Chinese media to both retain its credibility and become profitable. It did so by allowing a

*From taboo thinkers to thought leaders*  47

change of role for the Chinese media—the creation of a narrative that promoted more liberal values as well as a new national undertaking: building a wealthy and powerful China (Zhang 2016). Moreover, it has allowed the Party to capitalize on both of these while at the same time continue using the media to not only retain control domestically but also project its power and rise internationally.

For China's state-owned media, Chan (2007) argues that it has changed its role to an agenda-setting one in the 1990s, signaling the shift from propaganda to hegemony. The same can be said of foreign media, requiring China to reconfigure policies especially with regards to how the news was depicted and what outcomes it can produce in terms of public and international opinion. This narrative-forming ability has been easier to use due to the shift in media regulation policies.

The reforms have had unintended consequences for the Party-state and Chinese media. The opening up of the media to foreign networks have allowed the emergence of media outlets that have more autonomy compared to domestic networks, especially in airing and publishing views that are not necessarily similar in substance to the official views propagated by the Party.

The entry of foreign outlets such as NBC and CNN, where Baculinao and FlorCruz work, among others has also served dual purposes for China. First, it has served as additional windows with which the world can see China, or at least a version of China that the Party-state wants the world to see (He 2008). China has also cooperated with foreign media to offer spaces of publication domestically in exchange for rights to run state-media articles in foreign media, such as *The Washington Post, The Sydney Morning Herald*, and *Le Figaro* (Gan 2016), in order to boost soft power.

At the same time, it has also served as additional windows that can see past the pre-produced image that China wants to project and instead show the parts of Chinese society that the Party-state wants to remain hidden. The presence of relatively freer foreign media in China acts as a spotlight on Party-state activities for the rest of the world to see. In line with the watchdog role (Wang and Wang 2014), foreign media can influence actions of the Party-state from local to national levels.

On top of this, the introduction of the Internet and social media has made it harder for the State to control what news can be aired or not. Communication has now become instantaneous, and citizens have the power to report on news that the Party might otherwise find ill-suited for public consumption but have a very short time of controlling (Shirk 2011). The China Internet Network Information Center in 2008 found that people use the internet more for information than any other mass media outlet (Scotton and Hachten 2010). More than the fast flow of information, the internet affords an alternative to traditional "top-down messaging" (Mayer and Cornfield 2008).

This has made the internet a public hub of citizens with an enabling variable for changing power relations (Mayer and Cornfield 2008) between

48   *Jose Mari Hall Lanuza*

the citizens and the state. In China, internet and new media are seen as an alternative to mainstream journalism. This is understandable, given that scholars argue that journalism in China adheres to more of a lapdog than a watchdog role since 1989 and that journalists (save for a few others) mostly accept the limitations set by the Propaganda Department (Brady 2006).

In response, the Party-state has invested a large amount of funds for internet control mechanisms (He 2008) and surveillance technology (Walton 2001), with politics and pornography as the main targeted content online (Scotton and Hachten 2010). This makes sense on the part of the Party-state: all variables that can cause instability (or at least unwanted change) must be kept checked to preserve the status quo, which benefits the Party-state. This control manifests in the form of China's Golden Shield project (Walton 2001), a massive online policing mechanism and control system (He 2008). The government also has measures in place for bureaucratic controls, such as website licensing. In 1999, 250 websites applied to be one of the accredited websites that were allowed to display news content; of these, only 136 were approved (Brady 2006).

But China's responsive authoritarianism has enabled it to react beyond the censorship-freedom of expression nexus and instead move to control the discussion and the narrative through the use of state-sponsored internet commentators or what Han calls the "fifty-cent army" (Han 2015). Thus, the Party-state is able to control or at least affect discourse in the public sphere.

What is constant from China's unique interaction with the media is how it has continuously recognized the role of mass media for consolidation of power and influence, and adapted as a consequence. The relationship between the Party-state and mass media has evolved primarily as a consequence of China's political-economic development. As the Party-state's ideology evolved and became less abrasive about opening up, their control with the mass media—with moments of tightening grips in between—has also relatively loosened up, although more as a function of influence consolidation than democratization. While mass media has flourished from its days of simply being a Party mouthpiece, the process of opening the media up was seen as a chance at strengthening Party control, by painting mass media as a reliable and credible source of information again (Stockmann 2013).

This has allowed for a two-way dynamic between the Chinese state and Chinese mass media (Wang and Wang 2014), where media can become either a civil society watchdog or a lapdog for the state. Moreover, this has also resulted in a change with how China uses the media for its soft power. While it strives to maximize the gains from a mass media that is still somewhat controlled by the Party but remains credible, has international reach, and is profitable, China also becomes more careful of allowing this same mass media to report on its shortcomings or any other event that might be construed as contributory to the weakening of nationalism and loyalty to the Party-state (not necessarily the Party).

## China and the production of narratives

China's state mass media has been successful in weaving narratives that have largely been effective in maintaining the Party-state's influence. The processes that produce these narratives are not necessarily democratic or even transparent. That is not the purpose. These are narratives that are designed to make the Party-state look credible and efficient. In contrast, narratives made by non-state media are not always seen as beneficial or good to the Party-state, and for good reason.

According to Baculinao (2015), despite China's opening up to Western media in the 80s, China was still a very challenging beat for journalists then:

> many places were still off-limits to foreigners. In general, foreign media had to deal with lots of restrictions and other bureaucratic hurdles, especially if the stories involved travelling outside Beijing. Permissions had to be obtained in advance, and if the stories were deemed "sensitive" — politically, socially, militarily—permits would prove very difficult ... Reporting from China in the 80s—when Deng's open door policies were beginning to take effect—had two characteristics: one, the world was hungry for information about China and curious about where post-Mao China was heading toward. China news had a huge market, so to speak. Two, China's bureaucracy and the Western media were like strangers to each other, and news coverage had to contend with many tough and exasperating Chinese rules and restrictions.
>
> (Baculinao 2015:3)

This reflects the still-existent distrust that the Party-state has over non-state media, and more so for foreign non-state media. This distrust stems from the process of narrative production by the foreign media. Since they are less predictable and the news content is not filtered by the Party-state, it is easier for China to prohibit access and dissemination altogether, especially in times of vulnerability. As a response, the Party-state places more restrictions that hinder foreign media journalism. There are cases where foreign journalists are harassed and isolated from local scholars or opinion-makers (FlorCruz 2015; Wang 2017).

Furthermore, foreign media are also often targets of media blackouts and bans that prohibit them from broadcasting anything (Timmons and Huang 2016; Xu and Albert 2017). In March 2017, a crew from BBC China was attacked and forced by the police to sign a confession for trying to conduct an "illegal interview" on land reform in rural China (Haas 2017; Sudworth 2017). FlorCruz has also had similar experiences:

> We often encounter that when we travel in towns and cities to do unpalatable stories—fatal accidents, corruption cases, street protests or labor unrest, etc. Local officials do not want the media there because they

know that we are sniffing at unpalatable issues that, in their mind, will embarrass them, or will tarnish the image of their place, thus possibly turning off tourists or investors, or will simply get them into trouble with their higher supervisors. So sometimes, they employ local police or thugs to shadow, confront, or intimidate us ostensibly because we had no official permit. Or they come up with other excuses. In 2001, when we tried to do a story on the AIDS epidemic spreading in Henan villages because of the sale of blood for money, we had to sneak into a village with the help of Chinese NGOs. To get our stories, we had to play hide and seek with local officials and police so we could interview victims' families, shoot in the villages, and get out safely to tell our stories. In rare cases, harassment involved brief detention and questioning by local police whenever we got busted. That happened to our crew when we tried to cover labor unrest in Guangzhou, a sad story which involved cases of overworked and disturbed migrant workers committing suicide by jumping off buildings.

(FlorCruz 2015:10–11)

The Party-state's control over mass media's production of narratives—in an effort to create a good international image—can largely be seen as a success, as measured by the massive flow of foreign investments into the Chinese economy (He 2008). Although China has lost its position as the top destination for foreign direct investments to the United States and Hong Kong, it still ranks as the second-most attractive economy for multinational companies from 2016 to 2018, and foreign direct investment inward flows and stocks have been increasing from 2013 to 2015 (UNCTAD 2016).

A peaceful rise is most optimal for the case of China, a rising power (He 2016) since its focus is still on internal development rather than external conquest, and its culture favors moral strength over military power (Li and Worm 2011). For it to receive peaceful accommodation, it needs to put up a favorable image, one that is more in line with the standards of the current hegemon. In an international political realm that has sovereign states as the most basic unit, this means respecting sovereignty and maneuvering around established rules and boundaries. Therefore, it is important for China to maintain this favorable image.

One case study follows the 2011 Wukan rebellion and the role of foreign media in resolving the issue. Protests ensued in the village of Wukan in Guangdong Province following the death of a local village representative after meeting with local government officials. This resulted in an armed standoff between villagers and local police and anti-riot troops, which was covered by foreign media. The study showed that due to the pressure of being portrayed negatively in front of a global audience, higher ranking provincial officers negotiated a resolution with the protest leaders after days of conflict (Hess 2014).

*From taboo thinkers to thought leaders*   51

This shows that media can be political actors in the sense that their power to form public and international opinion is seen as a delicate variable by the Chinese Party-state, who is aiming to be seen as a peaceful and nonaggressive rising power. The unwanted international attention stems from the notion that China's development has two extremes: the remarkable growth of China's economy by international standards, and the increasing attention being given to the social costs of this growth, manifesting in domestic inequalities and environmental degradation (Hou 2014). These qualities are deemed unacceptable for a rising power aiming to be the new world hegemon. Thus, China tries its best to curb reports on these issues.

In general, foreign media portrayal of China has been perceived as mixed to negative, with perceptions to its political system and its actions on disputes as the main cause. According to Wang Qiu, a member of the legislature and head of a state-owned radio station, around 60 percent of all Western media can be seen as a negative campaign against China (Allen-Ebrahimian 2016).

Moreover, this has caused negative perceptions for China. In one case, Gallardo and Baviera found that the Philippine media had negative portrayals of China in light of the Philippines-China maritime disputes, and in effect the citizens echoed these sentiments (2013). There have also been international backlashes over certain incidents, such as the China's rare earths export trade dispute (Nikkei Asian Review 2016; Stahl 2015) and the questionable record on human rights (Calgary Herald 2008; Deutsche Well 2008). However, it is observable that in some cases, the Party-state made adjustments to its policies for appeasement purposes—whether for domestic or international opinions. China did drop its export restrictions in 2015, although after first struggling with the decision made by the World Trade Organization. Also as a response to both domestic and international concerns, China officially addressed its environmental problems, although the results have been criticized as inadequate (Silk 2013).

This is not to say that foreign media in China has only reported negatively about China. If anything, foreign media has tried its best to be objective in reporting. In the case of Baculinao and FlorCruz, they are seen as third-party media personnel—meaning neither Westerners nor West-influenced, nor purely Chinese. In addition to this, they have been in China since the days of the Cultural Revolution. These two factors award them a certain amount of trust. They cover news and current events for NBC and CNN bureaus in Beijing, respectively. They also maintain a strict policy on keeping neutral especially in public communication, as a sign of respect and loyalty to journalism. Although they do engage with the public as opinion-makers, they perform this role not only as media personnel but also as scholars, especially when engaging with outsiders on an informal basis.

Both of them engage with the public outside of China through talks and fora in schools and Filipino communities inside and outside the Philippines. In their case, their public engagements call for more understanding for

## 52   *Jose Mari Hall Lanuza*

China and greater improvement in bilateral relations (Baculinao 2015; Flor-Cruz 2015). These engagements affect perceptions of China by scholars and policy makers alike. For Baculinao, there needs to be more understanding on the side of the Philippines as to why China acts the way it does:

> There is so much ideological baggage that constricts our views of what possible strategies can be used to engage the Chinese and to win our case with China on our maritime disputes, successfully and peacefully. Sometimes I'd like try to explore different approaches and ideas, but I can immediately sense a sense of resistance.
>
> And I think maybe it's because nationalism is an important factor. It's natural to encounter resistance, especially if you challenge conventional positions; you run the risk of being called anti-nationalist or unpatriotic, even if it's not the case. I think the main difficulty of breaking through our restricted understanding of China is the fact that we are so passionate about our national interest—which is a very positive thing—that sometimes we neglect to see the weaknesses of our own positions, of our own understanding, which then leads us to very weak strategies or tactics; weak in the sense that they cannot conceivably lead to a peaceful negotiated outcome of our disputes.
>
> (Baculinao 2015:15)

Baculinao argued this point as well in a forum at the University of the Philippines last January 2016 on prospects of people-centered policy actions for Asian development and peace, where members of the academe and representatives from government agencies were in attendance.

Similarly, FlorCruz also stressed the fostering of greater understanding, more so by having more China watchers in the Philippines:

> I think understanding China is one of the pressing needs. We all agree that China will be important as a neighbor and as a global player. So obviously, we should know how to co-exist amicably with China, and the first step is to understand it. Hopefully China will seek to understand the Philippines as well. But on our part, I really hope that we can boost our knowledge about the country by developing more China watchers, people who really focus on the task of learning about it and then imparting the knowledge to the general population and sharing it to the policymakers. It is about time to do that, and one step to do that is through collective wisdom of our China watchers, who are too few.
>
> (FlorCruz 2015:13)

That two Beijing-based Filipino journalists from foreign media outlets promote more understanding of China is reflective of how fair foreign media can be. Foreign media are less impervious to Party-state influence, and thus are more able to portray aspects both favorable and unfavorable to Party-state agenda. Similar statements have also been echoed by other foreign

*From taboo thinkers to thought leaders* 53

journalists in China (Yuan 2010). Baculinao and FlorCruz are more unique than the other foreign journalists because of their long experience in China. Their exposure to the gradual reforming of China has granted them a lens which enables understanding despite being non-citizens.

## Closing remarks

The experiences of Baculinao and FlorCruz—living through the Cultural Revolution, witnessing first-hand the reforms following Mao's death, covering important moments in Chinese history—have given them a certain level of trust from the Chinese. They are not seen as complete outsiders devoid of understanding Chinese politics and society. Rather, they are third-country observers who are able to analyze China with a historical appreciation and understanding. Moreover, this deep understanding of China and the Party-state stems from China's attempts at opening itself up: first, to the world by inviting/accommodating young scholars, such as Baculinao and FlorCruz, to live in China in the 1970s; and second, to the media by allowing more leeway for reporting and data gathering. These initiatives have produced organic intellectuals and observers who can explain China's position in the international arena without being seen as Party-state puppets precisely because of their status as third-country observers.

Media can shape policy. Specifically, how mass media reports on a certain issue creates public and international opinion can shape both domestic and foreign policy. This in turn can be favorable or unfavorable for the state concerned, causing it to respond accordingly through policy formation or revoker. In the case of China, its peaceful rise is contingent on two things: the international image depicted by both its own media and the foreign media, and how convincing this image is for the international community. As such, there is more at stake for China in terms of ensuring positive mass media coverage.

Foreign mass media in China is able to affect Chinese policy because the Chinese Party-state has given it the power to do so, as seen in both the cases discussed above and in the experiences of Baculinao and FlorCruz. The prospect of mass media's potential as a catalyst for change was virtually nil during the days where it acted as a mere Party mouthpiece. However, major sociopolitical reforms and regional political interests required the Chinese Party-state to open up mass media and allow media outlets with more leeway into a brand of journalism which did not simply echo Party statements. The change in China's treatment of mass media resulted in the emergence of mass media's potential as both a destabilizing agent and a bridge to the outside world.

For Baculinao and FlorCruz, their ability to be media practitioners as well as thought leaders who advocate for greater understanding of China independently from the Party-state shows how China's change in mass media interaction has produced political actors which can be helpful to China's cause: a peaceful rise in the region. Baculinao and FlorCruz have been shaped by their experiences in a changing China, and they have been witnesses to the ideological shifts as well as victims to the Party-state's policies on mass media.

## 54 *Jose Mari Hall Lanuza*

More than this, their own worldviews were also influenced by the events surrounding China's reforms since these were *lived* experiences. The policy reforms have also helped Baculinao and FlorCruz see and understand China as a dynamic and changing society, with its own challenges and problems, rather than a monolithic entity controlled by the Chinese Communist Party. As such, they are able to see things from China's point of view without being blind to the interests of the Philippines and other countries with whom China has disputes.

### References

Allen-Ebrahimian, Bethany. 2016. "How China Won the War Against Western Media." *Foreign Policy.* Retrieved from http://foreignpolicy.com/2016/03/04/china-won-war-western-media-censorship-propaganda-communist-party/.

Alvaro, Joseph James. 2015. "Analysing China's English-Language Media." *World Englishes* 260–277.

Baculinao, Eric. 2015. "Interview by Jose Mari Hall Lanuza." *Department of Political Science, National Taiwan University: For China Studies and Cross Taiwan Strait Relations,* 3 November. Retrieved 1 March 2018 (http://www.china-studies.taipei/act02.php).

Brady, Anne-Marie. 2006. "Guiding Hand: The Role of the CCP Central Propaganda Department in the Current Era." *Westminster Papers in Communication and Culture* 3(1): 58–77.

Calgary Herald. 2008. "China's Un-Olympic Human Rights Record." *Calgary Herald,* 9 August. Retrieved from https://web.archive.org/web/20090625133402/http://www2.canada.com:80/calgaryherald/news/theeditorialpage/story.html?id=c06e4f24-ea77-467c-960e-abc94721e094.

Chan, Alex. 2007. "Guiding Public Opinion Through Social Agenda-Setting: China's Media Policy Since the 1990s." *Journal of Contemporary China* 16(53):547–559.

Chang, Wan Ho. 1989. *Mass Media in China.* Ames: Iowa State University Press.

Chinascope. 2011. "Party Official Promises to Protect the Rights of Foreign Media in China." *China Scope,* 29 September. Retrieved from http://chinascope.org/archives/2788.

Deutsche Welle. 2008. "Protesters Rally in Europe on Eve of China Olympics." *Deutsche Welle,* 8 July. Retrieved from http://www.dw.com/en/protestors-rally-in-europe-on-eve-of-china-olympics/a-3545274.

FlorCruz, Jaime. 2015. "Interview by Robin Michael Garcia." *Department of Political Science, National Taiwan University: For China Studies and Cross Taiwan Strait Relations,* 8 October. Retrieved 23 February 2018 (http://www.china-studies.taipei/act02.php).

Freedom House. 2016. "Freedom of the Press." Retrieved from https://freedomhouse.org/report/freedom-press/2016/china.

Gallardo, Sacha and Aileen Baviera. 2013. "Filipino Media and Public Opinion on the Philippines-China Disputes in the South China Sea: A Preliminary Analysis." *Philippines-China Relations: Sailing Beyond Disputed Waters: Chinese Studies Journal* 10:132–171.

Gan, Nectar. 2016. "Communist Party Mouthpiece Quotes China Daily as 'Foreign Media' to Reassure Public Over Slowing Economy." *South China Morning Post,* 16 December. Retrieved 12 March 2017 (https://www.scmp.

com/news/china/economy/article/2054515/communist-party-mouthpiece-quotes-china-daily-foreign-media).

Guan, Bing, Ying Xia, and Gong Cheng. 2016. "Structure and Media Autonomy in China: The Case of Southern Weekend." *Journal of Contemporary China* 26(104):233–248.

Guo, Suijan. 2013. *Chinese Politics and Government: Power, Ideology, and Organization*. New York: Routledge.

Haas, Benjamin. 2017. "BBC Crew Attacked in China and Forced to Sign Confession." *The Guardian*, 3 March. Retrieved from https://www.theguardian.com/world/2017/mar/03/bbc-crew-attacked-in-china-says-reporter.

Han, Rongbin. 2015. "Manufacturing Consent in Cyberspace: China's *'Fifty-Cent'* Army." *Journal of Current Chinese Affairs* 44(2):105–134.

He, Kai. 2016. "How Could China Bargain for a Peaceful Accommodation?" *Orbis* 60(3): 382–394.

He, Qinglian. 2008. *The Fog of Censorship: Media Control in China*. New York, Hong Kong, Brussels: Human Rights in China.

Hess, Steve. 2014. "Foreign Media Coverage and Protest Outcomes in China: The Case of the 2011 Wukan Rebellion." *Modern Asian Studies* 49(01):177–203.

Hong, Junhao. 2010. "Media Globalization in Asia." In *Global Communication: Theories, Stakeholders, and Trends*, edited by Thomas McPhail. Chichester, West Sussex: Wiley-Blackwell, 305–334.

Hong, Zhaohui and Yi Sun. 2010. "The Butterfly Effect and the Making of 'Ping-Pong Diplomacy'." *Journal of Contemporary China* 9(25):429–448.

Hou, Xiaoshuo. 2014. "Dissecting China's Rise: Controversies over the China Model." *China Perspectives* 2014(2): 61–67.

Kalathil, Shanthi. 2003. "China's New Media Sector: Keeping the State In." *The Pacific Review* 16(4):489–501.

Li, Xin and Verner Worm. 2011. "Building China's Soft Power for a Peaceful Rise." *Journal of Chinese Political Science* 61(1):69–89.

Lin, Mao. 2016. "'To See is to Believe?' – Modernization and U.S.-China Exchanges in the 1970s." *The Chinese Historical Review* 23(1):23–46.

Mao, Zedong. 1957. *Speech at the Chinese Communist Party's National Conference on Propaganda Work*. Peking: Foreign Languages Press.

Mayer, Jeremy and Michael Cornfield. 2008. "The Internet and the Future of Media Politics." In *Media Power, Media Politics*, edited by Mark Rozell and Jeremy Mayer. Lanham: Rowman & Littlefield.

Nikkei Asian Review. 2016. "China Crackdown Could Curb Rare Earths Outflow." *Nikkei Asian Review*. Retrieved from http://asia.nikkei.com/Markets/Commodities/China-crackdown-could-curb-rare-earths-outflow?page=1.

Nye, Joseph. 2006. "Think Again: Soft Power." Retrieved from Foreign Policy website http://foreignpolicy.com/2006/02/23/think-again-soft-power/.

Rawnsley, Gary. 2015. "Chinese International Broadcasting, Public Diplomacy and Soft Power." In *Routledge Handbook of Chinese Media*, edited by Gary Rawnsley and Ming Yeh Rawnsley. London: Routledge.

Romashkan, Dima. 2013. "How Countries Use the Media as a 'Soft Power.'" *Robert Bosch Stiftung*. Retrieved from http://www.bosch-stiftung.de/content/language2/html/51021_53676.asp.

Scotton, James and William Hachten. 2010. *New Media for a New China*. Chichester, West Sussex: Wiley-Blackwell.

## 56 *Jose Mari Hall Lanuza*

Shirk, Susan. 2011. *Changing Media, Changing China.* New York: Oxford University Press.

Silk, Richard. 2013. "China Weighs Environmental Costs." *Wall Street Journal,* 23 July. Retrieved from https://www.wsj.com/articles/SB10001424127887324879504578597462908226052.

Stahl, Lesley. 2015. "Modern Life's Devices under China's Grip?" *CBS News,* 22 March. Retrieved from http://www.cbsnews.com/news/rare-earth-elements-china-monopoly-60-minutes-lesley-stahl/.

Stockmann, Daniela. 2013. *Media Commercialization and Authoritarian Rule in China.* New York: Cambridge University Press.

Sudworth, John. 2017. "China Congress: BBC Team Forced to Sign Confession." *BBC,* 3 March. Retrieved from http://www.bbc.com/news/world-asia-china-39137293.

Tibetan Review. 2009. "China to Be More Open About Its Media Policy." *Tibetan Review* September 2009:35.

Timmons, Heather and Zheping Huang. 2016. "Beijing is Banning All Foreign Media from Publishing Online in China." *Quartz,* 19 February. Retrieved from https://qz.com/620076/beijing-is-banning-all-foreign-media-from-publishing-online-in-china/.

UNCTAD. 2016. *World Investment Report 2016.* Retrieved from http://unctad.org/en/PublicationsLibrary/wir2016_en.pdf.

Walton, Greg. 2001. *China's Golden Shield: Corporations and the Development of Surveillance Technology in the People's Republic of China.* Montreal: International Centre for Human Rights and Democratic Development.

Wang, Jianwei and Xiaojie Wang. 2014. "Media and Chinese Foreign Policy." *Journal of Contemporary China* 23(86):216–235.

Wang, Yaqui. 2017. "In China, Sources Face Harassment, Jail for Speaking to Foreign Media" *Community to Protect Journalist,* 24 February. Retrieved from https://cpj.org/blog/2017/02/in-china-sources-face-harassment-jail-for-speaking.php.

Wang, Zouyoe. 1999. "U.S.-China Scientific Exchange: A Case Study of State-Sponsored Scientific Internationalism during the Cold War and Beyond." *Historical Studies in the Physical and Biological Sciences, 30*(1):249–277.

Xu, Beina and Eleanor Albert. 2017. "Media Censorship in China." *Council on Foreign Relations,* 17 February. Retrieved from http://www.cfr.org/china/media-censorship-china/p11515.

Yamada, Ken'ichi. 2011. "China's Focus on External Publicity: The Impact of Changing Media Policy at Home and Abroad." *NHK Broadcasting Studies,* 9. Retrieved from https://www.nhk.or.jp/bunken/english/reports/pdf/11_no9_10.pdf.

Yuan, Yuan. 2010. "I am Broadcasting from China." *Beijing Review,* 11 March. Retrieved from http://www.bjreview.com.cn/culture/txt/2010-03/06/content_251817.htm.

Zhang, Xiaowei. 2016. "Mass Media in China." In *Understanding Chinese Society,* edited by X. Zang. New York: Routledge.

Zhao, Yuezhi. 1998. *Media, Market, and Democracy in China: Between the Party Line and the Bottom Line.* Chicago: University of Illinois Press.

# 4 Examining the challenges and possibilities in Tsinoy Studies

*Carmelea Ang See*

## Introduction: historical timeline of Chinese in the Philippines[1]

| | |
|---|---|
| 982 | First documented trade between Chinese traders and Ma-yi, identified as Ba'I in Laguna province, south of Manila. |
| 1521 | Portuguese explorer, Ferdinand Magellan, lands in the archipelago |
| 1542 | Ruy López de Villalobos names the islands *Las Islas Filipinas* in honor of Philip of Austria, who later became Philip II of Spain. |
| 1565 | Spain officially colonizes the Philippines |
| 1574 | Chinese pirate Limahong arrives in the northern part of the Philippines but is expelled by Spanish-led forces |
| 1585 | Binondo Church is built in the heart of the Chinese community |
| 1600s–1700s | Six incidences of massacres and violence occur against the Chinese in the Philippines |
| 1896 | Philippine revolution against Spain erupts |
| 1898 | Philippine independence is declared. Treaty of Paris is signed in Paris, France where the Philippines, Cuba, Puerto Rico are ceded to the United States as part of Spain's surrender after the Spanish-American War 1895–1898. |
| 1899–1901 | Philippine-American war |
| 1902 | Chinese Exclusion Law is applied to the Philippines. Only merchants and sons of merchants are allowed to migrate into the country. |
| 1921 | Chinese merchants are required to keep business records in either English, Spanish, or any Philippine dialect; later repealed by the US Supreme Court |
| 1941–1945 | Japanese Occupation of the Philippines Chinese guerrillas join Filipinos in fighting the Japanese. |
| 1949 | China closes its doors. People's Republic of China is born. Immigration from China to the Philippines was curtailed. |

58   *Carmelea Ang See*

|           | Relatives of the Chinese in the Philippines move to Hong Kong temporarily before coming to the Philippines. |
|-----------|---|
| 1950s     | Congress passed a series of Filipinization laws that discriminate against aliens (read: Chinese) |
| 1954      | Retail Trade Nationalization Law disallows non-Filipino citizens from engaging in retail trade. Majority of the Chinese are in retail, and have nowhere to go except into wholesaling, import-export, manufacturing. |
| 1972      | President Ferdinand Marcos declares Martial Law. |
| 1975      | Establishment of diplomatic relations between China and the Philippines<br>LOI (Letters of Instruction) 270 issued by President Marcos grants easy access to naturalization through administrative means to Chinese residing in the Philippines |
| 1986      | The Philippines successfully deposes Marcos in a bloodless People Power Revolution. |
| 1987      | Kaisa Para Sa Kaunlaran (Unity for Progress) is formed on August 28. |
| 1993      | Protest rally at the funeral of Charlene Sy in January and at the National Summit on Peace and Order became significant milestones in the Chinese-Filipino community history. |
| 1990s–2000s | Spate of kidnappings terrorizes members of Chinese-Filipino community, peaking from 1996 to 1998. |

## Life histories

Early years and education

### *Go Bon Juan* 吳文煥

At the core of Go Bon Juan's research on all things, Tsinoy (Chinese Filipino) is a social activism borne out of his concern for the poor and a loyalty to his motherland, the Philippines. His primary advocacy is the integration of the Chinese into Philippine mainstream society and the Chinese Filipinos' contribution in uplifting the plight of the poor. This lifelong commitment has fed Go's research and study on the Chinese in the Philippines. This outlook begins in his primary school years at Kiaotiong (Philippine Chinese High School 菲律濱華僑中學, now Philippine Cultural College 菲律濱僑中學院)[2] and continues in his writings and advocacies.

Go was born in 1949 in Shenhu (深滬 more popularly known in its Hokkien term Chimho), Jinjiang, Fujian, China, where the people were mostly fishermen. The family lived in China and Hongkong before going to the Philippines in 1960. Go and his family arrived in the Philippines when he was around 12 years old and about to finish elementary school. However, since he was educated in Hongkong, his equivalency for English was only at

Examining the challenges and possibilities in Tsinoy Studies   59

the third grade level. Go thus finished Grade 12 from Chinese class, but only finished Grade 10 for English class.[3] He first studied in Yorklin (Northern Rizal Yorklin School) for elementary and eventually completed high school in Kiaotiong.

Go attended the National University (NU) for one semester and then transferred to the University of the East for another semester. He took a degree in Education at NU and commerce at UE.

He considers himself self-taught as his research into Philippine society and the Chinese in the Philippines are all self-learned. When the Go family arrived in the Philippines, his father was already in the business of making the little tags attached on the inside neckline of T-shirts. Even at an early age, Go says in retrospect, he had social consciousness: "When we arrived in the Philippines, my father's workers were poor and I sympathized with their conditions" (Go 2015:2).

### *Richard Chu* 吴興奇

Richard Chu describes his path to history as somewhat accidental and quite circuitous. After nearly two decades in the field, mining primary sources, Chu feels the lack of experts and the need for more scholars to focus on the field of diasporic studies.

Dr. Richard Chu's beginnings came some 20 years after Go. Like 90 percent of the Chinese in the Philippines, Chu's clan migrated to the Philippines from Jinjiang County in the Minnan region of Fujian. His paternal grandfather came into the Philippines using Chu Ongco on his *tua di mia* (大字名),[4] while his real name was Go Taco. By using somebody else's papers, Go Taco was able to enter and stay legally in the Philippines. Family members would be brought into the Philippines over the years with majority of the household arriving in the 1930s, when the conditions in China were very bad. Family members would go back and forth to China until about 1949, when the Communists took over.

Chu's father was one of eight children who came to the Philippines at the age of seven and grew up in Binondo. He went to Mapua Institute of Technology and got a degree in Civil Engineering. He was 27 years old when he married Chu's mother, Agustina Tan, then 19.

Like majority of the Chinese in the Philippines at that time, Chu's parents lived within Chinatown. The Chu family, including aunts, uncles, and cousins, were cramped together in a big compound on Soler Street in Binondo, where they also ran the grandfather's lumber business, known as Gotaco. Chu was born in 1965 and spent only his first year in the family compound. With five children, Chu's immediate family moved to Pasay City where his father worked for another employer. Four years later, they had moved into a bigger house and the elder Chu started his own plywood business. With Chu's older sisters spending a lot of their younger years in Chinatown, they are very proficient in Hokkien. Meanwhile, Chu and his younger sisters

60   *Carmelea Ang See*

grew up in a neighborhood with Filipinos. They had to consciously learn Hokkien and did not develop a high level of proficiency.

Chu spent his primary and secondary school years at Xavier School, an all-boys school founded by foreign Jesuits, who were expelled from China and could no longer do missionary work there after 1949. They moved to the Philippines and opened in 1956 a school for the children of Chinese immigrants in the Philippines. Many of these priests were fluent in Mandarin; a number came from North America, with some coming from Europe, particularly Spain. Chu considers his education in Xavier School very well-rounded in that the school emphasized not only academic achievement but also excellence in sports, music, and arts. The students had 2 hours of Chinese language instruction from Monday to Friday. Most of the teachers came from Taiwan or trained in Taiwan.

Chu entered Ateneo de Manila University on full scholarship granted to students who graduated valedictorian from a Jesuit high school. His parents had wanted him to enroll in a business-related course, but Chu was quite hesitant to pursue that direction. Instead, he pursued a degree in Legal Management that served as a compromise. After one semester of law, he switched to Interdisciplinary Studies, which allowed him to obtain degrees in philosophy and education.

## Research interests and advocacies

### Go Bon Juan

The ethnic Chinese community in the 1950s to the 1970s was divided into two groups—pro-Kuomintang and pro-mainland China. Both groups see the local Chinese community as "foreigners" even when the second generation of this period was born in the Philippines (Ang See 2004). Go saw this as social issue that had to be addressed—who are the Chinese in the Philippines and what is their place in society? Thus began his foray into reading and writing about social issues, especially those related to the Chinese in the Philippines. Go discovers "the Chinese problem" and focuses on this.

Both the pro-Kuomintang and the pro-China groups would not think of identity as an issue at all. They saw themselves as Chinese who simply happened to be in the Philippines. Meanwhile, those who were pro-mainland China imagined a strong China that will protect their interests when the community is oppressed. By the 1970s, the ethnic Chinese community foresaw the solution to the Chinese problem upon the establishment of diplomatic relations between China and the Philippines in 1975 (Ang See 1990).

These desires do not reflect the realities happening in the country. The People's Republic of China replaced the Republic of China (Taiwan) in the United Nations in 1971. In a little more than 4 years, Philippine president Ferdinand Marcos issues LOI 270 (Letters of Instruction) granting mass naturalization to the Chinese in the Philippines in April 1975. This

## *Examining the challenges and possibilities in Tsinoy Studies* 61

campaign was created in preparation for the establishment of diplomatic relations between China and the Philippines in the same year. Marcos did not want a group of alien Chinese to owe loyalty to PRC. At the end of the application period, by the mid-1980s, approximately 95 percent of ethnic Chinese in the Philippines had become Filipino citizens.

For the elder generation pro-mainland China, they suddenly had to face the reality that their motherland could not "protect" them. China did not intervene, as a matter of policy, on local affairs. Neither does it recognize dual citizens. The pro-Taiwan faction was in the same boat. With the United Nations officially declaring a one-China policy, Taiwan is no longer in a position to assist their supporters. Both groups realize that their futures lie in the Philippines and promoting Philippine national interests will also hasten their own successes (Ang See 1990).

Sometime in the 1980s, Go's interest was piqued by a series of articles in Orient News 東方日報, under the banner *Crossroads*, by Professor Chinben See 施振民, Teresita Ang (now Ang See) 洪玉華, Rosita Tan 陳巧琦, Lily Chua 蔡麗麗, and Victor Go 吳勝利. All the writers' points of view stemmed from their identities as Filipinos. He sought out Victor Go, who then introduced him to Chinben See. Go's views on the overseas Chinese issue solidified during and after discussions with See. It is also during this time that Go began feeling the dearth of information on the Chinese in the Philippines.

Go recalls, "He [Prof. See] pulled out two books and gave them to me. From this point, I never stopped reading up on the subject because the field is very broad. The more I read, the more I learned." (Go 2018:2).

Go's continuing research expanded as he felt his reading and research were never enough. The research had to be contextualized within Southeast Asia and extended to compare the Philippine condition with that of the United States, Canada, Japan, Europe, and Africa. Go posited that only through comparative study can one discover more about the Philippines.

Furthermore, the wide expanse of overseas Chinese studies demands that scholars also become familiar with economics, social sciences, sociology, culture, and anthropology. Go, in fact, recommends that these in-country studies be compared with that of other countries to find out how the local Chinese are similar or different.

It is through these comparative studies that researchers may find out the uniqueness of the ethnic Chinese minority in their own country. Go feels that there are many areas of Chinese studies that need more in-depth study. However, he also realizes that very few people have the passion and the willingness to sacrifice monetary income. Scholarly pursuits here in the Philippines do not earn money but the resources needed, before, during and after conducting research, are immense. He acknowledges that it is quite lonely but necessary work.

The conditions are slightly better for scholars attached to universities, as their primary duty is to conduct research. However, after more than a decade of attending and speaking at conferences, Go felt more strongly that

## 62  *Carmelea Ang See*

there are a myriad aspects of study that are not touched upon (做不了). Admittedly, there are always proposals on how to truly resolve issues, but the influence and the network of scholars is too small to be of major influence. From experience, Go observed an average of two to three people devoted to Chinese studies in a particular country. As well, for many, the goal of research is to widen the knowledge base and to further the field along. In contrast, Go wishes that the ultimate goal of research and scholarly output is policy change or specific action. Go proposes that the best scenario is for every country to have a local Chinese to conduct Chinese studies because they would be more knowledgeable of the problems of their own country. Preferably, they should have both the intellectual capability to discover the issues, analyze them, offer solutions, and the political or societal capability to influence policy or action (做事情).

This severe lack of scholars in the field of the Chinese in the Philippines stems from the fact that the emergence of Chinese-Filipino intellectuals focusing on this field is quite late beginning only in the 1950s and 1960s.

One of the first scholars was Tan Taybin, who began speaking and writing about the path of the sojourners (huaqiao 華僑) in the 1950s. As Go wanted a bigger picture of the 華僑 and Chinese Filipinos and needed to delve beyond history and learn about the Chinese community's economic, social, and cultural situations, he realized, "I have to depend on myself, because there are very few people who have done studies in this field. For Chinese Filipinos, there are only a handful."

Go enumerates this handful of experts who mostly wrote about the history of the Chinese in the Philippines: [Names are written first in Hokkien as these are the names they are known by in the Philippines/Pinyin/Chinese characters]

- Tan Tay Bin/Chen Tai Min/陳臺民 (1961)
- Tan Diat Hu/Chen Lieh Fu/陳烈甫 (1958 and 1981)
- Tan Siu Kok/Antonio Tan/Chen Shou Guo/陳守國 (1981 and 1984)
- Lao Chi Thian/Liu Zhi Tian/劉芝田 (1952)

Tan Taybin wanted to write ten volumes of the history of the Chinese in the Philippines but came out with only two volumes in the 1960s on the early Spanish period. At that time, he was working at the *Chinese Commercial News* (*Siong Po* 商報), which then created a discussion revolving around Tan's book regarding "the future of the Chinese community" (Chen 1961). The other volumes did not see fruition when *Siong Po* stopped operations.[5]

Meanwhile, Antonio Tan was mainly a historian who concentrated on the American period and the Chinese political awakening (1984) and one book on the Japanese occupation (1981). He did not consider the issue of integration of the ethnic Chinese into Philippine mainstream society. As well, both publications came out in the 1980s, not during the critical period

## Examining the challenges and possibilities in Tsinoy Studies    63

of the 1960s and 1970s when the Chinese community was seeking their place in society.

The question of identity and place has been floating slightly above community consciousness since after the war, particularly when China closed its doors in 1949. The Chinese saw themselves suddenly in a foreign land, dealing with foreign laws, but with no protection from their country of origin. There were no indications that China will open up again in the next few decades.

Thirty years later, it is a younger generation local-born Chinese, as members of the Pagkakaisa Sa Pag-unlad,[6] who brought up and openly discussed the concept of integration. This coincided with the period of China's return to the global arena, as well as LOI 270. The Chinese in the Philippines began to accept the idea of belonging to the Philippines. Integration is hastened when sometime between 1982 and 1985, the majority of the ethnic Chinese population in the Philippines officially became naturalized Filipino citizens.

Freedom from dictatorship is restored in 1986 and 1 year later, Kaisa Para Sa Kaunlaran (Kaisa) is formed as the only research organization within the Chinese-Filipino community. Compared to other Chinese community organizations that have other interests, Kaisa has positioned itself within the community to be spurred by research to push its advocacy of integration of the Chinese, as well as to push the community into more meaningful social development work. The research orientation of Kaisa Para Sa Kaunlaran is geared toward identity formation and social activism—both to increase awareness on the ethnic Chinese minority within the larger Philippine society and to tap the potentials of the Chinese-Filipinos to engage in social development work (Alejandrino 2005; Ang See 1990, 1996, 1997, 2004, 2007, 2013; Kaisa Bridges; Kaisa Lessons). All research Go has done under Kaisa is to guide and provide some sort of direction, to give community members a real sense of Philippine social and political development.

Go continues to lament the constraint faced by researchers that there is nowhere to find ready materials. In many instances of his studies, he accidently finds information as a footnote in an unrelated publication. Go cites his discovery of information regarding Chinese who built a dam in Calamba, Laguna, in 1640 (Hilberto 1985). It is an ancient tidbit of history that nobody knows about.

Go knows there is still much material to be mined from Archivo General de Indias, housed in the ancient merchants' exchange of Seville, Spain. The Lonja de Mercaderes is the repository of extremely valuable archival documents illustrating the history of the Spanish Empire in the Americas and the Philippines. No one has yet delved deeply into the archives of the University of Santo Tomas founded in 1611. Another large source on the Philippines is Mexico's archives and possibly the national archives of Brunei Darussalam.

Sadly, there have been and are more international scholars researching on Chinese in the Philippines. Almost all seminal works in this field were done

64  *Carmelea Ang See*

by non-Filipinos like Edgar Wickberg (1965, 2000) for the last 50 years of the Spanish period, Khin Myint Jensen's dissertation on the Chinese in the American period (1956), Jacques Amyot's study on Chinese families and lineage (1973), Gerald McBeath (1973) on political integration, Robert Tilman (1974) on integration, and Fr. Charles McCarthy on sociopolitical integration (1971) and historical studies (1973).

Even exhaustive studies on the Chinese in different Philippine regions were conducted by international researchers. John Omohundro of University of Oregon lived in Iloilo for 1 year so he could write authoritatively about the topic (1981). Missionaries Hubert and Harriet Reynolds lived in the Ilocos and produced a comprehensive ethnographic study, Chinese acculturation in Ilocos in 1964, formally published in 1998.

Large-scale comprehensive studies cannot be expected because there is either little interest or diverse interests. Little pockets of research have yet to be consolidated into a comprehensive whole to attempt a bird's eye view on the entire community, its direction, and racial problems. Furthermore, Go returns to the lack of data. He cites the misconception in the Philippines that all Chinese are good in business and that the ethnic Chinese minority controls the economy. The reality is that the Chinese are not major players even in the retail economy as people perceive. But reliable data is very limited.

The common misconception is that the local Chinese community control 60 percent of the economy. There is no statistic to confirm this. Go relates how this percentage came about.

In the 1970s, a renowned Japanese economist, Kunio Yoshihara (1971), made a study regarding the Philippine manufacturing industry. He got the top 1000 corporations and extracted around 250 manufacturing firms and analyzed these. The manufacturing firms were divided into three categories—domestic (purely local), Chinese, foreign—with each category approximating 30–35 percent. If foreign-owned firms are disregarded and only Chinese-owned and domestic are considered (approximating a half-half division), then the Chinese-owned firms comprise 56.2 percent of the shares. Researchers and the media began referencing this limited data set and over the years, it has evolved into an interpretation that Chinese control 60 percent of the Philippine economy.

Continuing with his theory that researchers need to find information in not-so-obvious sources, he recommends that those who want to study the economy get data from car sellers, builders of high-rise condominiums, and developers of gated communities as more reliable sources of information. Other data sets that could be mined for information are the number of Tsinoys who purchased property and houses in China, as well as the number of Southeast Asian Chinese who have bank accounts in Hong Kong.

The Chinese in the Philippines are, admittedly, mostly businessmen, who were primarily concerned with their own survival and the success of their enterprises. As a group, they were not concerned with pointing out solutions

*Examining the challenges and possibilities in Tsinoy Studies* 65

to the huaqiao problem. Even the largest Tsinoy organization, the Federation of Filipino-Chinese Chambers of Commerce and Industry, Inc. (FFCCCII), formed in 1954, was formed mainly to "control" the community. The FFCC-CII was established by the Kuomintang, it never pointed to integration as a solution to Chinese identity issues.

When Pagkakaisa Sa Pag-Unlad brought it up, it was a novel idea for the ethnic Chinese community; it was a different argument altogether. At that time, the local Chinese did not fully understand the concept of integration and were not ready to accept it.

Pagkakaisa was initially formed to push for an amendment in the Philippine citizenship law—to allow for *jus soli*, or citizenship by location of birth. This would have enabled children of Chinese-citizen parents to automatically become Philippine citizens. The organization saw itself as "an organ of service and information conducting research into the historical, social, economic, legal and cultural factors which contribute to healthy integration of resident minorities." (McCarthy 1971: ix).

Unfortunately, Pagkakaisa had to close shop because of Martial Law. A strong sense of country motivated Go to gather different people from different groups to form Kaisa Para Sa Kaunlaran[7] in 1987. The former members of Pagkakaisa were already gathering themselves to reorganize the organization into a new group when Go approached them. Go connected them with a sponsor who also wanted to put up an organization to give a voice to the Chinese community. Go then invited friends from 僑中, Xavier School (光啓學校), and Chiang Kai Shek College (中正學院).

Kaisa's thrust in the early years was to continue the work that Pagkakaisa began more a decade prior—to study how to influence the community and society. While there have been many inroads in recent decades, there is still much to be done.

Just in the first few years of this new organization, integration has become a byword. Three years into its work, however, a new problem arose— kidnapping-for-ransom. Beginning the 1990s up to the present, Chinese Filipinos became favorite targets of kidnapping syndicates in the Philippines. They were "easy" targets because they paid monetary ransom quite quickly and never reported to the police. The kidnapping problem has not yet been solved, but, at a height of one kidnapping incident every other day between 1996 and 2004, the statistics from 2005 onward average at 60 cases per year.

The kidnapping problem made the local Chinese realize that they have to depend on themselves in cooperation with Filipinos to figure out how to end crime. It brought to the fore the idea that the Chinese community can no longer stay as bystanders within the confines of Chinatown and that they have to venture into the mainstream society—working with the Philippine justice system to solve the kidnapping problem. Kidnapping thrust Kaisa into the forefront of the community's consciousness in 1993 when it organized a funeral-protest march for a child victim, Charlene Mayne Sy[8] (Kidnap Watch 2007).

## 66   *Carmelea Ang See*

Addressing the kidnapping issue and providing support to victims of crime took up Kaisa's energies for close to a decade. However, other societal problems come to the fore, and Go's hopes for the community to respond grows deeper.

After year 2000, many new organizations have cropped up and are still cropping up. Go notes the Chinese newspaper where launchings of new organizations are announced quite often. If the existing organizations could already solve community issues, then there is no need for new groups. Go observes that the dynamics of these organizations, old and new, are quite competitive in the "showing-off" arena.

A cursory look at the names of the leading organizations in the community reveals that majority use 總會 (federation) to portray and emphasize their leadership. Meanwhile, even in the 1980s and 1990s, when an up and coming leader of an organization is bypassed and not elected into his desired position, a break-off would ensue and a new group is formed. This has happened a number of times in both large and smaller organizations.

The most ostentatious form of "showing off" is during organizations' anniversaries and induction of officers, usually conducted every 2 years. Most of these organizations expend so much resources on grand celebrations at five-star hotels spending millions of pesos.

Go wishes those millions are instead spent on processes to help solve societal problems and in cultural work. At most, the local Chinese community organizations' social development work focuses on *sampo* (三寶), the three treasures, all under the auspices of business organizations around the country—the volunteer fire brigades, free medical clinics/medical missions, barrio schools. The latter are local public schools provided with new school rooms donated by business organizations mainly through the FFCCCII. Go also wishes that the community automatically adds a fourth treasure—the Bahay Tsinoy, museum of Chinese in Philippine life. Sadly, community interests are focused on business and networking and barely on culture and history.

Go diagnoses the community as having "become selfish," and thus, unwilling or unable to do deeper and more meaningful development work. It also does not help when the Philippine government blames the Chinese in the Philippines for a myriad of concerns to divert citizens' attentions from real issues.

What Go truly wants is for the Chinese Filipinos to show gratitude to the country that allowed their ancestors live, develop, and become successful. Go perceives that doing good things for the country is not saying that one is just helping the people but it is paying back the country for the successes the local Chinese have reaped.

Kaisa's efforts in pushing for integration have generated results very slowly. There are a number of Tsinoys who, upon reading some of our publications, especially Go's articles in World News, choose to donate their

*Examining the challenges and possibilities in Tsinoy Studies* 67

funds to Kaisa instead of holding a wedding anniversary or birthday party. It seems like a small step, but it is this awareness of the needs of the poor that Go pushes for.

The repeated call for more meaningful work in Go's articles became reality after Typhoon Ondoy in 2009, when seven of the biggest organizations in the community decided to consolidate resources.

Traditionally, different organizations issue their own calls for donations in the Chinese newspapers. Even World News, the largest Chinese daily in the Philippines, issues its own call for donations. Members of the community thus will have to "choose" which group to donate their monies to. Upon consolidation, Kaisa Para Sa Kaunlaran was called upon to join the group of seven as a "consultant," in recognition of its expertise in straddling both the Chinese community and Philippine mainstream quite comfortably. Kaisa has acted as a conduit for these donated monies to serve communities in need.

It is also a strong sense of country that drives Go to write about the Philippines in Chinese for the local Chinese community. Writing as Hua Ching 華清 in World News, he wants to help the local Chinese discover and learn about the Philippines. In the early years of his writings, Go covered complicated Philippine issues to help the Chinese understand and analyze the country's economy, politics, elections, and current events. His efforts have borne fruit as more and more leaders and members of Chinese organizations have accepted the idea of integration and more meaningful social development work.

Since 1987, Go produces a one-page Kaisa supplement (in Chinese) published on Sunday in World News. The page, titled "Integration (融合)," contains his views on a myriad of issues affecting the Tsinoy community, the Philippine society, and world events, such as globalization, economic crisis, free trade liberalization, and other important topics that have far-reaching and significant impact. The more important articles have been combined into three volumes (Go 1990, 1997, 2001). Go also writes fortnightly columns for Tulay Chinese-Filipino digest. The first issue is titled "Gems of History," and the second is titled "Soul of China"—one touches on Philippine historical figures and events and the other on China's folk heroes and events.

Some of Go's Chinese publications, intended especially for the elder generation as well as new migrants, are translations in Chinese of Teodoro Agoncillo's *History of the Filipino People* (1996), Renato Constantino's *Miseducation of the Filipino* (2001), and O.D. Corpuz's *Filipino Revolution in our Collective Memory* (2000). Go wrote *Myths about the Ethnic Chinese "Economic Miracle"* (1996) to debunk the popular belief that all Chinese in the Philippines are engaged in business.

Changes are apparent by just looking at the current Chinese dailies in the country. When World News, the leading Chinese daily, started in 1981, front page news stories were only copied from China's newspapers. Go was

## 68 *Carmelea Ang See*

editor-in-chief of World News, so during the 1986 People Power revolution, he attempted to put the news on the front page and got the ire of the owners. On the last day of the revolution, February 25, Go stayed at World News until past midnight and was able to put Corazon C. Aquino's photograph on the upper half of the front page—no news but with one caption identifying Aquino as the new president of the Philippines. The owners again were extremely angry. Thirty years hence, World News now publishes local Philippine news in the first three to four sections of the newspaper. News from China is now labeled foreign news.

Nation building has always been the core of Go's advocacy and research. For him, it is not just about donating money, or a barrio school, or fighting fire (as volunteer fire brigades). With poverty statistics looming large, Go recommends that national development focus on health, education, and infrastructure. While yes, the Chinese contributions are large, they could offer so much more. Go and Kaisa's views on poverty alleviation differ from the community at this juncture. There should be a specific direction and a different level of awareness. At this point, no one has yet thought of how to organize these resources. "What if they build one entire infrastructure? Or develop one industrial park? That is what has impact" (Go 2018:12).

To combat inaccurate information and/or the lack thereof, Go proposes to look at data as a whole. He views the wealth of the local Chinese as the wealth of the Philippines. The research should show both the Chinese-Filipino community and Filipino mainstream society how tightly knit the relations are. Hundreds of years of intertwining history and destiny have already revealed that the two peoples are in each other's lives and cannot be separated. He sees no need to separate the two. Separating the information on the Chinese from the overall country's information is detrimental to the Chinese Filipinos and their cause for integration. When research continues to segregate, it feeds into the consciousness of the people that there is so much wealth in the country contained in the small Chinese community. Go fears for the time that this view will lead again to racial riots because of perceived inequalities.

> Why do we need to say/differentiate you from us? There is no need to do that. We realize that we are close. We avoid the concept that the Chinese are not Filipinos, or that you are Filipinos, we are Chinese. If we cannot resolve this identity issue, then the two peoples cannot become close, racial problems cannot be resolved.
>
> (Go 2015:17)

### Richard Chu

Upon graduation, Chu considered becoming a Jesuit priest. He first became a member of the JVP, Jesuit Volunteers of the Philippines, the volunteer program of Ateneo de Manila University and taught religion (the Old Testament

## Examining the challenges and possibilities in Tsinoy Studies   69

and morality) at the Sacred Heart School for Boys in Cebu for a year. At the same time, he was also a guidance counselor for first-year students there.

During his JVP year in Cebu, Chu attended a lecture on the history and state of China's Catholic Church, and what the challenges were for Catholics in China. This lecture was part of the China mission workshop set up by two Jesuits—Father Ismael Zuloaga and Father Jose Calle—to try and spread Catholicism in China again, as China had already started to open up to the outside world. The workshop gave Chu an interest in participating in the propagation of Catholicism in China.

After his JVP program-year ended in 1987, Chu went to Xiamen University (廈大) on scholarship for a year and a half brush up on his Mandarin and to learn more about Fujian. China at that time was just turning around—coming out of the age of Mao Zedong and of Deng Xiaoping, going into its early stages of modernization. Roads were still filled with bicycles and no cars; people still dressed up very conservatively, with a lot of grays and blues in the rural areas. Chu reminisces, "It was still a very far cry from what China is today" (Chu 2016:6). Toward the end of his studies in China, Chu decided to apply to become a Jesuit but was unsuccessful. He thus began to think of a way to start a career

Chu's first job upon his return to the Philippines was as a program assistant to the director of the Chinese Studies Program of Ateneo de Manila University. While working as the program assistant, Chu also taught basic and intermediate Chinese. When the program director, Dr. Manuel Dy, went on sabbatical, Chu became the acting director. Upon his return, Chu became the assistant director of the program.

While there, he was advised by senior faculty not to hold administrative positions at such a young age and encouraged to pursue graduate studies if he planned to have a career in academia. It was at this time that he decided to pursue a master's degree in East Asian Studies abroad. Father Calle recommended Stanford University where Chu took graduate courses in history and anthropology on China. Chu's adviser was Harold Khan, who was an expert on the Qing Dynasty. Chu also took classes with Al Dean, ancient China historian at Stanford; Lyman Van Slyke, a modern China historian; and Hill Gates, a Chinese anthropologist.

After completing his master's degree, Chu decided to pursue a doctoral degree, and that his research was going to be about the Chinese in the Philippines. He was contemplating on whether to go into the field of anthropology or history. While passionate about anthropology, he was concerned about the discipline's requirement at the time for anthropologists to focus on studying a society or group of people *other than* one's own (which would then already disqualify him from studying the Chinese in the Philippines) and on adhering to a particular theoretical framework when choosing a research topic. He found the emphasis on theory to be constraining. Therefore, Chu decided to go into history, even though he had never imagined himself to be a historian. At least, as a historian, he could still

## 70  *Carmelea Ang See*

utilize anthropological methods of inquiry and theoretical frameworks for his study. Furthermore, there were more jobs available in history than in anthropology departments. Chu sought the advice of the late Dr. Edgar Wickberg of the University of British Columbia before applying to history PhD programs. Wickberg recommended applying to the doctoral program of the history department of the University of Southern California (USC) and working with John Wills of the University of Southern California, whose expertise on maritime Chinese history overlaps with Chu's own research interests.

During Chu's coursework at USC, his other adviser, Charlotte Furth, an expert on modern China, introduced him to *Making Ethnic Choices* by Karen Isaksen Leonard, a historian who eventually became an anthropologist. She studied the Punjabi Mexican families in the Imperial Valley in California. These families were formed during the early part of the 20th century, when Indian men from the Punjabi region in India came to work in the fields of California. Since they did not bring along their women, they ended up marrying Mexican women who were also laborers or farmers (1992). The ethnographic study of these bicultural families fascinated Chu, the fathers were Sikh, and the mothers were Catholics with their children growing up in this bicultural environment.

Inspired by Leonard's work, Chu decided to focus on the Chinese and Chinese mestizos. His main research question back then had to do with identity. He had read, under his professors both at USC and Stanford, works on ethnic identity or ethnicity and was particularly interested in the intersection of nationalism and ethnicity—that is, how nationalism leads to the construction or invention of national identities that are oftentimes rarified, homogeneous, and static (Hobsbawm 1983). Chu wanted to study how the ethnic identity of the Chinese in the Philippines, and that of the Chinese mestizo, had been constructed and reconstructed over time (Wickberg 2001).

Because Chu was born and raised in the Philippines, he knew and had experienced for himself how ethnic categories had been applied to the ethnic Chinese in the Philippines, and how these affected his own self-identity. The local Chinese were commonly called "*Intsik*," a word that had derogatory undertones, especially during the 1960s to the 1980s. Chu's experience with being labeled *Intsik* made him feel slighted when all along, he had thought of himself Filipino. This kind of "dual" identity or "conflicting" identities led Chu to want to study how Philippine society came up with such a term for the Chinese, and how the Chinese had equivalent terms for the Filipino— and why there is an ethnic tension between the two. Chu wanted to go into the historical roots of that phenomenon.

That meant his research had to go back to the period before the 20th century or at the very least to the turn of the 20th century, during the latter part of the Spanish colonial period, and the beginning of the American colonial period. This is when many Tsinoys today trace their history of migration to

## Examining the challenges and possibilities in Tsinoy Studies 71

the Philippines. This was also the period when the epithets—the names being used by Filipinos for the Chinese, like *Intsik*, and the Chinese words for Filipinos, like *huana* or *chutsiah* to refer to Chinese mestizos—had become more popular in usage and had acquired the sort of connotations that these words have today.

Using Leonard's approach (1992), Chu decided to study the lives of the Chinese and their Chinese mestizo children, and to approach the study from a bottom-up perspective. He was not only interested in the origins of these terms, but also in how the Chinese and their children themselves understood these terms and used them. Chu's examination into the lives of the Chinese and Chinese mestizos was a way to critique the use of nation-based ethnic identifications to exclude others.

The result was his first major monograph *Chinese and Chinese Mestizos of Manila: Family, Identity, and Culture 1860s–1930s* (2010, 2012), in which he not only examined the everyday practices of these merchant families but also traced the historical origins of the division between the *huana* and the *Intsik*.[9]

The epithets used against each other like *huana* and *Intsik* were all influenced by nationalism, both by Philippine and Chinese nationalisms. In their effort to create a, sort of, "imagined community" that Benedict Anderson (1991) talks about, nation-states resort to exclusionary and inclusionary policies and help build stereotypes around certain groups of people. Chu goes on to explore the "history" or the "genealogy" of such ethnic constructions in the Philippines, as they pertain especially to Chinese and Chinese mestizos.

Chu's research journey has been constantly evolving. Whereas he imagined archival research as being buried in old documents, in dusty or dark-lit rooms, he realized later that archives were not dark, cavernous rooms. Chu trained himself to be proficient in reading both Chinese and Spanish.

Like Go, Chu discovered that tidbits of history were buried in obscure places. Chu has always described doing archival work like detective work—while there is a hypothesis and questions, the researcher does not know exactly what the answers are nor where they may lie. When trying to find answers in the archives, he would unexpectedly come up with information about a particular person, which would lead to other information.

Doing the research for his dissertation and writing it took about 5 years. The pleasure came from seeing that historical data were gradually proving his hypothesis: that the ethnic identities of Chinese and Chinese mestizos were more complex than what had been said in history textbooks, or even in Edgar Wickberg's analysis of Chinese and Chinese mestizo identities, which came from a macro-historical perspective (Wickberg 2000). Chu wanted to demonstrate that, from a micro-historical point of view, people often lived out and understood their identities in ways that did not usually conform to what the government, for example, or what other dominant groups wish to propagate. As Chu's dissertation was focused on the Chinese in the

## 72  *Carmelea Ang See*

Philippines and not so much on China, he started veering toward more expertise on the Chinese *in* the Philippines, or on the Chinese diaspora, and not on the Chinese in China.

The field of Chinese diasporic studies, which in earlier times was called overseas Chinese or Chinese overseas studies, has been a marginal part of China Studies. China or Chinese studies were formed out of the Cold war era, and all the other area studies—such as Philippine studies, Russian studies, Latin American studies—were all areas created in order for the United States government to be able to understand the enemy, or "The Other," better (Ong 1997). The focus, really, was on trying to understand their culture as a way to control them. People who were trained in area studies had to be very proficient in the language of the people they were studying, and to focus on a particular country's people, and not on the people in the diaspora.

Chu's venture into this new area of Chinese diasporic studies is evidenced, over the years, in the kind of conferences that he has been attending. China Studies scholars attend the Association for Asian Studies conferences, which Chu regularly attended. Beginning in 1992, when the International Society for the Study of Chinese Overseas (ISSCO) was established, Chu began to attend those conferences instead. Although Chu still attended Association for Asian Studies conferences, he found that there was more common interest or overlap in his research interests with people who attended the ISSCO conferences. Chu views this as a reflection of how his identification as a scholar had begun to veer from China Studies and shifted specifically toward Chinese diasporic studies.

Life events also conspired to secure his position as a scholar of Chinese diaspora and not Chinese studies. Of the thirty jobs applications that he sent out after completing his PhD program, twenty-nine were for positions on Chinese history. But one, from the University of Massachusetts-Amherst and the Five Colleges Consortium[10], specifically advertised for a scholar with an expertise in the US empire in the Pacific and with a subspecialization in Asian American studies. Having taken some graduate courses on Philippine history with Michael Salman at University of California, Los Angeles (UCLA), and having taught Philippine history at the University of San Francisco while finishing his dissertation, Chu felt that he was qualified to apply for this position as the Philippines was the biggest colony of the United States in the Pacific. Furthermore, he had done a field in Asian American studies with USC professor Lon Kurashige. He thus applied for this position and chose to teach at UMass/Five Colleges over other universities that wanted to hire him. Teaching at UMass/Five Colleges also afforded him to teach a course on Chinese diasporic history. Thus, both in research and teaching, Chu has become more associated with the field of Philippines studies, Asian American studies, and the Chinese diaspora. His research journey brought him into directions that he did not really plot."

*Examining the challenges and possibilities in Tsinoy Studies* 73

He has been invited to give lectures in different countries like Japan, Singapore, Hong Kong, Germany, and Spain about the Chinese and the Chinese mestizos, especially as they pertain to the Spanish colonial period in the Philippines. His studies on the Chinese mestizos also led to presenting his research at conferences that were interested in Spanish colonial Philippines. Even his participation in Asian American studies conferences now focuses on the "Chinaman question" in the Philippines and how it relates to the "Chinaman question" in the United States. Meanwhile, his presentations at the ISSCO conferences, as well as Philippine Studies conferences, concentrated on the Chinese diaspora. Chu envisions himself continuing research on the Chinese in the Philippines but thinks his next book project will identify with Asian American studies as he compares the experiences of the Chinese in the Philippines with the Chinese in the United States during the American colonial period.

Chu derives satisfaction from being a scholar when he sees his work being appreciated by the people he is in direct contact with every day. While his first book, which focused largely on the Chinese in the Philippines during the Spanish colonial era and then early American colonial era, is appreciated, for example, by people in the Philippines, by those who are in Spain, or those in China diaspora studies, it has little, or a very indirect application to Americans. Chu's research interests are also dictated by the need for relevance and application. Since he lives part time in the United States and part-time in the Philippines, he desires to be relevant to both societies. Hence, his next book project will identify him closer with Asian American studies, as he is comparing the experiences of the Chinese in the Philippines during the American colonial period with the Chinese experience in the United States.

Like Go, however, Chu feels frustrated with the dearth of research being done on the Chinese in the Philippines. At UMass/Five Colleges, he primarily teaches undergraduates, and the graduate students he advises are doing research in the field of US empire and Asian American studies. All is not that bleak, however. In other universities, there are graduate students who *are* studying about the Chinese in the Philippines, and, in a few cases, he has sat on doctoral committees of these students and advised them. One example is Phillip Guingona from the State University of New York (SUNY)-Buffalo, who did research on the lives of Filipinos living in Shanghai and some Chinese in the Philippines, like Albino Sycip during the first half of the 20th century. Another student he is advising is Chien Wen Kung from Columbia University who is working on Taiwanese-Philippine and Kuomintang-Filipino-Chinese relations from 1946 to 1975.

Chu says, "that's kind of the irony there, that there are more people abroad doing that instead" (2016:14). Chu recalls one study by Clark Alejandrino, whose first monograph was on the Chinese Exclusion Act of 1902.

## 74 *Carmelea Ang See*

But now Alejandrino has become more of a China scholar, studying natural calamities in China. It would still be an asset to the Philippines if Alejandrino decides to return to the country, but then his research is not focused on Chinese in the Philippines anymore. However, all is not lost. Under a Fulbright grant in 2015, Chu taught a number of history master's degree students at the Ateneo de Manila University. Some of the students wrote excellent research papers and, in 2016, presented these at a conference on the Chinese in the Philippines he co-organized with Teresita Ang See and Carmelea See of Kaisa Para Sa Kaunlaran, and co-sponsored by the Ricardo Leong Center for Chinese Studies at Ateneo de Manila. One of the research papers is also being considered for publication in an anthology on LGBTQ studies he is co-editing with Mark Blasius, a professor from the City University of New York. He hopes to continue teaching graduate students from Philippine universities during his summer breaks so that he can help train a new generation of Philippine-based scholars.

Every year, Chu makes a conscious effort to visit the Philippines in June and in December, during his summer and winter breaks from teaching. From these regular visits, Chu has gained some insights on the Chinese-Filipino community. He sees members of the community involved in many sociopolitical or civic activities, but very few of them really want to do in-depth research, not only about their history, or even about contemporary issues. Chu surmises that many young ethnic Chinese in the Philippines do not feel the need for research; they feel that they are very integrated already in Philippine society. Other national issues take the primary attention over the need to understand themselves more or understand history more. Furthermore, he has observed that, save for a few, members of the older Chinese-Filipino community are not also interested in investing money to support research on the Chinese in the Philippines. This is unfortunate because he ardently believes that in order for society to improve, there is a need to know and understand the past. Chu senses that their way of thinking about their ethnic identifications is still influenced by nation-based narratives, where there is a thirst for either-or propositions and an attempt to create clear markers of identifications, even though the term "Tsinoy"[11] had been coined.

Even though "Tsinoy" tries to blur those lines, the movement behind the construction of such a term is still fueled by the integrationist paradigm found in modern-day nationalism. While not opposed to the goal of integrating the Tsinoys into Philippine society, he is worried that these efforts will lead to a kind of sanitizing the image of the Tsinoy at the expense of excluding other people. In other words, those working for the acceptance of the Tsinoy into Philippine society may choose to focus only on the "positive" aspects of the Tsinoys or construct an image of the "Tsinoy" that may mask or hide the heterogeneity and complexity of the ethnic Chinese population in the Philippines. For instance, many Tsinoys tend to look down on or dissociate themselves from the *xinqiao*, new immigrants

## Examining the challenges and possibilities in Tsinoy Studies   75

from China. Some *xinqiao* have been accused of illegal activities, such as the smuggling contraband goods. Unfortunately, many Filipinos tend to think that the Tsinoys and the *xinqiao* all belong to the same group. Consequently, Tsinoys concerned with selling a "positive" image of themselves to the larger Filipino community may do so at the expense of "othering" the *xinqiao*, which runs the risk of repeating the very thing that the movement behind the creation of Tsinoy is fighting against—discrimination toward "others."

From a historical perspective, Chu is interested also to see whether history does repeat itself. In the past, even in other countries, when immigration stopped, a second- and third-generation integrated offspring appeared because there was no infusion of new migrants. When that changes, what happens? For instance, back in the 1850s, when immigration policies of both Spain and China were more relaxed, a new infusion of Chinese came to the Philippines. How did the old-timers, and Chinese mestizos, view this huge influx of newcomers? After World War II, a similar phenomenon occurred when China became Communist and Chinese immigration to the Philippines trickled down.

Chu grew up in a generation when there were very few *xinqiao*. He feels this new infusion would be interesting to study—how the *xinqiao* affect the Tsinoy community and how the older generation of Chinese in the Philippines view them. In effect, the Tsinoys are like the Chinese mestizos before of the 1860s and 1870s, looking at the newcomers. But then, these newcomers now have their own children who are also more integrated than their parents. So how do older generation Chinese Filipinos look at this new generation of Chinese Filipinos, whose parents came to the Philippines in the 1980s–1990s?

The efforts of academics and scholars, as well as Kaisa Para Sa Kaunlaran (of which Chu has been a member since its founding in 1987), in pushing for integration, have paved the way for smoother transitions. This generation of *xinqiao* has not gone through what the elder generation of parents had gone through. The most difficult time for the ethnic Chinese was in the 1960s, when they were often threatened with deportation unless they paid bribe money to extortionists. These *xinqiao* children are embedded in school, primarily with Tsinoys. Many of them can navigate three communities with ease—Philippine mainstream, Tsinoy communities, and their parents' communities, and, to varying extents, their own home communities in China.

As interesting as this new phenomenon is, Chu sees research directions from scholars as a changing-of-the-guard perspective. There is a generation gap between those who are doing research on the Chinese overseas and the Chinese diaspora. Scholars of Chinese overseas studies include Wang Gungwu, Teresita Ang See, Tan Chee-Beng, and Leo Suryadinata. These are all people who belong to the earlier generation. They have a different approach to the study of the Chinese in terms of theoretical perspective.

## 76  *Carmelea Ang See*

Most of them are still concerned with issues of national integration, which younger scholars are not necessarily concerned with. Some of them prefer to use the term "Chinese diaspora" instead of "Chinese overseas" to focus on the flows of capital, information, technology, and bodies—processes that are part of what affect, influence, or shape of what it means to be "Chinese" today, while at the same decentering "China" as the foundation of what constitutes "Chineseness."

Despite the differences between the older and younger generation of scholars, the field is certainly growing. For example, years back Brill Publishing started a series on the Chinese overseas. Chu's book, *Chinese and Chinese mestizos in Manila, Family, Identity, and Culture, 1860s–1930s*, was the first one that came out of the series, and there have been several others that followed. The National University of Singapore, together with Brill, has established the *Journal of the Chinese Overseas* for ISSCO. So, there is continued interest in the subject matter.

The direction of the field is certainly interesting. Where it is headed depends on the changing of the guard. Furthermore, a new generation of scholars from China or Taiwan interested in studying the Chinese overseas are beginning to reshape the field as they bring their own perspectives that are different from Western-educated scholars.

### Conclusion

The landscape of the study on the Chinese in the Philippines is definitely changing, in both the people involved in it, as well as the foci of studies. While there is not a strong momentum in the field, both Chu and Go hope that the younger generation of Chinese Filipinos, as well as the universities in the Philippines, would continue to encourage people to do more scholarship. The Kaisa Para Sa Kaunlaran to date has published 58 titles mostly on the Chinese in the Philippines. Though many are not strictly academic, they fulfill Kaisa's role as social activists in enlighting both Tsinoys and mainstream Filipinos as to the realities happening in the Tsinoy community. The organization's *Tulay* Fortnightly Chinese-Filipino Digest likewise has significant impact among the young generation who cannot read Chinese anymore. Both Chu and Go hope that the successor generation can continue to contribute to such scholarship. As well, the field needs to expand as the community and its members evolve into more complex relationships and identities.

### Notes

1 Agoncillo 2010; Alejandrino 2005; Chu 2010; Felix 1966, 1972; Ang See 1996; Tan 1981.
2 Popularly known in the Chinese-Filipino community as Kiaotiong 僑中, the formal legal name was Philippine Chinese High School (菲律濱華僑中學),

*Examining the challenges and possibilities in Tsinoy Studies* 77

established in 1923. The name changed to Philippine Cultural High School in 1976 and is now Philippine Cultural College (菲律濱僑中學院).

3  Elementary school in the Philippines is from Grades 1 to 6. High School is comprised of 4 years equivalent to Grades 7–10. The educational system changed in 2012, and year 2016 saw the first batch of Grade 11 students. However, Chinese language education up until the early 1970s was still up to Grade 12. This was reduced to 10 grades so students proceeding to university would also have "graduated" from their Chinese language classes.

4  The大字名 was literally a large piece of paper (12 × 16 inches) entitled Landing Certificate of Residence. This certificate indicated the name of the migrant, his origins in China, and his relatives (usually the father) in Manila. More often than not, the certificate would also show the Chinese characters of the migrant's name. The Chinese Exclusion Act of 1902 only allowed Chinese migrants who were merchants or sons of merchants to enter the Philippines. As such, any Chinese who desired to come into the Philippines, but had no relatives living there, found neighbors or friends or uncles to stand in as a father on paper. Hence, the legal English name is often not the migrant's real family name. Chu's ancestors are from the Go clan.

5  The first time *Siong Po* ceased operations was during the Second World War when it refused to be used as Japanese Propaganda. The editor, Yu Yi Tung, was executed and the newspaper shut down. The second time was when president Ferdinand Marcos declared martial law in 1972 and shut down all media outlets.

6  Pagkakaisa Sa Pag-unlad (Unity for Progress/菲律濱華僑問題研究論集) was formed in 1970 to encourage and promote assimilation and integration of alien minority groups into mainstream Philippine society; promote the belief that integration of minority groups shall benefit the Philippines; cooperate with other organizations to serve directly in worthy social charitable and civic projects which develop communication and collaboration between Filipinos and members of other ethnic groups.

7  Kaisa Para Sa Kaunlaran (Unity for Progress) 菲律濱華裔青年聯合會 is a leading resource organization that advocates the proactive and sustainable participation of the Tsinoy community in local and national development. (We are Kaisa, 2015)

8  Charlene Mayne Sy, 13, was abducted on her way to school. Police pursued the kidnappers and a gunfight ensued. The child was slain in the cross fire. At this time, Kaisa has already been calling for more than a year for police and other government agencies to solve the kidnapping problem (Kidnap Fever, 1992; Breakthrough, 1993).

9  Aside from this book and numerous articles, Chu published *Chinese Merchants of Binondo in the Nineteenth Century* (2010), edited *More Tsinoy Than We Admit* (2015), and co-edited with Caroline Hau of Kyoto University a special forum on the Chinese in the Philippines published by *Kritika Kultura* (2013).

10 The Five Colleges Consortium consists of UMass Amherst, Amherst College, Smith College, Mount Holyoke College, and Hampshire College. Chu was hired at UMass Amherst with a joint-appointment at the Five Colleges, thereby teaching one course at UMass every semester but teaching his second course in one of the four colleges.

11 Tsinoy was a term invented by Kaisa Para Sa Kaunlaran in 1992. It combines two Filipino words—*Tsino* for Chinese and *Pinoy*, a colloquial term for Filipino. It serves as an alternative to *Intsik* and also as a challenge to the monolithic, either-or *Intsik* vs. Filipino/*huana* binary, because to be Tsinoy is to be both Chinese and Filipino.

## 78 Carmelea Ang See

## References

Ang See, Teresita. 1990. *Chinese in the Philippines, Problems and Perspectives*. Vol. 1. Manila: Kaisa Para Sa Kaunlaran, Inc.

Ang See, Teresita. 1996. *The Ethnic Chinese in the Philippine Revolution*. Manila: Kaisa Para Sa Kaunlaran, Inc. [Filipino edition translated by Joaquin Sy. Chinese edition translated by Go, Bon Juan].

Ang See, Teresita. 1997. *Chinese in the Philippines, Problems and Perspectives*. Vol. 2. Manila: Kaisa Para Sa Kaunlaran, Inc.

Ang See, Teresita. 2004. *Chinese in the Philippines, Problems and Perspectives*. Vol. 3. Manila: Kaisa Para Sa Kaunlaran, Inc.

Ang See, Teresita, ed. 2007. *Tsinoy: The Story of the Chinese in Philippine Life*. Manila: Kaisa Para Sa Kaunlaran, Inc.

Ang See, Teresita. 2013. *Chinese in the Philippines, Problems and Perspectives*. Vol. 4. Manila: Kaisa Para Sa Kaunlaran, Inc.

Agoncillo, Teodoro A. and Milagros Guererro. 1970. *History of the Filipino People*. Quezon City: Garcia Publishing.

Alejandrino, Clark L. 2005. *A History of the 1902 Chinese Exclusion Act: American Colonial Transmission and Deterioration of Filipino-Chinese Relations*. Manila: Kaisa Para Sa Kaunlaran, Inc.

Amyot, Jacques S.J. 1973. *The Manila Chinese: Familism in the Philippine Environment*. Quezon City: Institute of Philippine Culture, Ateneo de Manila University.

Anderson, Benedict. 1991. *Imagined Communities: Reflections on the Origin and Spread of Nationalism*. London: Verso.

"Breakthrough ... But Who's Next?" 1993. *Tulay, Chinese-Filipino Digest* 5(8): 6–13.

Chen, Lie Fu. 1958. 菲律賓歷史與中菲關係的過去與現在 [*History of Philippines and Chinese Filipino Relationships: Past and Present*]. Taiwan: Zheng Zheng Books Printing Company (in Chinese).

Chen, Lie Fu. 1981. 菲律賓的民族文化與華僑同化問題 *[Chinese Filipino Education]*. Manila: Chinese Filipino Educational Publishing Company (*in Chinese*).

Chen, Tai Min. 1961. 中菲關係與菲律賓華僑第一冊 [*Sino-Philippine Relations and Philippine Overseas Chinese*]. Manila: Yi Tong Publishing House (*in Chinese*).

Chu, Richard. 2016. "Interview by Carmelea Ang See." *Department of Political Science, National Taiwan University: For China Studies and Cross Taiwan Strait Relations*, 14 January. Retrieved 23 February 2018 (http://www.china-studies. taipei/act02.php).

Chu, Richard. 2010, 2012. *Chinese and Chinese Mestizos of Manila: Family, Identity, and Culture, 1860s–1930s*. Leiden and Boston: Brill; Pasig City: Anvil Publishing House.

Chu, Richard. 2010. *Chinese Merchants of Binondo in the Nineteenth Century*. Manila: University of Santo Tomas Press.

Chu, Richard, ed. 2015. *More Tsinoy than We Admit, Chinese-Filipino Interactions over the Centuries*. Quezon City: Vibal Foundation, Inc.

Chu, Richard T. and Caroline Hau, eds. 2013. *Forum Kritika: Regional Studies of the Chinese Diaspora in the Philippines*. Kritika Kultura 21/22.

Felix, Alfonso Jr. 1966. *The Chinese in the Philippines, 1570–1770*. Vol 1. Manila: Solidaridad Publishing.

*Examining the challenges and possibilities in Tsinoy Studies* 79

Felix, Alfonso Jr. 1972. *The Chinese in the Philippines, 1770–1898*. Vol 2. Vancouver: University of British Columbia.

Go, Bon Juan. 2015. "Interview by Carmelea Ang See." *Department of Political Science, National Taiwan University: For China Studies and Cross Taiwan Strait Relations,* 18 November. Retrieved 23 February 2018 (http://www.china-studies. taipei/act02.php).

Go, Bon Juan. 2001. *Long Live the Filipino People*. Manila: Kaisa Para Sa Kaunlaran, Inc.

Go, Bon Juan. 1996. *Myths about the Ethnic Chinese "Economic Miracle."* Manila: Kaisa Para Sa Kaunlaran, Inc.

Go, Bon Juan. 1990, 1997, 2001. *Rong He (Integration),* three volumes (in Chinese). Manila: Kaisa Para Sa Kaunlaran, Inc.

Hilberto, Demetrio L. 1985. *Calamba in War and Peace: A History of the Heroes' Hometown*. Manila: LACS Graphic Corporation.

Hobsbawm, Eric and Terence Ranger, eds. 1983. *The Invention of Tradition (Past and present publications)*. Cambridge: Cambridge University Press.

Jensen, Khin Khin Myint. 1975. *The Chinese in the Philippines during the American Regime: 1898–1946*. San Francisco, CA: R and E Research Associates.

Kaisa.org.ph. 2015. "We Are Kaisa." Retrieved from www.kaisa.org.ph.

Kaisa Para Sa Kaunlaran Research Division, ed. 2001. *Bridge-builder in our Midst*. Manila: Kaisa Para Sa Kaunlaran, Inc.

Kaisa Para Sa Kaunlaran Research Division, ed. 2001. *Lessons Written in Blood*. Manila: Kaisa Para Sa Kaunlaran, Inc.

"Kidnap Fever Intensifies in Manila." 1992. *Tulay, Chinese-Filipino Digest* 4(7):6–7.

"Kidnap Watch: A Summing Up For 2006." 2007. *Tulay Fortnightly, Chinese-Filipino Digest* 20(15):3.

Leonard, Karen Isaksen. 1992. *Making Ethnic Choices, California's Punjabi Mexican Americans*. Philadelphia, PA: Temple University Press.

Liu, Zhi Tian. 1952. 華僑與菲律濱 *[The Overseas Chinese and the Philippines]*. Manila: Kong Li Po (in Chinese).

McBeath, Gerald. 1973. *Political Integration of the Philippine Chinese*. Berkeley, CA: Center for South and Southeast Asia Studies, University of California.

McCarthy, Charles J. 1971. *Philippine-Chinese Integration*. Manila: Pagkakaisa Sa Pag-Unlad.

McCarthy, Charles J. 1973. "The Chinese in the Philippines." In *Philippine-Chinese Profile: Essays and Studies,* edited by Charles McCarthy. Manila: Pagkakaisa Sa Pag-Unlad.

Omohundro, John. 1981. *Chinese Merchant Families in Iloilo: Commerce and Kin in a Central Philippine City*. Quezon City and Ohio: Ateneo de Manila University Press and Ohio University Press.

Ong, Aihwa and Donald Macon Nonini, eds. 1997. *Ungrounded Empires: The Cultural Politics of Modern Chinese Transnationalism*. London and New York: Routledge.

Reynolds, I. Hubert and Harriet Reynolds. 1998. *Chinese in Ilocos: 1950s–1960s*. Manila: Kaisa Para SaKaunlaran, Inc.

Tan, Antonio S. 1981. *The Chinese in the Philippines during the Japanese Occupation, 1942–1945*. Quezon City: University of the Philippines Press.

## 80  *Carmelea Ang See*

Tan, Antonio S. 1984. *The Chinese Mestizos and the Formation of the Filipino Nationality*. QC: Asian Center, University of the Philippines.

Tilman, Robert O. 1974. "Philippine-Chinese youth. Today and Tomorrow." In *Philippine-Chinese Profile: Essays and Studies*, edited by Charles McCarthy. Manila: Pagkakaisa Sa Pag-unlad.

Wickberg, Edgar. 2000. *The Chinese in Philippine Life, 1850–1898*. Quezon City: Ateneo de Manila University Press. (First published in 1965 by Yale University Press)

Wickberg, Edgar. 2001 *The Chinese Mestizos in Philippine History*. Manila: Kaisa Para Sa Kaunlaran, Inc. (with Chinese translation by Go Bon Juan).

Yoshihara, Kunio. 1971. "A Study of Philippine Manufacturing Corporations." *The Developing Economics* 9(3):268–289.

# 5 Narratives and identity
## Active agency and the formation of counter-narratives

*Yvan Ysmael Yonaha*[1]

## Introduction

The concepts of "Filipino-ness" and "Chinese-ness" have had a complex relationship in the Philippines. Wickberg (1964: 63) explains that as early as the Spanish occupation of the islands legal distinctions have already been enforced between the "Indio," the Chinese, the Spanish, and the Chinese *mestizo*. The government of the colonial population, he continues, has been informed and reinforced by these distinctions: the "Indio" pays less tribute than the Chinese *mestizo* and the *mestizo* pays less tribute than what the Chinese pays for. Moreover, the first two groups are also forced to supply labor for the Spanish government while enjoying significantly more rights like mobility and participation in local governance.

It is made apparent in Wickberg's (1964) discussion that the development of the Chinese *mestizo* is brought about by a mixture of economic indispensability, political security, and religious fervor. He continues that the Chinese inhabitants of the country were found to be economically important by the Spaniards upon their arrival in the islands given the network of trade that they have developed across the archipelago. Nevertheless, the Chinese inhabitant's considerable population and their cultural differences with the Spaniards created a culture of mistrust without abrogating their economic necessity. The Spanish response was to encourage these inhabitants through incentives to settle permanently in the colony, convert to Catholicism, and marry—usually to the native population because of the lack in Chinese women. This policy is thought to create a new segment of the population that is both loyal to Spain and could be facilitative to advance missionary activity in China. It is thus that the Chinese *mestizo* is born in the Philippines and their legal distinction became formalized in 1741, reaching a total of 120,621 (Wickberg 1964; Comyn in Wickberg 1964). He continues that at the time, these mestizos were usually engaged in landholding and wholesale trading; activities that would eventually lead to the economic and social prominence of the Chinese mestizo in the Philippines due, in part, because of the capital inherited from their Chinese parent and because of the Spanish-imposed geographical limitation upon the Chinese which stifled competition.

## 82  Yvan Ysmael Yonaha

In an effort to make the Philippines into a profitable colony, the Spaniards would eventually liberalize the economy, ban Spanish officials from participating in trade, and relax rules on Chinese immigration and settlement in the country which enlivened the economic competition between the Chinese and Chinese *mestizo* (Wickberg 1964). More importantly, the Chinese *mestizo* were undergoing a process of social change that he called social Filipinization—an emergent cultural consensus drawn from a mixture of Indio and Spanish culture—where he believes the Chinese mestizo played an important role. He continues that the previous system of tribute which segmented the population into Indio, Chinese *mestizo,* and Chinese were also becoming more untenable because of the then economic restructuring in Philippine society which eventually led to its abolition in the 1880s and the application of a general property tax to the entire population.

Wickberg (1964) claims that the breakdown of the tribute system has rendered the legal distinction between Indios and *mestizo* unenforceable. The categories in due course evolved to include only Spanish, Filipino, or Chinese. In turn, the *mestizo* chose to identify as Filipino due to their shared "'Hispanicized' and 'Catholic Heritage'" and their participation in the revolution is an indication that they have begun to identify their interests with that of the Indio (Wickberg 1964; Wickberg [1965] 2000 in Chu 2010:5). This would have lasting effects in the future as when the United States ushered in its rule in the Philippines, the mestizos were categorized along with the Filipinos while the Chinese remained as aliens and the old distinction between Indio, Chinese, and Chinese *mestizo* gave way to Filipino and non-Filipino alien (Wickberg [1965] 2000 in Chu 2010).

While the previous work traced the development of the Chinese *mestizo* since it acquired legal status in 1741 until this legal status gave way in the face of changing economic, political, and social structures up until 1989, Chu (2010) overlaps and continues the conversation by looking at the 1860s to the 1930s. For the purposes of this chapter, the discussion will begin in Chu's (2010) arguments regarding American imperialism in the Philippines and its subsequent effect on Chinese ethnicity. To him, American imperialism in the Philippines saw the hardening division between segment of the population considered Chinese and those considered Filipino due to a combination of American policies regarding foreigners and the Chinese and the emerging Filipino and Chinese nationalism.

One instrument that the Americans immediately imposed in the Philippines was the Chinese exclusion act which "was designed to restrict the entry of both skilled and unskilled Chinese laborers" (Chu 2010:282). Its proclamation by General Otis and its eventual ratification of the US Congress, he argues, was because of race, economics, and politics. Racially, the Chinese were considered heathens and Chinese *mestizos* were viewed with suspicion having been significant figures in the revolution. Economically, Chinese laborers were thought of as competition to "native" labor while also difficult to govern because they transfer from work to work and have

## Narratives and identity 83

many names. Politically, the Americans were suspicious of China because of its potential to developing as a superpower like Japan. In the end, the US Congress would extend the Chinese Exclusion Act to both the Philippines and Hawaii preventing Chinese unskilled laborers while allowing the Chinese from better strata to enter under certain conditions. He writes,

> Ultimately, the decision to exclude the Chinese was based on the different arguments presented above, including the desire to show their new colonial subjects and anti-imperialists in the metropole that the goal of the United States in annexing the Philippines was to preserve "the Philippines for the Filipinos," as well as to prevent the Chinese from using the Philippines as a stepping stone to the United States.
>
> Chu (2010:288)

The Chinese in the Philippines then also had to contend with the new citizenship laws imposed by the Americans. Chu (2010), drawing from Azcuna (1969), Jensen (1975), and Hau (2000), explains that the Philippine Bill of 1902 and the Chinese Exclusion Laws both promulgated by the American government created a situation where Chinese *mestizo* already born in the Philippines and whose parents remained Chinese subjects (as opposed to Spanish subjects) were themselves considered "Chinese" unless they elected to be "Filipino" upon their age of majority, in effect marking the abrogation of Chinese *mestizo* as a legal category. Eventually, Chu (2010:290, see also Aguilar 2011) continues that

> [i]n 1916, Section 4 of the [Philippine Bill of 1902] was amended to authorize the Philippine Legislature to grant Philippine citizenship to specific classes of persons, and this was re-enacted by the Philippine Autonomy Act or Jones Act of 1916. In 1917, the Philippine Supreme Court changed the citizenship law by ruling that anyone, whether born of two Chinese parents or of mixed Chinese-Filipino parentage, was, by the principle of jus soli, when born in the Philippines a Filipino citizen (Jensen 1975, 163). In 1920, the Philippine Legislature enacted the first naturalization law under Act No. 2927 which provided for the naturalization of those "native" to the Philippines but did not possess Filipino citizenship.
>
> (Chu 2010:290)

Additionally, and following the same source, Chinese nationalism both in the Philippines and in China has also contributed to the developing divide between "Filipino" and "Chinese" in the country. Chu (2010) refers to Chinese nationalism as

> the ideology spread by leading thinkers in China during the late nineteenth and early twentieth centuries that focused on "saving China" from being destroyed or overtaken by Western or Japanese powers, and

84  *Yvan Ysmael Yonaha*

encouraged patriotism among the Chinese. This type of nationalism also involved the construction of a "pure" Han racial identity based on an invented tradition and long history of shared values, attributes, habits, and culture.

(2010:314)

One way that the embattled Qing government did in the promotion of this kind of nationalism, according to Chu's (2010) citing Douw (1999), was by reaching out to the *huaqiao* (華僑) or "overseas Chinese" in order to reignite their connections with China even if their history in the "host" country included more than one generation.

In the Philippines, according to Chu (2010), this nationalism took the form of establishing consulates and professional organizations both through the aid of the Chinese government and the initiative of Chinese merchant families. Eventually, he informs us that this relationship has reached a point that the Chinese government has granted citizenship to Chinese living abroad, regardless of their area of birth, through the principle of *jus sanguinis*. In fostering a separate identity from the "host" country, he claimed, these movements of the Chinese government were supported by the anti-Chinese treatment received in their host countries including the Philippines.

The Philippine form of nationalism built upon the anti-Chinese policies promulgated by the Americans (Chu 2010). Though vetoed by the American executive or struck down by the American Supreme Court, the Philippine Legislature then enacted laws such as the Bookkeeping Act and an immigration bill. He explains that the Bookkeeping Act was meant to require Chinese businesspersons to write their records in "English, Spanish or any Philippine dialect" (2010:323), while the immigration bill requires all Chinese residents in the country to be registered within the year it was promulgated. Chu (2010) citing Hau (2000) mentioned that the Chinese were also accused of only trying to acquire citizenship because of possible economic gain. It is the combination of these factors: American imperial government, Filipino nationalism, and Chinese nationalism, Chu (2010) argues, that ossified the distinction between "Chinese" and "Filipino."

After the American period, the circumstances surrounding those with Chinese descent and their relationship with the Philippines remain to be an evolving issue. This chapter will provide an overview of two contemporary issues. First are two of the actions of the Philippine government under the Marcos dictatorship which provided a crucial step in the integration of those with Chinese descent in the Philippines, namely, LOI 270 and Presidential Decree 176 (Ang See 1989; Crossroads 1988; Ang See 2007). Second are the new Chinese immigrants or the xinqiao (Ang See 2007).

Philippine dictator Ferdinand Marcos (1975 & 1973) promulgated Letter of Instruction 270 s. 1975 and Presidential Decree 176 s. 1973 that would both have significant implications on the lives of those with Chinese descent in the country. LOI 270 or *Naturalization of deserving aliens by decree* provides specific guidelines for the naturalization of aliens that have had a long duration of stay in the country and have exhibited their allegiance and "usefulness" to the country. LOI 270 was issued before the Philippines opened its ties with the then nascent People's Republic of China and was issued to avoid

> the substantial number of Chinese nationals [in the Philippines] to be legally under the jurisdiction of a communist regime but also had the effect of hastening the integration of those of Chinese descent in mainstream Filipino society because of the sheer number of accepted applications.
>
> (Ang See 1989; Ang See 2007:141)

The same motives are ascribed by Ang See (1988) to Marcos's drive for the Filipinization of Chinese Schools. Presidential Decree 176 s. 1973 or *Implementing Section 8 (7), Article VX, of the New Constitution* banned the teaching of foreign curricula within the country. She noted that this move is an attempt by the dictator's government to minimize the possibility of foreign interference in the education of children residing in the Philippines and instead turn their allegiance to the Philippine state. While Ang See notes that these have been followed to the letter by the Chinese schools, she notes that there is a continuing need to assess the success of the program of inculcating allegiance to the Philippine state.

Ang See (2007) has also made distinctions between what she calls the xinqiao (new immigrants) and the jiuqiao (old immigrants). Paraphrasing Go Bon Juan (2002), Ang See (2007:141) makes the following distinctions between the two groups based on their "reasons for migrations, hometown of origins, means of immigrations (transportation used), 'quality' of the immigrants (like level of education, manners and civility), and relations with the local Chinese." The xinqiao tend to go to a foreign country not because of socioeconomic necessity but because they are looking for more opportunities abroad, despite the rise of China as an economic power. This is contrasted with the jiuqiao that had to migrate out of socioeconomic necessity in a China then struck with hardships. The jiuqiao also have had negative experiences with the xinqiao despite the latter enjoying better educational status. This is because the former finds the xinqiao "uncouth, ill-mannered and uncivilized (2007:142)," and they are even avoided within Chinese-language schools, being perceived by their classmates as "quite spoiled, are bullies and unruly, prone to cursing, and even in high school, many have been disciplined for gambling and smoking (2007:142)." After making this distinction, Ang See draws the attention of the reader to the implications of illegally staying xinqiao in the country. To put it succinctly, illegally staying xinqiao becomes a new group of people eyed by predatory immigration agents for corruption. Efforts by the government to curb this kind of activity through raids are also a cause of concern for human rights because of indiscriminate arrest of people who 'look Chinese' thus implicating even the

## 86  Yvan Ysmael Yonaha

local Chinese-Filipino population. This implication extends even to the general population of the cultural minority because distinctions are not made between the jiuqiao and the xinqiao by some law enforcement agents.

The preceding discussion provides the context for the continuing complex relationship between "Filipino-ness" and "Chinese-ness." This chapter offers a modest contribution by looking at the realities of being Chinese Filipino in contemporary Philippines from the life experiences of senior China experts including the counter-narratives they formulated to battle stereotypes, correct government policies or in completing stories. The intention here is less about developing explanations for certain realities (e.g. racism) and more on creating a systematic understanding of the imaginary of the senior China experts. As scholars, activists, and writers, the senior China experts offer a unique take because of their involvements (e.g. leading the Philippine Association for Chinese Studies, editing an anthology of Chinese-Filipino Writing) with institutions and agents that are influential to the lives of the Chinese and Chinese Filipinos in the Philippines. This chapter maps out their perspectives on matters that they themselves discuss, systematize the similarities, and lay down their discussed contribution to counter-narratives on ethnicity without claiming generalizability to the entire population concerned.

### Framework and methodology

This chapter utilized the generated transcripts of the interviews of Caroline Hau (2015), Charlson Ong (2016), and Teresita Ang-See (2015). The transcripts were coded to separate personal encounters; public encounters; and the counter-narratives generated through their activities, publications, and organizations. Table 5.1 provides the definition for the *a priori* codes used.

*Table 5.1* A Priori Codes

| Code Name | Description | Examples |
|---|---|---|
| Public encounters | Events that pertain or the senior China experts believe to pertain to issues of communal or national significance which are external or they perceive to be external to their (or their immediate circle's) experience | Nationalization of education, opening of ties to China |
| Personal encounters | Events that pertain to senior China experts' (or their immediate circle's) direct experiences which may or may not be reflective of national issues | Studied abroad, visited China |
| Counter-narratives | Actions or discourses (or events which assist in the creation of these actions or discourses) which challenge actual or perceived characterizations of their perceived community | Reflexive identities |

Originally, *public encounters* were called *national issues*, while *personal encounters* were called *personal issues* and were coded accordingly. Changes in the label were done post-coding to better reflect the realities that were present in the transcripts. For example, some events such as founding an organization could be coded *personal issue* which may unnecessarily add a perception that a problem exists when there is none. It has been decided that the term *encounter* is superior in describing the segments that were coded. The use of the word *national* was dropped because some coded segments were not national issues but were instead of *public* concern.

At the same time, separating *personal encounters* and *public encounters* does not assume a separation between the personal experience of the senior China experts and public issues in the country or community. In fact, as the reader would see, the problems encountered on the personal level may also be matters of pertinence in the public sphere. The separation is simply for conceptual clarity to emphasize the thoughts of the senior China experts about their own lives and their takes about matters that are important to a larger community.

After using the codes from Table 5.1, the text segments are subjected to open coding or "[t]he first coding of qualitative data that examines the data to condense them into preliminary analytic categories or codes" (Neuman 2011:511). Codes were usually derived from the transcript themselves. The third step was to subject the codes developed from open coding into *axial coding* or the "second stage of coding of qualitative data during which the researcher organizes the codes, links them, and discovers key analytic categories" (Neuman 2011:512). The main themes presented here are the result of axial coding.

## Community and identity

This section looks at the commonalities that could be found in the experience of the senior China experts regarding the importance of networks and institutions; their experience of being sensitized to ethnic differences; and the enduring pertinence of China, as a field, in their thinking.

### *Networks and institutions*

The networks of the senior China experts in the form of university partnerships, epistemological communities, and professional associations have had a substantial impact on their intellectual development having served as a facilitative factor in their journey of attempting to understand China, problematize nationalism, and completing communal narratives. This could be in the form of resources pooled, mentorships provided, or as an incentive for the continuation of their work.

Kyoto University has been instrumental to Hau's (2015) intellectual development through its grants, research support, and institutional linkages

## 88 *Yvan Ysmael Yonaha*

aimed to deepen understanding about China and Southeast Asia. The university, she claims, has supported her research initiatives and created connections with leading Chinese and Philippine higher education institutions such as Xiamen, Chi Nan, Sun Yat-Sen, the Asian Center of the University of the Philippines, San Carlos University, and Mindanao State University. Its Center for South East Asian Studies has also served as a secretariat for the Consortium for Southeast Asian Studies in Asia (SEASIA) and invited Chinese scholars working on the field of China and Southeast Asia to attend in their 2015 Conference. Similarly, Ong (2015) has been able to use the writing grants of the (Philippine) National Commission for Culture and the Arts (NCCA) as an additional incentive to novelize his detailed screenplay. Though he was unsuccessful in winning the NCAA grant, his entry for the grant yielded *Banyaga: A Song of War*; a novel which has attempted to intersperse the story of the Chinese and Chinese Filipinos in Philippine history through fiction.

Noninstitutional networks also prove instrumental to the senior China experts' engagement with China as an object of inquiry. Hau (2015) served as one of Ong's (2015) reader and critique and both are involved in the publication of *Instik: An Anthology of Chinese Filipino Writing*. Meanwhile, Teresita Ang See, Go Bon Juan, Joaquin Sy, Wang Gungwu, Wang Hui, and Jun Aguilar served as mentors for Hau (2015). They have, according to her interview, inspired her intellectual journey through their research, their personal mentorship, and have facilitated her publications. Jun Aguilar of Ateneo de Manila University, as editor of the Philippine Studies Journal, marshalled her works on Chinese Filipinos to publication while she draws inspiration from Ang See's strength as an advocate against the rampant kidnappings of Chinese nationals back then while also benefitting from the extensive publication work Ang See is engaged in. Hau states,

> I was active in Kaisa Para Sa Kaunlaran, which is an organization where Teresita Ang See, Go Bon Juan, Joaquin Sy were also active with, so I was lucky enough to have had a chance to meet these *three very influential people who really shaped my life and my thinking that early*, even before I went to, or maybe when I was just starting in, college.
>
> (Hau 2015:4, *emphasis added*)

The discussion above renders clear that communities are important factors in the development of Philippine scholarship—within which See, Hau, and Ong belong as Filipino Chinese scholars—on China, the Chinese in South East Asia, and the Chinese Filipino. A formation of a vibrant community of scholars that tackle China issues within the academe can provide an arena of conversation to enrich cultural and strategic understanding of varying issues at hand. Also, as Hau (2015) argues, language instruction that is able to bridge the gaps among different language communities—or in this case the

*Narratives and identity* 89

Philippines and China—will be useful to deepen the understanding among different academic traditions.

### Sensitizing differences

Even as the senior China experts are able to utilize their connections to further their understanding of China, they remain agents subjected to a web of power relations in communities that they are embedded in. During the course of their lives as Chinese Filipinos, they have had experiences, which sensitized them to ethnic differences which construed them as an "Other" in a backdrop of an imagined homogenous Philippine nation. This homogenization is especially seen in a postcolonial setting where, as Aguilar (2011:433) states, "citizenship was seized upon by ruling elites to promote a narrow, conservative, and homogenizing nationalism." Ong (2016), Hau (2015), and Ang See (2015) shared a similar circumstance of living in the archipelago and being educated in the University of the Philippines (UP) and yet have had very different dealings with *citizenship rights*. Ong had no problems relating to citizenship when he was studying in UP because he is a natural born citizen. Hau and Ang See have had similar experiences of sensitization in UP albeit in varying degrees. Hau (2015) recounted that her experience in UP nuanced her understanding of herself in relation to her classmates and subsequently provided one of the impetus for her scholarship on identity. On the other hand, Teresita Ang See's exposure to education in UP has served as a pivotal moment on her views on ethnicity and the state's enforcement of citizenship. Ang See was considered a Chinese citizen until her age of majority and one marker of her difference is having to pay an Alien Registration Fee when she was studying in UP. Moreover, because her family is not engaged in business, she reveals that she was not conscious that being a Chinese citizen then could pose considerable disadvantages.

If citizenship served as the formal process of imposing difference, there were also *informal mechanisms* by which this is reinforced. Caroline Hau (2015) recalls an instance when she was mockingly mimicked by children while speaking Hokkien in public—one of the moments that she feels ethnic differences are etched in her consciousness. Chu (2010) recalls a similar fate. In his Introduction to his book *Chinese and Chinese Mestizos of Manila: Family, Identity, and Culture, 1860s to 1930s*, he narrates that part of his interest in studying the relationship between the "Filipino" and the "Chinese" has been borne out of his experience in university, when he was referred to as *Intsik* and *not "Filipino,"* despite having identified as *both Filipino and Chinese* when he was younger and having performed symbolic gestures, such as the recitation of *Panatang Makabayan* (Patriotic Oath); cheering for Filipino basketball teams; studying Filipino history; speaking Hokkien, English, and Filipino at home; and writing down "Filipino" in forms asking for citizenship.

## 90   *Yvan Ysmael Yonaha*

To be sure, the mechanisms which enforce differences are not only per-petuated by "mainstream Filipino society" against a perceived "Other" but are also reinforced by mechanisms from within the Chinese-Filipino community such as, but no limited to, *Chinese schools.* Chu (2010), drawing from Tan (1972), explains that the then nascent Republic of China sought to inspire "Chinese-ness" among those living abroad through Chinese schools that encompass programs similar to those prescribed by the Republic's Ministry of Education. Ang See (2015) problematizes the functioning of Chinese schools *in the past*—whose instruction, she believes, involves loyalty to China instead to the Philippine state. She explains that studying within Chinese schools then isolated Chinese Filipinos from their larger context. Her own education from the Anglo-Chinese School and the Chiang Kai-Shek College created, for her, a sheltered environment. For Ang See, these schools are "bastions of ultraconservatism and ethnocentrism" (T. Ang See and C. Ang See 2013/2014:11). Her pivotal moment that would deepen her understanding of ethnic issues would come later within the heterogenous confines of the University of the Philippines. Ong (2016) did not experience outright discrimination because he studied in Xavier School for Basic and Secondary Education which according to him is a Chinese-majority school and while Hau (2015) did not comment on how Chinese schools can shelter from discrimination, she herself studied in St. Stephens High School, a "Chinese" school.

### China as an enduring source of identity

Before discussing how China remains an enduring source of identity, it is important to explain the way "China" is understood in this chapter. This chapter takes the cue from Hau's (2015) discussion on how China as a source of heritage is not necessarily tied to the concept of the nation-state or to its current government. The quote from the following transcript shows the nuances of China as an object of study:

> Many scholars have debated China or what China is. There's no consensus on what China is: Is it the current government? Is it the nation-state? Is it the civilizational process? Is it Cultural China? "What is China?" has been one the biggest questions. Is it the Kuomintang-led government that used to call itself the Republic of China? What about the people who prefer to call themselves Taiwanese? Is it the communist state?
> (Hau 2015:20)

The same predicament has been expressed comprehensively by Hau (2014) in another work.

> But what does it mean to identify oneself as "Chinese" and with "China"? Is "China" the mainland state known as the People's Republic of China,

*Narratives and identity* 91

as the Philippine government has officially acknowledged since the establishment of diplomatic relations in 1975? Is it the Republic of China based in Taiwan, which had been an anticommunist ally of the Philippines during the Cold War era and whose Kuomintang branch had played an active role in Chinese-community affairs in the Philippines? Is it a "Greater China" defined in terms of the combined markets of China, Hong Kong, and Taiwan (plus Macau and perhaps Singapore)? Is "China" a civilization or a nation-state? Or is it "Cultural China" (Tu 1991), a way of expanding the definition of "Chinese" beyond a single nation-state by including those who identify themselves as Chinese; those who are called Chinese; those who subscribe to "Chinese" values, ideas, "traditions", and patterns of behavior (in whatever ways these are defined); and also those who study Chinese and China...? What does it mean to say that one is "pure Chinese" if one means not only ancestry, based on the "myth of blood" (Dikotter 1992, 116) but also access to something called "Chinese culture"?

(Hau 2014:24)

Drawing from these, China as an object of study may be divided into different components. Some understand China as the nation-state, others see China as those who are descended from peoples from China, and some think of China as a cultural resource autonomous from the nation state. This chapter uses the term China, in this discussion, to mean the third definition. This chapter emphasizes this to avoid essentialist notions on Chinese and Chinese-Filipino loyalties especially in the context of contemporary territorial disputes. In other words, this chapter uses the term China to refer to its dimension as a cultural resource from which the senior China experts continued to draw from as part of their heritage.

China as an enduring source of identity is primarily secured by family customs such as parental influences, domicile practices, and family lore. Hau's (2015) family of flour retailers decided to pursue traditional Chinese painting in the Ling Nan tradition which exposed her to Chinese arts and letters. She recalls her childhood as consisting of stories about China, exposed to books and art materials, and the lively network that her parents maintained in their career in the arts. In fact, and she narrates, her parents invited Chinese artists in the Philippines for an exhibition and were, in turn, invited by the People's Exhibition Agency for their work which was eventually published by the People's Publishing House in an album. According to her, at home, they speak Hokkien, Tagalog, and English. Perhaps unsurprisingly, literary critique would become one of her mediums in the problematization of the concept of nation in the Philippines.

Family lore and its inextricable ties with China served as basis for parts of Ong's (2015) work. Ong recalls that one of his stories in *Banyaga: A Song of War* is based on the relationship between his grandfather and grandmother. Ah Beng and his mother's story in the novel, where they traveled to

## 92   Yvan Ysmael Yonaha

the Philippines without their patriarch's instructions, were drawn from the story of his grandfather deciding to send his grandmother back to his natal home in China. It resulted to conflict when his grandmother returned to the Philippines after giving birth without the instructions from the patriarch. Some other themes from his work such as the Chinese as a merchant and having multiple wives as a sign of wealth have also been drawn from his own family. In a sense, family lore continues to connect the senior China experts to China as a cultural source.

Choice of domicile for her brother and language formed the links Ang See (2015) had to China as a geographical reality. She relates that her eldest brother lived in China for 2 years at the insistence of their paternal grandmother during the family's first visit to China. The brother was brought back to the Philippines because of the Communist Revolution in 1949 (Ang See 2015; T. Ang See and C. Ang See 2013/2014). Due to this, Ang See's (2015) brother initially had difficulty in pronouncing the letter "r" and was subsequently teased as a child because of his "inappropriate" pronunciation of Filipino words. She narrates that though they did not perceive this as a race issue at the time, it shows that language has become an important marker of identity. At home, her Filipina mother was able to speak Hokkien fluently. This, she believes, may have been influential to the acceptance of her mother among their relatives. She, however, has never visited China until 1988 and visited her father's hometown for the first time in 2003.

In fact, the Greater China Area is a space where the senior China experts have interacted or continue to interact on a regular basis. One of the short stories written by Ong (1999; 2015), *Another Country*, draws from his experience working in Taiwan as an editor. He (2016) traveled to Taipei after the EDSA Revolution[2] and returned to the Philippines after a 7- to 8-month stint. There were also instances, he continues, when he returned to the mainland as a translator for *Hari sa Hari, Lahi sa Lahi* (1987), a film co-produced by the Philippines and China. The same can be said for Hau (2015) whose family have taken up lives in Zhangzhou, Xiamen, and Shenzhen while China, for her, has become an area for academic exploration.

Notice how even events in China are still interspersed within the lives of the senior China experts. Ong (2016) perceives that his father, who was a Kuomintang sympathizer, was not alone in his support for the Kuomintang among those of Chinese descent in the Philippines because of its characteristic as a merchant community. In the case of Ang See, family choices have been made and undone because of unfolding events in China. It was already mentioned that in the case of her brother, when in the outbreak of the Communist Revolution, her brother was brought back into the Philippines. Similarly, Ang See's father, Jose Ang, immigrated to the Philippines "when he was just twelve at the height of the civil unrest, warlordism, and skirmishes between the Communist and Kuomintang armies" (T. Ang See and C. Ang See 2013/2014:7). Living in the Philippines, in fact, does not mean that institutions in China are unable to interact with the senior

*Narratives and identity* 93

China experts. Ong (2016), to illustrate, recounts his experience when he visited China on the invitation of the Chinese government owing to a program which seeks to maintain links with people of Chinese descent, even if the person lived his or her life on a "foreign" land, and even if this person hardly speaks Chinese. Ang See (2015) has also attended similar events organized by the China Overseas Exchange Association but is not particularly active in associations like this. However, Ang See insists that for the younger generation, the Kuomintang-Communist split has no relevance because many (like her students at the Ateneo de Manila University) cannot even distinguish who Sun Yat Sen, Chiang Kai Shek, Mao Tse Tung, and Chou En Lai were. For example, Paul Stephen Lim (1982 in Ang See 1989:7) writes,

> I am Chinese but I do not sympathize with Chiang Kai Shek ... I am Chinese, and yet I take no pride in Mao Tse Tung ... I am Chinese yet my roots are Philippine. So, why is it that I have never identified (and continue to feel that I will never be able to identify) completely with Filipinos? I know only one thing-everyday, I feel the alienation growing.

## Public encounters

Public encounters in this chapter are events that pertain or the senior China experts believe to pertain to issues of communal or national significance. Another qualification is that these events should be external or are believed to be external from themselves or their immediate circles' experiences. In this chapter, these public encounters are divided into two major themes: historical viewpoints and academia.

One important historical viewpoint, from the imaginary of the senior China experts, is the way the imperialist powers treated the ethnic Chinese in the Philippines. Ong (2016) draws from passed on stories and his personal imagination to characterize how the Chinese nationals and those of Chinese descent in the Philippines were treated by both the Japanese Occupation Government and the anti-Japanese guerillas during the Second World War. People of Chinese descent who engaged in the junk trade, in his work, were torn between the heavy restrictions imposed by the Japanese and the demand for support by anti-Japanese guerillas who perceive non-cooperation as implicit support for Japanese imperialism. This encounter is vividly painted in the lives of the characters of Ong (2006) in *Banyaga: A Song of War*. This characterization of a hostile environment is in stark contrast to Ong's (1999; 2006) portrayal of Manila as a land of promise and China as a place to return to.

Similarly, Ang See (2015) recalls the 1987 Angeles Anti-Chinese Rally led by the "furniture industry" suffering from the logging ban at the time. She continues that the national policy on logging ban was being blamed on the

Chinese and alleges that this is a diversionary tactic perpetrated by a foreign power to create an "Other" to serve as the new enemy. She decries that there has been very little effort from the said power to understand the nuanced position of the Chinese Filipinos. For example, she claims that the Filipino-Chinese Chamber of Commerce only switched sympathy from Taiwan to China in 1999 (Ang See 2015). She mentions the statement of sociologist Randy David claiming that racism could be a vehicle for a particular political end goal. Chu (2010) citing Ang See (2005), McCoy and Roces (1985), and Wong (1999) have also narrated a similar experience when Chinese traders were blamed for the rice shortage in 1919 produced by hoarding not only by the same Chinese traders but also by Filipino landholders, farm and import mismanagement, and the demand for food among the Allied Forces in Europe.

Still, discrimination does not only come from without but may also be from local social structures. Hau (2015) uncovered documents from the Katipunan, a revolutionary group that sought to overthrow Spanish colonialism in the Philippines, describing the Chinese in a negative light. Hau says,

> I was also bothered when I first came across the foundational documents of the Katipunan and found a very important passage where they basically said, you can't learn anything from the Chinese because they know only trickery, thievery and misery, the Chinese are not capable of imparting anything enlightening that you can learn from ... The kind of anti-Chinese sentiment that shaped the Katipunan's foundational documents bothered me greatly, because I always thought of myself as Filipino.
>
> (Hau 2015: 6)

Through time, however, she noted that sentiments regarding the Chinese and Chinese Filipinos have been changing with anti-Chinese sentiments becoming harder and harder to articulate in public. She recalls the attempts at integration during Pres. Corazon Aquino's time when many Chinese *Mestizos* acknowledged openly their Chinese descent.

Nationally, the interactions with the Philippine state is a mixed bag. Ang See (2015) notes the circumstances of some people of Chinese-descent in the Philippines before the normalization of the diplomatic relations with the People's Republic of China and the former. Lacking formal citizenship, they were barred from practicing the professions that, she believes, could have had an integrative effect among different ethnic groups ("Filipinos" and "Chinese" because of inter-group interactions). Instead, she continues, those of Chinese descent would only be able to engage in business. Ong (2016) also mentioned the Retail Trade Nationalization Law which sought to curb Chinese domination of the retail business. Kidnapping has been a particular concern for all three senior China experts. Hau (2015) is concerned with the

*Narratives and identity*  95

kidnappings of Chinese Filipinos in the 1990s which Ong (2000b) alluded to in his short story *Mismanagement of Grief.* Chu (2010), paraphrasing Ang See (1997), noted that the Philippine government has given less priority to Chinese-Filipino kidnapping victims compared to people from Japan and the United States.[3] Still, and more positively, Hau (2015) also notes that there is a fundamental change in the attitude of the Filipinos in relation to the ethnic Chinese Filipinos. She posits that this may be due to the phenomenon of more and more Filipinos traveling abroad which in turn cultivates values of pluralism and tolerance in society.

Lastly, the promises and challenges in academia retain a certain pertinence with the senior China experts; not only with their individual lives but also to the ethnic community in general. For example, education can still be a potent source for division between the ethnic Chinese and "mainstream" Philippine society. When asked to provide an explanation for the disconnect between the "facts" that some of those with Chinese descent were born here in the country and yet maintains an attitude of "returning" to China, Ang See (2015) answered thus:

> I think the biggest disconnect lies in the school system, the way we were brought up. All the teachers were graduates of National Taiwan University, or if it's Cultural, the Q*iao Zhong* (桥中; abbreviated Chinese for Philippine Cultural College) maybe graduates from Jimei (集美) [University] in China. So, the sentiments are all towards China. I would say it's the upbringing and the education.
>
> (Ang See 2015:5)

To be sure, there is a need to nuance this attitude of "returning." As early as 1989, Ang See (1989) has already described signs of integration such as in changes in perceived parental attitudes on intermarriage, religious beliefs, and food choices. Nevertheless, Academia as a potent tool for socialization may still lead to certain disconnects between the actual geographical "home" of those of Chinese descent and what they perceive as "home." In higher education, even academic programs that comprehensively tackle certain subject matters need to question the traditions from which they draw knowledge. Hau (2015) explains that Philippine Studies has not been able to expand much to include in its subject matter its neighbors in Asia because its tradition is drawn from an American-Western tradition. She cites as proof the limited number of scholars adept at Japanese and Chinese Studies especially in its original language. This is not to say that there has been minor change in the way Filipinos tried to understand or interact with neighbors. Looking at larger socioeconomic changes, Hau (2015) claims that Filipinos like the Aboitiz learn Hokkien in aid of business interests. She admits, however, that academic exploration of the Philippines' Asian neighbors still has a long way to go especially if compared to Japanese Sinology, which is being read even within China.

## Counter-narratives

Counter-narratives are actions and discourses (or events which assist in the creation of these actions or discourses) which challenge actual or perceived characterizations of their perceived community. This discussion is divided into three sections: vehicles of counter-narratives, elaboration on regional connections, and problematizing the nation.

### *Vehicles of counter-narratives*

Kaisa Para sa Kaunlaran (Kaisa) remains to be one of the important vehicles for counter-narratives in the lives of the senior China experts. Ang See (2015) was there during its transition when it was still called Pagkakaisa into Kaisa which is a nuance born out of the discernment that integration is already underway. She had to accept the presidency of the new group to avoid division in its current ranks. In her own words,

> That is why at the end, I had to reluctantly accept the presidency. I was crying when they finally elected me ... Because I was a young widow at that time, they could see how bad I've felt. But I've realized also that nobody could foil [him (pertaining to a China-oriented member who badly wanted to lead) ] ... except me because I was the one who tied up all the groups together—the group of Bon Juan (English name of Go Bon Juan—吳文換, one of the founding members of Kaisa Para sa Kaunlaran) in Kiao Tiong (Hokkien spelling of Philippine Cultural College); the group of Xavier ... Harry Chua and Alex Tee; the group of ... Lolita Lim, attorney Juanito King were our colleagues in Ling Hui (Hokkien name of Grace Christian High School—菲律賓基督教靈惠學院); and then the Pagkakaisa group, Nancy Herrin, Alfred Pineda, Robert Tsai, was the key components of the organization ... I was the tie that got them all together, so there was no choice. Bon Juan dinned it on me, *"Chiu Na Lai Bo Ho, Lao Kao Ching Ong"* (Hokkien of "森林裡無虎, 猴子稱王 which means "Without a tiger in the forest, even a monkey can be king") the equivalent of the country of the blind.
>
> (Ang See 2015:9)

After assuming the Presidency, Ang See (2015) shepherded Kaisa into brainstorming sessions to create a new vision for the future. Some of the directions that were taken, she states, were heritage, development, and continuing research. She continues that included in the development work (during Pagkakaisa) are some exposure programs for young Chinese Filipinos to depressed areas that they would not be able to visit otherwise because of their privileged economic status.

As an organization, Kaisa was also facilitative of Hau's (2015) writings. *Tulay* (Bridge) is one of the venues through which she shared her thoughts to the public. Within the organization too she narrates her engagement with editing a collection entitled *Voices/Mga Tinig*. For Hau, "[her] involvement in Kaisa has a lot to do with learning to speak out as a Filipino while remaining aware of one's Chinese ancestry and heritage" (2015:5).

Creating works drawn from their personal experiences is another vehicle which facilitates their counter-narratives. Recall the previous sections discussing how Ong (2015) draws from family lore to paint a picture of the lives and struggles of people of Chinese descent. For him, the purpose is to draw a "sense of identity." Asked whether he had motives about writing his character or he only draws from the collective imagination with no ulterior motive, he replied, "It's where I'm coming from and the work of fiction or literature is also towards defining that sense of identity. At some point, the personal and your sense of community merge" (Ong 2015:2).

Interestingly, the same can be said for Hau (2015) who drew from stories of the war and sees her work in fiction and in the academe also as a way of understanding her position in society.

> My interest in things Chinese was a way to understand myself, my family, what sort of community I grew up in, and also to understand ethnic Chinese relations in Southeast Asia. It was less about China, and more about Chinese in the Philippines and Southeast Asia
>
> (Hau 2015:3)

Her grandfather served as a war guerilla in Laguna and Quezon during the Second World War and she took stories from that. In fact, she claims that her first love is fiction and she wanted to write instead of being an academic. She narrates that during her undergraduate years, she was already writing about Chinese Filipinos in *Tulay*; her fiction is a way to make sense of things. Later in life, Hau (2000) would write a (true?) story that tackles attachment to geography of those with Chinese descent who lived in the Philippines but longed for China. Ending her story on Ah To after his visit to China, Hau (2000) tells,

> What Ah To could not understand—and I had to wait until I was grown up to hear Ah To confess this and to figure out what it meant—was why he could not bring himself to let go of the shred of earth and sky, not the one he had brought back with him from Tsinkang, but the one he had had all along, the one he mistook for a replica, the original of which he had sought in China. He had gone into the swamps of Candaba understanding that he was ready to die for a place he could no longer, even then, remember clearly. And years later, when he tried to summon these images in his mind to fill in the tedium of being on the run, he had to admit to himself the (sic) he might have remembered the white sands, pristine waters, and curving eaves from his travels across Luzon and the Visayas.

## 98   *Yvan Ysmael Yonaha*

> ... Whenever I light joss sticks to the thirteen generals and their reti-
> nue in the temple on Tomas Mapua Street ... I light some for Ah To and
> for all the old men of my childhood who called up the spirits to watch
> over them, and their wives, and their children, *in a land that they do not
> know is their own.*
>
> (Hau 2000:133, *emphasis added*)

Aside from organization work, the senior China experts are also engaged in
debates in literary and academic circles in terms of their narratives about
people of Chinese descent. Ong (2015) continues to write fiction including
*Of That Other Country We Now Speak and other Short Stories* and a new
novel about a Chinese-Filipino surgeon whose stories tie with that of the
Black Nazarene and White Lady. In this chapter's view, especially in this
final work, Ong attempts to offer a multifaceted picture of reality by com-
bining factors drawn from Filipino piety and superstition combined with
the presence of the Chinese Filipino.

Owing to Hau's (2015) literary studies background, one of her main research interests is looking at how written and visual work relate to issues of
ethnicity of people of Chinese descent in Southeast Asia. To her, she offers a
take which overturns perspectives that centralizes the Chinese nation-state
and its influence on Overseas Chinese identity. Instead, she offers a view on
how regional and international relations between China and Japan, Southeast Asia, and the Anglo-Pacific regional system shape China itself. In the
case of the Philippines, Hau (2015:11) helps shape the literature "from the
margins" and avoids what she refers to as "canonical works" in Philippine
literature. The purpose of which is to look at the margin's implications on
Philippine nationalism. For Chinese Studies, she engages in a work of "retrieval" and tracks the changes in the literary world by looking at media
through the works of Charlson Ong, Bai Ren, Jose Angliongto, and Du Ai.
She states,

> I see my research as partly a work of retrieval, but also as work that
> tracks the changes in popular understandings of, and sentiments to-
> ward, the Chinese. But the focus has been mainly on literary and cine-
> matic works, and to a lesser extent, on history and politics.
>
> (Hau 2015:18)

She is convinced that a Philippine perspective can offer a unique way of
looking at China; stating that Southeast Asia has been the destination for
migrating Chinese, perspectives from Southeast Asian can offer a new and
profound perspective in understanding Chinese ethnicity in particular and
even ethnicities in general. She particularly notes that the legal recognition
of the Chinese *mestizo* during the Spanish colonization in the country, discussed earlier in Wickberg (1964), is a unique situation in Asia.

*Narratives and identity* 99

## Elaboration on regional connections

In their works, the senior China experts have sought an elaboration on regional connections, argued for the re-evaluation of the Philippines' assumed position in the globe, and called for the realization of the country's rootedness in Southeast Asia. They criticize the overly Western imaginary that always paints the country in terms of the colonizer—Spain and the United States—instead of the connections it has within the region. Ong (2016) states,

> An Embarrassment of Riches is more consciously political because it was for the PH centennial. Although I started writing the book before the centennial contest was launched. I wanted to come up with a book with a feel of a hundred years after 1898, to locate the imagined community in Southeast Asia, because I thought a lot of our literature especially in English from Nick Joaquin down paints us as Latin, Hispanic, Catholic. I wanted to write a Philippine novel where the imaginary is located in Southeast Asia because we've never done that. I think it's practical, or even more appropriate because our economy is really Southeast Asian. I wanted to write as well about the Chinese in Southeast Asia.
>
> (Ong 2016:2)

Ong (2015) believes that institutions such as the Asian Center of the Philippines should do more in terms of strategic planning as regards our relationship with China and serve as think tank for developing our China policy. He finds fault in hosting "soft-power projection" institutes within state universities such as the Confucius Institute because "[o]ne can never discount the possibility of political influence building in their activities" (2015:16).

Regional connections were also tackled by Hau (2015). She states that the territorial dispute between the Philippines and China requires more experts that are able to grapple with and explain the complexity of the situation. The increasing geographical and economic linkages in the region, she believes, make such scholars more pertinent. In relation to the territorial disputes, she believes that people to people interaction may also be productive in creating understanding in tandem with state to state talks.

Even more interesting is the interest their work has garnered in the international scene as some of their work has been translated into Chinese. Some of Ong's (2016) stories have been translated into Chinese by a student from China, who studies at the De La Salle University. Meanwhile, *Intsik: An Anthology of Chinese Filipino Writing* has been translated by Go Bon Juan, Joaquin Sy, and Anita Sy (Hau 2015). Some of her essays from the *Chinese Question* have also been translated to Chinese. She sees this as an opportunity for their work on the Chinese and those of Chinese descent in Southeast Asia to cross the language divide into Chinese-speaking academia.

## 100    *Yvan Ysmael Yonaha*

### *Problematizing the nation*

Lastly, a common problematique for the senior China experts is the nation; its composition and the position of the people of Chinese descent within. Citizenship rights play as a key component in integration from the perspective of Ang See:

> Until 1975, the lack of citizenship was the biggest stumbling block to the full integration of the local Chinese into mainstream society. Majority of the local Chinese did not have legal recognition as Filipinos before 1975, even if they were born in the Philippines, grew up, and were educated in the country; therefore, it was understandable that their sense of identification with the Philippines would also suffer.
>
> (T. Ang See and C. Ang See 2013/2014:15)

Citizenship rights based on the *jus soli* principle were part of Ang See (2015) and *Pagkakaisa sa Pag-Unlad*'s campaign that would have granted some of those of Chinese descent citizenship rights. At the time, they believed that there was no other direction for Chinese Filipinos to take but to integrate and this has led to some negative reception from their target audience. One such instance she (2015:4) recalls is when during a lecture in Chiang Kai-Shek College her husband was "almost literally thrown out" after discussing the need for Filipinization of Chinese Schools through an inculcation of loyalty and identification to the Philippines instead of toward China. Ang See (2015) believes that if the community has chosen to participate or take initiative in the Filipinization of Chinese schools, they may have been able to influence the process to reach more agreeable terms such as the continued explorations of Chinese culture without sacrificing loyalty to the Philippines. She believes that the same could be said of the Retail Trade Nationalization Law, had the Chinese-Filipino community been willing to cooperate, because they would be part of the process.

Despite this, Ang See (2015) recalls successful engagements with the Philippine government. She narrates that the late Miriam Defensor-Santiago was the discussant of her paper interrogating whether the Chinese Filipinos are assets or liabilities for the Filipinos. Ang See (1988) states that during the colonial governments of Spain and the United States in the Philippines, they have been able to exploit the Chinese as assets due to the trade networks that they are able to develop within the archipelago though they remain subject to periodic massacres or as political scapegoats. Moreover, she noted that the policies regarding the Chinese in the colonial period usually revolved around that of discrimination or accommodation—the former looking at the Chinese as liabilities and the former as assets. At the time she delivered the lecture, she claimed that Philippine policies regarding those of Chinese descent need not be limited to the assets or liabilities. She states that the relationship between the Filipinos and the Chinese calls for something beyond just accommodation or a relationship of convenience – it should not be taken in the same vein as the Chinese relationship with the colonials of the past. A relationship based on mutual trust and confidence should prevail. However, it is a two-way process. For instance, helping the Philippines develop its national economy is an obligation of the Chinese as a Filipino citizen and as an ethnic minority. On the other hand, accepting the Chinese as part of the Filipino mainstream and tapping their vast potentials is the responsibility of the Philippine administrators

(Ang See 1988:131)

Defensor-Santiago ended up drafting amnesty for illegal aliens[4]. Hau (2015) also had a similar encounter when she wrote an essay about the kidnappings of Chinese nationals in the Philippines published in the front page of a national broadsheet.

In literature, Ong (2015) challenged preconceived notions of what the nation is composed of and sought to expand the reader's understanding of the subject matter.

[T]he idea is to broaden or to deepen the idea of nation and community. I think that's the main work—to deepen and broaden the idea of community, of nation, of ethnicity, to problematize it, and then to broaden and help people understand it. I think that's the work.

(Ong 2016:15)

He believes that his thoughts are already sufficiently articulated on the literature he has produced and does not see the need to engage in debates directly. He likens his work to those of Muslim Filipinos writing literature whose purpose is to be able to include in the narrative the lives and stories of misrepresented or underrepresented segments of Philippine society. According to Ong (2016), his writing is partly fueled by a sense that there were very little representations of the Chinese Filipinos in mainstream Filipino media during his time except for some unfair caricatures. Pagkakaisa produced a movie titled Dragnet (renowned scriptwriter Ricky Lee's first movie script) to provide a counterbalance to the painting of Chinese Filipinos in a negative light in the movies (Ang See 2015).

Academic explorations were also part of their repertoire of actions. The Philippine Association for Chinese Studies (PACS) is one organization that Ang See is active in. Ang See (2015) suggests that one of the reasons why PACS was created is to provide a venue to discuss issues and concerns on Chinese Studies, China, Taiwan, and the Chinese in the Philippines not just in the university level but in the NGO and other civil society groups. Kaisa, with PACS, has used academic means to promote better understanding through exposure trips of Filipinos to China, forums and conferences

## 102   *Yvan Ysmael Yonaha*

on the Chinese in the Philippines to promote integration and to serve as counterbalance especially to the Anti-Chinese rallies that were held. PACS, she states, along with the Center of Integrative and Development Studies of the University of the Philippines was also instrumental in crafting a 10-day Philippine Studies module for experts from China to promote mutual understanding. Meanwhile, Hau (2015) sees her work as part of the ongoing process of exploring matters that pertain to people of Chinese descent in the country. She considers herself in conversation with Edgar Wickberg, Richard Chu, and Teresita Ang See. Some of the topics she looked into are the sources of anti-Chinese sentiments of some segments of the Filipino elite despite being descended from the Chinese. She has recently been engaging with a public debate with F. Sionil Jose's (2015) public sentiments about the Chinese Filipinos. She has also been involved in research regarding Chinese returnees to the mainland. Some of her respondents are from the Philippines who have produced novels to narrate their experience. These include writers like Bai Ren who wrote Nanyang Piaoluiji and Li Bin, widow of Du Ai who wrote a novel about the Wha Chi Guerillas in the Philippines. For Hau (2015), her hope is that her work would be read by experts who could transform them into policy.

## Conclusion

This chapter sought to map the imaginary of senior China experts along the lines of personal and public encounters as well as the counter-narratives they formulated to battle unjust stereotypes.

Narratives are powerful tools that can have real implications to the lives of the population involved. The history of the Chinese and Chinese Filipinos in the country is a testament to the capacity of narratives and interests to oppress, to encourage to flourish, and to direct the lives of segments of the population.

Their personal encounters showed the importance of institutions, formal and non-formal networks in facilitating conversations and the utilization of these spaces has resulted in collaboration in common areas of concern and in rearing future experts in the field. Still, the cohesiveness of these groups is confronted with mechanisms that establish differences between the Chinese and Chinese-Filipino community and the larger society that continues to "Other" through formal and formal mechanisms. Their firsthand experiences may be said to be reflective of this enduring "Othering" even in the national stage. The public encounters that they have identified are societal manifestations of these imposed distinctions which create opportunities and constraints for the population.

That their personal encounters draw from China as part of its sources shows the continued struggles and immensity of the Chinese-Filipino Heritage. For this chapter, the senior China experts are in a constant tension between observance of a heritage nourished by family practices and history

*Narratives and identity* 103

and whose expression should not be curtailed in a truly plural society and the realization that this observance can be a cause for differentiation and suspicion. The navigation between these tensions varies among groups. The senior China experts have resolved this by rejecting the bifurcation between what is Chinese and what is Filipino. Ang See's leadership and Hau' participation in Kaisa is a testament to this. For example, Hau (2015:5) says that her "involvement in Kaisa has a lot to do with learning to speak out as a Filipino while remaining aware of one's Chinese ancestry and heritage." While Ang See (2015:4) reiterates that at their time "the Pagkakaisa pioneers Chinben See and Bernard Go were pushing for integration, that you cannot have double loyalty, and they were trying already to prove that you can be culturally Chinese but politically Filipino." Chinben See (1980), in an article entitled Culture and Political Identity, argues that

> although the Chinese are racially (sic) and culturally different, they can still be part of this pluralistic society. The Philippine policy towards the culture of the minorities – that the Philippines respects and will help preserve minority cultures has been clearly expressed on several occasions. Hence, as long as the Chinese can establish a strong political identity with the *Filipinos, they can secure for themselves a position as a cultural minority of the Philippines and preserve their cultural traditions and identity.*
>
> (See 1980:24, *emphasis added*)

Similar arguments have been expressed by Ang See (1979). Situating her response against the backdrop of a fear that integration would require giving up the cultural practices of those of Chinese descent living in the Philippines, she assures that

> integration does not bring with it a concomitant extinction of what is good and fine in Chinese culture. On the contrary, the best of traditional Chinese culture enriches the existing national culture of the Philippines.
>
> (Ang See 1979:9)

Additionally, she states that

> The Chinese influence on Filipino culture is all-pervasive. Through the years, instead of forcing the Chinese to give up the traditions and customs they hold dear, Filipinos in fact have upheld and accepted them as part of the national culture of the Philippines.
>
> (Ang See 1979:11)

Finally, their counter-narratives have found a variety of vehicles but a singularity in purpose. Kaisa has become a potent vehicle for mobilizing and

## 104  *Yvan Ysmael Yonaha*

supporting initiatives of Chinese Filipinos in integration—requiring the problematization of the nation and elaboration on regional connections for the purposes of challenging old formulations and completing narratives. The work of the senior China experts complexifies the position of being Chinese in the Philippines by situating them in historically important contexts of the country—even in works of fiction. Philippine History, rather than a monopoly of active Malay characters, becomes the joint result of struggles of ethnically different groups. As described by Ong,

> So too the Chinese Filipino writer has declared the death of Akong and sought to replace him with representations more truthful and honest … He knows that the Chinese is not just victim or outsider. That he is no longer pirate and neighborhood store keeper. He has become Henry Sy, Claudio Teehankee, John Gokongwei, Jose Mari Chan as well as Dewey Dee, Rolito Go and Kenneth Ng Li. Capitalist, entrepreneur, professional, artist, swindler, murderer, kidnap victim. *All these are representations of the Chinese Filipino. Anything less is suspect.*
>
> (Ong 2000a: xiv–xv)

### Notes

1 The author would like to express his sincere thanks to Ms. Honeylet Santos and Mrs. Edna Yonaha for all the support they have provided in writing this article. Special thanks also to Dr. Tina S. Clemente and Ms. Pamela G. Combinido for the guidance and patience they have extended to the author. The author's deep gratitude also to Ms. Teresita Ang See, Dr. Caroline Hau, and Mr. Charlson Ong for all the comments and feedback given for this chapter. This would not have been possible without their invaluable input.
2 EDSA Revolution refers to the broad movement that toppled down the Marcos dictatorship. It earned the name because massive protests were held in Epifanio de los Santos Avenue or EDSA.
3 For a more personal take, see Ang See, Teresita (2000). "Vignettes in the Life of an Anti-Crime Crusader." In: Hau, Caroline (ed), *Intsik: An Anthology of Chinese Filipino Writing*. Pasig City: Anvil Publishing Inc., pp. 240–245.
4 See United Press International. (1988). Aquino backs embattled immigration officer. *United Press International*. Retrieved from http://www.upi.com/Archives/1988/10/19/Aquino-backs-embattled-immigration-officer/2740593236800/

### References

Aguilar, Filomeno. 2011. "Between the Letter and Spirit of the Law: Ethnic Chinese and Philippine Citizenship by Jus Soli, 1899–1947." *Southeast Asian Studies* 49(3):431–463.

Ang See, Teresita. 2015. "Interview by Reynard Hing." *Department of Political Science, National Taiwan University: For China Studies and Cross Taiwan Strait Relations*, 6 November. Retrieved 23 February 2018 (http://www.china-studies.taipei/act02.php).

## Narratives and identity 105

Ang See, Teresita. 2007. "Influx of New Chinese Immigrants to the Philippines: Problems and Challenges." In *Beyond Chinatown: New Chinese Migration and the Global Expansion of China,* edited by Mette Thunø. United Kingdom: NIAS Press.

Ang See, Teresita. 2000. "Vignettes in the Life of an Anti-Crime Crusader." In *Intsik: An Anthology of Chinese Filipino Writing,* edited by Caroline Hau. Pasig City: Anvil Publishing Inc., 240–245.

Ang See, Teresita. 1989. "Integration and Identity: Social Change in the Post-WWII Philippine Chinese Community." In *Chinese in the Philippines: Problems and Perspectives v1,* Teresita Ang See (1997). Manila: Kaisa Para sa Kaunlaran. 1–19.

Ang See, Teresita. 1979. "Integration is not Extinction." In *Crossroads: Short Essays on the Chinese Filipinos,* edited by Teresita Ang See and Lily T. Chua (November 1988). Manila: Kaisa Para Sa Kaunlaran, Inc.

Ang See, Teresita. 1988. "The Chinese in the Philippines: Asset or Liabilities." In *Chinese in the Philippines: Problems and Perspectives v1,* Teresita Ang See (1997). Manila: Kaisa Para sa Kaunlaran, 122–136.

Ang See, Teresita and Carmelea Ang See. 2013/2014. "Navigating Cultures, Forming Identities." *Kritika Kultura* 0(21/22):353–372.

Chu, Richard. 2010. *Chinese and Chinese Mestizos of Manila: Family, Identity, and Culture, 1860s to 1930s.* The Netherlands: Brill.

Crossroads. 1988. "Introduction." In *Crossroads: Short Essays on the Chinese Filipinos,* edited by Teresita Ang See and Lily T. Chua (November 1988). Manila: Kaisa Para sa Kaunlaran, Inc.

Hau, Caroline. 2015. "Interview by Jose Mari Hall Lanuza." *Department of Political Science, National Taiwan University: For China Studies and Cross Taiwan Strait Relations,* 5 November. Retrieved 23 February 2018 (http://www.china-studies.taipei/act02.php).

Hau, Caroline. 2014. *The Chinese Question: Ethnicity, Nation, and Region in and Beyond the Philippines.* Quezon City: Ateneo de Manila University Press.

Hau, Caroline. 2000. "The True Story of Ah To." In *Intsik: An Anthology of Chinese Filipino Writing,* edited by Caroline Hau. Pasig City: Anvil Publishing Inc., 126–133.

Sionil, Jose. 2015. "A Memoir of War (Then) and China (Now)." *The Philippine Star,* 7 June. Retrieved from http://www.philstar.com/sunday-life/2015/06/07/1462943/memoir-war-then-and-china-now.

Marcos, Ferdinand. 1973. *Presidential Decree No. 176, s. 1973 or Implementing Section 8 (7), Article XV of the New Constitution.* Manila: Official Gazette of the Republic of the Philippines. Retrieved from http://www.officialgazette.gov.ph/1973/04/16/presidential-decree-no-176-s-1973/.

Marcos, Ferdinand. 1975. *Letter of Instruction No. 270, s. 1975 or Naturalization of deserving aliens by decree.* Manila: Official Gazette of the Republic of the Philippines. Retrieved from http://www.officialgazette.gov.ph/1975/04/11/letter-of-instruction-no-270-s-1975/.

Neuman, Lawrence. 2011. *Social Research Methods: Qualitative and Quantitative Approaches 7th Edition.* Boston, MA: Allyn and Bacon.

Ong, Charlson. 2016. "Interview by Yvan Ysmael Yonaha." *Department of Political Science, National Taiwan University: For China Studies and Cross Taiwan Strait Relations.* 18 January. Retrieved 23 February 2018 (http://www.china-studies.taipei/act02.php).

Ong, Charlson. 2006. *Banyaga: A Song of War.* Manila: Anvil Publishing Inc.

Ong, Charlson. 2000a. "A Bridge Too Far: Thoughts on Chinese Filipino Writing." In *Intsik: An Anthology of Chinese Filipino Writing*, edited by Caroline Hau. Pasig City: Anvil Publishing Inc., ix–xv.

Ong, Charlson. 2000b. "Mismanagement of Grief." In *Intsik: An Anthology of Chinese Filipino Writing,* edited by Hau, Caroline. Pasig City: Anvil Publishing Inc., 106–116.

Ong, Charlson. 1999. *Men of the East and Other Short Stories.* Quezon City: University of the Philippines Press, 45–74.

See, Chinben. 1980. "Culture and Political Identity." In *Crossroads: Short Essays on the Chinese Filipinos*, edited by Teresita Ang See and Lily T. Chua (November 1988). Manila: Kaisa Para Sa Kaunlaran, Inc.

United Press International. 1988. "Aquino Backs Embattled Immigration Officer." *United Press International.* Retrieved from http://www.upi.com/Archives/1988/10/19/Aquino-backs-embattled-immigration-officer/2740593236800/

Wickberg, Edgar. 1964. "The Chinese Mestizo from Philippine History." *East Asian Series* Reprint No. 10. Kansas: Center for East Asian Studies. Reprinted from *The Journal South East Asian History* 5(1) 62–100.

# 6 China watching and China watchers in the Philippines
## An epistemological note[1]

*Chih-yu Shih*

## Introduction

The social and cultural positions of scholars and scholarships are key to understanding human knowledge and our knowledge of humans. This notion is true in modern China, which challenges not only the existing knowledge on the Chinese nation, Chinese people, and Chinese civilization but also the identity or self-identification of China watchers with these positions (Brook and Blue 2002; Culp, Eddy, and Yeh 2016; Hillemann 2009; König and Chaudhuri 2016; Manomaivibool and Shih 2016; Vukovich 2012). In other words, the identity of those who watch China, the Chinese people, and Chinese civilization make a difference in understanding the subjects and their objects. The challenge is surely different for watchers who watch China in an imagined external position and those who possess a certain type of self-perceived "Chineseness." Another challenge for the latter is if they watch China outside the territorial, legal, and institutional barriers of the People's Republic of China. The emerging identity crisis in postcolonial Hong Kong and Taiwan in the 21st century seemingly indicates a trend among those possessing Chineseness to seek an epistemologically external position. However, the lingering identity politics pertaining to a culturally, territorially, and economically diverse Chinese population in Southeast Asia illustrates no such definitive trend (Tagliacozzo and Chang 2011; Wang 2002).

Contrary to the effort to establish an external position of watching, American, Japanese, Vietnamese, and Russian watchers of China, as a few noticeable examples, have been reflecting on their epistemological capacity to understand China from within. Instead of the issue of transcending the Chinese identity of (once) self-regarded Chinese scholars, the epistemological hurdle in studying China, the Chinese people, and Chinese civilization elsewhere is to overcome the imagined difference, which causes some to view "Orientalism" (Katzenstein 2012; Shih 2013; Tanaka 1993). Japan's China studies appear to be a successful case of epistemological migration out of the Chinese intellectual trajectory after 150 years of study, evolving the identity of Japan from a Sinological state into a nation state by itself.

## 108  *Chih-yu Shih*

Ironically, the call by late Mizuguchi Yuzo (1932–2010) to move beyond the Japanese national conditions while studying China suggests his regretful reflection of such epistemological migration. I will argue in the ensuing discussion that the trained adoption of a sympathetically internal perspective for the West to understand China, lauded as China-centrism (Cohen 2010) as opposed to an otherwise imagined externality, is not the same as watching China from an innately internal position because an exit is relatively easily available to the (Western) former. Their dual ability to bridge and disconnect distinguishes them from ethnic Chinese scholars.

The study uses the case of China watching in the Philippines to further argue that the desire to move from the internal position is social and psychological. The reflections of the Philippines' China experts reveal a politics of identity that most would consider irrelevant given the effective integration of Chinese Filipinos into the indigenous community. However, ethnic Chinese scholars continue to ponder on the question of how the integration of Chinese Filipinos can be further improved, for example, by seriously considering the interests of the entire Philippine nation or contributing to the welfare of the indigenous population, in addition to caring merely the benefits provided for the Chinese-Filipino community. Integration can be perceived by some Filipinos as incomplete as long as distinctive routes of reconnection with Chinese elsewhere, with the People's Republic of China (PRC) probably being the most significant, are registered among Chinese Filipinos. Such presumably distinctive routes of reconnection conspicuously exist in other Chinese Southeast Asian communities, alluding to a significant challenge posed by the project of integration.

The current study relies on the social psychological notion of altercasting and the anthropological notion of post-Chineseness to appreciate the positions of the Philippine's China watchers. Basically, the case study suggests that the attainment of the sympathetic capacity to understand China can enrich the knowledge of those China watchers coming from an external position. However, adhering to an internal position of China watching may lead to backlashes in the indigenous community. Therefore, in the long run, the trend is for all ethnic scholars to navigate internal and external perspectives in watching China.

## Post-Chineseness, altercasting, and self-altercasting

### *Emerging post-Chinese agenda*

I will use the concepts of post-Chineseness and altercasting, including those adopted by Filipino scholars, to study the intellectual perspectives on China and the Chinese people. Post-Chineseness not only informs the variety of Chineseness but also considers the choices of identity strategy made necessary by post-Chinese conditions. Post-Chineseness indicates the resources and the processes incurred to achieve reconnection with the

*China watching and China watchers in the Philippines* 109

notion of Chineseness. Altercasting in this study indicates the role expectations of China or anyone acting on its behalf to adhere to such a role that arise from the enactment of reconnection (Epstein 2012; Wehner 2015). For those watchers who culturally or politically identify themselves with China, such as Chinese Filipinos who mind their Chinese identities, altercasting is actually self-altercasting, which induces a role identity in their own understanding.

In theory, post-Chineseness constitutes the self-identities of China watchers because they unilaterally discover some type of Chineseness in the population under study that makes sense mainly in relation to their own conditions, socially as well as intellectually. In practice, post-Chineseness triggers mutuality of connection across all types—between watchers and China, between different watchers, and between watchers and their readers everywhere. Although the conventional ownership of Chineseness everywhere is predominantly premised on some imagined kinship, post-Chineseness allows anyone who owns non-racial Chineseness, that is agreed upon reciprocally, to enact reconnection. One such example could be European Sinologists who faithfully subscribe to Confucian values and can make an intellectual history subject out of cultural China. Given that Chineseness can either symbolize cultural centrality in the Confucian condition or ironically sensitize differences between Chinese populations in an ethnic condition, post-Chineseness enacts strategic reconnections between anyone as well as everyone through altercasting for whatever incongruent and inconsistent purposes (Nyíri and Tan 2016; Wang 2014).

Altercasting, for example, is the process of encouraging another Chinese to express Chineseness, recognized as such, to maintain social relationships (Michalski and Pan 2016; Thies 2015; Wong 2010). The narrator should be able to communicate with the other person such that the latter self-identifies with such Chineseness (Callero 1994; Thies 2012; Wasson 2015). As an epistemological privilege, China watchers apply indirect altercasting at best, as watchers do not systematically communicate with the population under study. Nevertheless, China watching engenders a macro discursive condition, in which China and those acting on its behalf have to correspond to remain socially connected.

Self-altercasting, for example, conveying the message that a Chinese like me should or should not be doing something, is the process in which China watchers imagine an expectation of their own role by the studied population and to such expectation (Hastings 2000; Kai and Feng 2015; Valenta 2009). Self-altercasting occurs when China watchers are by themselves self-regarded Chinese who watch China from an internal position. In this peculiar situation, China watchers are also pressured to conform as their studies immediately implicate on their own role identity. Self-altercasting in academics is much more direct when compared with altercasting, as watchers induce their own conformity alongside their expectation of China. When self-altercasting occurs outside territorial China, for example, in migrant or

## 110 *Chih-yu Shih*

ethnic Chinese communities, self-altercasting that generates the pressure to conform to Chineseness necessarily makes a statement of difference from the hosting society. Under this circumstance, China watching reconnects China watchers to their target population as one single group. In other words, self-altercasting reproduces Chineseness in China watchers.

Post-Chineseness that is beyond the scope of imagined kinship allows one to enact the process of re/connection between a Chinese and a potential Chinese. This notion could apply to a self-defined non-Chinese that owns characteristics that are regarded as essentially Chinese. Post-Chineseness could similarly enable a self-defined Chinese to re/connect with a could-be Chinese or a once Chinese whose identity has intellectually been lost. Post-Chineseness has an ontological dimension, which is related to whether the initiation of reconnection comes from a self-regarded in-group actor or out-group actor. Any Chinese-Southeast Asian narrator whose loyalty goes to one of China's Civil War rivals is an example of a self-regarded in-group actor. A re/connection initiated from an external position similarly re/constructs a role identity that unavoidably brings forth expectations that are informed to a degree by certain out-group perspectives, thereby altercasting. An in-group re/connection has the function of reconfirming one's sense of belonging in particular ways and entails a role identity that necessarily generates self-expectations, thereby becoming a type of self-altercasting.

Resources available to enact reconnection through altercasting and self-altercasting of role identity point to what the people under study do or should do, as well as who they are or who they should be. Who they are is related to the physical condition defined by race, network, and site. What they do requires interpretation, and thus, a shared meaning is critical. Accordingly, resources to incur reconnection with the people under study can be material or constructive, depending on the purpose of the reconnection and the conditions of the target to be reconnected. Thus, the process of post-Chineseness involves an epistemological dimension, which pertains to, discursively, whether the resources enlisted are material or interpretive.

A material (or objective) dimension involves criteria that are primarily ostensibly objective and usually spatially definable, such as citizenship, color of skin, or residence, which arise from traveling experiences, living conditions, or objective observation. By contrast, the interpretive (or subjective) dimension is most plausibly embedded in the trajectories of their intellectual growth, as well as the historical, civilizational, and ideological knowledge of the people under study. These trajectories involve primarily temporal evolution, contrary to the spatial scope that defines who they are in terms of territorial, racial, residential, and organizational membership, among others. An interpretive dimension requires the participation of the people under study, at least indirectly, to determine how they own Chineseness. Specifically, one should make judgment in each case by understanding their background and self-identity.

## China watching and China watchers in the Philippines 111

To illustrate how categories of post-Chineseness enable a scholar to position his or her relations with the object of study—China, Chinese, and Chineseness, the following discussion attends primarily to how positions stay or shift. Categories are therefore results of strategic positioning according to the choice of the scholar at the time. They are not given structures that constrain choices continuously. Categories do not apply to individuals, accordingly. Categories emerge in narratives. It is only proper to surmise how scholars choose between categories, not how categories fix scholars. After all, post-Chineseness is processual, fluid, and political. It reflects agency. It does not label people.

Figure 6.1 notes six categories accordingly: "cultural Chineseness" that is enacted by imagining a shared culture and values; "experiential Chineseness" that is enacted by recalling past living with Chinese; "Sinological Chineseness" that is enacted by bridging differences of China and another; "ethnic Chineseness" that is enacted by caring expectations of both China and at least one other imagined motherland; "civilizational Chineseness" that is enacted by assessing China on a subjective scale; and "scientific Chineseness" that is enacted by treating China as a comparable object. The notion of post-Chineseness thus engenders a research agenda that studies how Chineseness as (1) an unquestionable ontology is reproduced through its constitution of either in-group or out-group self-identity anywhere; (2) an unsynchronized epistemology

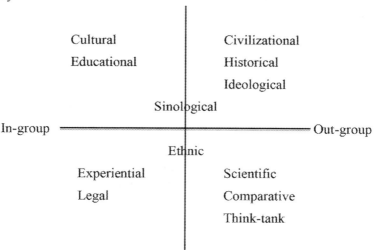

*Figure 6.1* Two Dimensions of Post-Chineseness.

## 112    *Chih-yu Shih*

is supportive of contradictory identity strategies everywhere temporally and spatially; (3) a cultural methodology is destabilizing to nationalist mobilization; and (4) an intellectual project is necessarily composed of individualized cycles of life.

The following discussion will rely on the oral history interviews of senior scholars of China and Chinese Studies in the Philippines to gather different intellectual paths that reflect identity strategies of various types pertaining to Chineseness. The concept of Chineseness is no longer analytically productive because it mainly emphasizes difference and is therefore socially impractical. Post-Chineseness balances its obsession with the deconstruction of the unified Chinese identity by reconnecting discursively differentiated populations toward socially as well as strategically proper relationality that is nevertheless embedded in no definitive destiny or scope.

## Theoretical propositions of post-Chinese agency

The social psychological literature does not confirm the designation of a positive emotion or affect to a relationship constituted by the greater self. Within the scope of Chinese social relationality, the greater self is literally a Confucian notion of collective identity, the contents of which varies depending on the encountered social context (Ho and Chiu 1998; Hwang 2012; Hwang, Francesco and Kesslear 2003). The social psychological translation of the greater self points to the incurring of the relational self such that the roles taken by one constitute one's self-identity (Barbalet 2014; Qi 2011). The greater self is therefore a sociological necessity everywhere despite the fact that the Chinese culture injects a distinctive moral significance into the conscious celebration of its prevailing (Hsu 1971; Yang Kuo-shu 1995). Nevertheless, social identity theory consistently demonstrates that the sheer belonging to an artificially constructed group is sufficient to incur behavior that favors the in-group and discriminates against the out-group (Oldmeadow and Fiske 2010; Stephan and Stephan 1985). This condition partially explains the rationality of constructing a greater self and securing one's membership regardless of context. The greater self-consciousness is thus not uniquely Chinese, although the Chinese culture pertaining to the greater self is arguably more sophisticated than the Western one. Feeling for others is nonessential to the enactment of role identities; on the contrary, feeling concerned with how others regard the fulfillment of the role identity maintains social harmony and order (Barbalet 2001: 108). The emotional stress incurred renders the relevance of the indigenous population because migrant and minority groups, with their imagined difference, are a target of loyalty or merit check.

The literature suggests that, under the condition of relational self, the emotional aspect of role identity is easily registered in anxiety or stress (Burke 1991; Simon 1992). The self-discrepancy in one's performance of a role, as evaluated by the counterpart, is a major source of anxiety (Higgins 1987;

*China watching and China watchers in the Philippines* 113

Roseman 1984). Moreover, symbolic interactionism and dramaturgical sociology concur with the observation that significant others hold the key to one's emotional state of stress (Turner and Stets 2006:26–32). The relational turn in psychoanalysis similarly points to the important subject of separation anxiety (Dimen 2012: 396; Renolds 2007), thus implying the dreaded loss of a role partner. In addition, studies of Chinese psychology note the critical function of relationships in the maintenance of mental health (Hwang and Chang 2009; Lin, Tseng, and Yeh 1995). A role is constantly examined externally to cause stress (Hsu 1985:100). As such, a stable relationship might momentarily generate a positive effect, but this situation is a rarity, especially for anyone acting on behalf of a national actor. On the contrary, relationality as a process of constant adaptation is the condition of altercasting and self-altercasting.

From the emotional aspect, Chineseness that is imagined as essential engenders a different type of self-identity in comparison with Chineseness that is consciously acquired. A self-image of innate Chineseness compels one to assess one's own performance from an imagined internal Chinese perspective and reproduces the difference between Chinese and non-Chinese. A greater self embedded in shared values and rituals exists to encompass mutual role expectations between one and other in-group members (Ho 1998; Hwang 2012; King 1985). Self-altercasting becomes inevitable as Chineseness is registered in the duty of being a member. For self-regarded Chinese, an emotion of anxiety is immediate wherever Chineseness is incurred. The same was most apparent during World War II (WWII), which is a period in which many Chinese-Southeast Asians supported China in resisting Japan. Anxiety is strong in the condition of a split in the greater self because the split compels one to choose sides and to work on reintegration, without which selfhood constituted by Chineseness, qua greater selfhood, becomes void. This effect was observed during and after the Chinese Civil War, which resulted in the split of Chinese-Southeast Asians into being either pro-Communist or pro-Kuomintang.

Self-regarded Chinese may face another pressure of self-altercasting as they interact with indigenous communities because they may perceive a role identity vis-à-vis the indigenous population, a role identity that they believe is a reflection of their higher status economically as well as culturally, and interact accordingly. In other words, they think that local communities expect Chinese to be socially and economically advanced. In summary, two processes of self-altercasting simultaneously occur. One induces the self-regarded Chinese-Southeast Asians to act patriotically toward China, and the other induces this group to differentiate their identities from the hosting communities. Both processes generate psychosocial pressure to perform to release the worries that the perceived motherland, that is, China, or the indigenous population may consider them to be doing lower than expectations.

By contrast, acquired Chineseness complicates one's self-identity through learned or practiced values, rituals, and languages, among others. Such

114    *Chih-yu Shih*

complication gives rise to an intellectual capability to understand and interpret both sides. Such intellectual capability, if exercised, similarly complicates the criteria of self-evaluation of both sides once a different set of criteria is introduced to them. In the process, one's own standing in either group may be jeopardized if neither side appreciates one's effort of bridging the gap. In the situation in which one's in-between position is acquired, for example, in the case of a Sinologist, an anthropologist, an expatriate, a China-based journalist, or a diplomat, the wide discursive scope attained may enable the narrator to achieve strong self-confidence. On the contrary, in cases in which such in-between position is socially imposed, for example, in the case of a migrant citizen, he or she may suffer incompatible role expectations coming from both sides.

A migrant or an ethnic citizen is in one sense similar to self-regarded Chinese to the extent that both carry identities that are given, except where the actor is an ethnic citizen, in which case he or she has more than one given identity. An ethnic Chinese-Southeast Asian faces double altercasting. Unlike Sinologists who preach to both sides about how the other understands the world, ethnic citizens are not discursively prepared to preach. On the contrary, the situation can be embarrassing if they have to meet the expectations of both sides. Double self-altercasting does not reproduce the same sense of difference as in the case of a self-regarded Chinese who can perform consistently, although anxiously, in an environment such as Chinatown/Binondo (Kwang 1996). For ethnic citizens living in a large group, they ought to occasionally perform inconsistently to meet the inconsistent expectations caused by their in-between positions. If one standard to be met already causes anxiety, then double altercasting can only aggravate the situation.

The contrast of the Sinological and ethnic types suggests that the Sinological type is ultra-stable, whereas the ethnic type is ultra-unstable. An ethnic narrator can improve his or her discursive position by taking an in-group position that privileges the Chinese identity and yet reproduces mutual discriminatory condition in the midst of the indigenous population. A frustrated narrator in the mainstream condition could strategically choose to take shelter in Chinatown, whereas others may opt for a determined struggle for equal citizenship. This condition is nearly true everywhere, such as in the States, Southeast Asia, or even the Chinese Hong Kong and Taiwan. By contrast, a Sinological narrator may face similar double pressures from both sides but is able to understand their limitations. He or she is intellectually confident and discursively prepared to either refute the one-sided criticism or simply remain calm without feeling the need to engage political correctness. However, in the long run, the return to Chinatown guarantees no continuous reward unless one runs into a new age of the PRC that may give new meanings of belongingness to a distinctive Chinese category. Even with the rise of the PRC, the retrieval of Chinese identity may generate

## China watching and China watchers in the Philippines   115

considerable pressure of self-altercasting to an extent that the PRC on the rise may fail to appreciate.

On this basis, the chance of reverting from an out-group position to an in-between or in-group position exists in cases in which politics of identity retrieves unpleasant memories of discrimination, stereotyping, and stigmatization or in cases in which, with the rise of China, reconnection with the PRC triggers a sense of enhancement, familiarity, or relaxation that revitalizes a silent and silenced cultural memory embedded in an imagined string of Chineseness. However, this condition is difficult because citizenship denoted by pragmatic considerations of rights and equality is always locally oriented. Nevertheless, in the case of Hong Kong or Taiwan that lacks dominant cultural alternatives to Confucianism, other than the colonial British and Japanese legacies, the population may be relatively vulnerable to the influence of cultural reconnection. Nevertheless, since their alleged difference from China is primarily undergirded by a distinctive, and colonially superior, site outside of the PRC, the rise of China could appear unattractive to that extent.

Anxiety is not a comfortable affect, and the intellectual capacity, cultural memory, and social distinction of the later generations of a migrant population to retain in-group cohesion necessarily diminish over time; thus, one can predict a historical trend that moves away from the positions that require self-altercasting as incurred by the imagined belongingness to China or the Chinese people. Such a trend indicates the objective to adopt an out-group position such that one's assessment on the Chinese nation, Chinese civilization, and Chinese people simulates indigenous Filipino perspectives. The Chinese relationality that constitutes the identity of a self-regarded Chinese or an ethnic Chinese Filipino evolves into an object to be assessed from the vantage point of the Philippines' national interests, as well as a certain Philippine historiography. In this development, the enthusiasm or calm of being able to objectively reconnect with Chinese targets, be it a sovereign state, a social network, or a cultural asset, substitutes for anxiety caused by the in-group consciousness. On the other hand, the sense of belonging to the indigenous group may engender another source of self-altercasting, though.

Accordingly, a few plausible propositions, particularly about individualized tracks, emerge to assist in the reading of the evolution of intellectual history in general. Please refer to Figure 6.2 for an illustration of these propositions. I contend that these propositions can be generally applied to any place where non-Chinese identities prevail in the mainstream, although the later section relies primarily on Philippine interviews.

Proposition I. 1. The general trend is for any narrator to shift from an in-group perspective to an out-group perspective in the long run.

Proposition I. 2. The auxiliary proposition is that the movement from an out-group perspective to an in-group perspective is impractical.

116  *Chih-yu Shih*

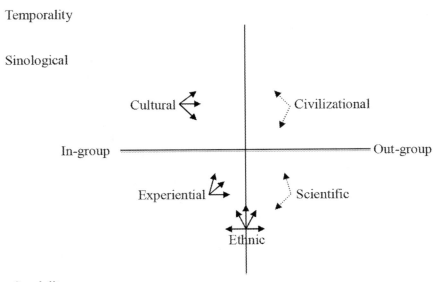

*Figure 6.2* Post-Chinese Evolution in the Long Run.

Proposition I. 3. The third-order proposition is that the movement from an out-group perspective to an in-group perspective is only possible in cases in which re-incurred discrimination compels a narrator to carry an ethnic stigma again. (This proposition is absent in the case of the Philippines.)

Proposition II. The Sinological perspective is ultimately stable. A Sinological type of narrator will not shift to other positions.

Proposition III. The ethnic perspective is the least stable. An ethnic type of narrator always seeks opportunities to practice an in-group or an out-group perspective.

## Epistemological shifts illustrated

The scholars of Chinese Studies in the Philippines include indigenous scholars who study China and Chinese-Filipino scholars. They make two ostensibly ethnic groups. Chineseness constitutes their self-identities professionally and culturally. The three propositions suggest that the evolution of China watching for Chinese-Filipino scholars moves toward an out-group position.

*China watching and China watchers in the Philippines*   117

### *Proposition I. 1: in-group Chineseness moves toward out-group Chineseness in the long run*

Theresa Cariño (2015) is a Chinese Singaporean moving to the Philippines. She has been intensively involved in development projects affiliated with a religious foundation and in the development of the curricula for Chinese Studies in higher education. Unlike her experience in Singapore, she realized that being Chinese made a difference in the Philippines after her arrival. However, she has not attempted to enter a hybrid position to bring her own Chineseness into her career. In fact, her perspectives on China shift from ideological to scientific Chineseness, with the former registered in Maoist romanticism when she was much younger such that China had acquired an exotic ideological understanding, although on the positive side. Her later involvement in exchanges with Chinese NGOs and Chinese development projects has led to a scope of observation defined by the state boundaries of the PRC. She cautions against the cultural explanation of economic success in Confucian societies by looking at economic policies. In international relations, she recommends a pragmatic policy to cope with the China-Taiwan rivalry. These approaches are not ethnic in the sense that Cariño's analysis is not guided by how either China or indigenous politics assesses her.

A case of experiential Chineseness moving toward scientific Chineseness is vividly present in the interview with Jaime FlorCruz, whose advice for the contemporary, after living in China and becoming "mature and patient," is to "[s]pend time in understanding China. And then, share it with the population" (FlorCruz 2015:13). What this advice implies for the population is "to go and visit China even though for a short time because I experienced myself what a big difference it made to see it, to feel it, to smell it, and to personalize China" (FlorCruz 2015:8). He also warns against racism and advises with noticeable comparative objectivism, "strip away the ideology or the color of the skin, or the shape of our eyes, we Filipinos and Chinese are all the same" (FlorCruz 2015:8). His own task is to report on China, providing timely and accurate information. However, his experiences in China win him trust as an in-group member such that he always speaks, inquires, and sits in on behalf of a large international media group in China. The Chinese audience of his lecture welcomes him because he can compare modern China and China 40 years ago, witness the changes taking place, and appreciate the "incremental" as opposed to the drastic speed of change (FlorCruz 2015:13). As he is a China watcher who "never miss[es] an appropriate chance to say that I am a Filipino," his scientific Chineseness seems to spontaneously evolve out of his experiential Chineseness:

> For over 30 years, China has been successively my refuge, my training ground, and my home. Living and working in China pose genuine difficulties: language barriers, culture shock, pollution, bureaucracy, and home-sickness. However, China has an inherent charm that draws me to stay on. Its diverse culture and long history is a bottomless mine to

118    *Chih-yu Shih*

> explore and study. It is a huge country in a state of flux, and watching it change—and even experiencing the changes myself—is exhilarating as a China-watcher. On a personal level, what draws me to China are "three Fs": friends, food, and foot massage.
>
> (FlorCruz 2015:12–13)

The pressure of ethnic Chineseness to generate self-role expectations from both sides can be reduced if one can physically evade the supposedly monitoring environment. Despite monitoring by the Kuomintang and the anti-Chinese attitude resulting from the Philippine nationalism, Caroline Hau's (2015) journey from Binondo, to Filipino communities, and then to the United States and Japan eases the potential tension of being ethnic. She is aware of owning some Chineseness, and she thus feels no position to speak for China because of her lack of sufficient knowledge. She is determined to understand her Chineseness. However, this goal creates no self-assessing pressure. On the contrary, she reverses the usual schema of understanding Chineseness from the PRC standpoint by appreciating PRC Chineseness being adaptive and nuanced in itself through her own path of becoming differently Chinese. Hau similarly enjoys visits to the Philippines despite her academic alert at an anti-Chinese potential at home. She discovers that internationalization is conducive to the alleviation of such potential.

Hau's ethnic Chineseness causes a distinctive example of relaxed ethnicity. Self-altercasting is particularly weak in her self-reflection because she could calmly hope someone else who understands Chinese positions to clarify situations on the South China Sea, assist in the Chinese-Filipino integration without committing activism, and exempt from usually intense exchanges while engaging in public identity debates. In other words, she lacks bridging sensibility that is often observed in Sinological Chineseness. Hau shows no urgency in preaching each side how one side perceives the other. She learns from both sides through visiting China and the Philippines but transcends the anxiety toward recognition. This behavior has much to do with her adoption of a comparative perspective through an exit in Japan, where she enlightens her target of research regarding each of the countries historically shaped and changing identities. This characteristic actually illustrates a derivative of civilizational Chineseness attained in an ethnic Chinese identity.

### *Proposition I. 2: out-group Chineseness does not move toward in-group Chineseness*

Aileen Baviera (2016) represents the epistemological stability of an out-group watcher in international relations, a task she enjoys while watching China being defined territorially by the sovereign borders. She is concerned with the formation of the coherence in the Philippine foreign policy sectors, composed of analysts and the policy makers. In the Chinese counterparts, she cautions against too much intellectual investment unless the other side

## China watching and China watchers in the Philippines   119

demonstrates open mindedness. She shows slight intention to bridge the gap or preach the PRC Chinese scholars on the outside world for enlightening. With her expertise on Chinese foreign policy, her involvement in the Philippine Association for China Studies, composed of experts on the Chinese-Filipino Studies and overlapped with Kaisa Para Sa Kaunlaran (Kaisa), fits the Kaisa's overall goal of breeding an integrated and national consciousness among the Chinese Filipinos. Consistently throughout her career, she realized the importance of China to the Philippines. Curiosity and pragmatism appear to catch the spirit of her agenda.

Santa Romana (or Sta. Romana) similarly demonstrates the stability of an out-group perspective, initially leaning toward civilizational Chineseness as his evaluative schema has been Maoism. He started with an ideologically romantic view of China with a strong comparative sensibility. In his 15 years of stay in China, he discovered that ideology is irrelevant for him to understand China. In retrospect, he compares China and the Philippines to completely bypass the thinking of China model. The issue is not "whether we can use the China model" but rather "to see what we could learn from China" (Santa Romana 2016:15). According to Romana, "Filipinos are a little more spontaneous and freewheeling. The Chinese, on the other hand, are ritualistic and Confucian values are very strong" (Santa Romana 2016:11). In addition, he finds "certain aspects of Filipinos' religion, culture, and politics, which make it difficult for authoritarianism to take root" (Santa Romana 2016:11). Moreover, "they are a mainland or continental country, while we are an archipelago" (Santa Romana 2016:15). Romana warns against any quick judgment from the surface:

> You have to see the situation from there; and the bottom line is that you have to understand that human beings are influenced by all these cultural and historical forces. We are the same but yet we are different. We have our own culture and our own history. It is just that I do not expect it to be easy to understand China. I mean you could experience it yourself. If you live in China, there are certain things you have to get used to, which is not so easy. Basically, we have to find our own way of understanding and navigating in China, but also need to consider their experiences.
>
> (Santa Romana 2016:15)

Romana's experiences in China have retrained him to reconnect China through a mix of civilizational and scientific sensibilities. His job as a foreign journalist, who had to explain the situation in China to an international audience, reinforces this tendency of staying objective while gathering information and reporting the news. He is consciously "an outsider" who enjoys a "detached view" while benefiting physically being an insider who "got to know people's sentiments and talked to them" (Santa Romana 2016:12). In addition, an insider detects forces not within the media and reads between

120    *Chih-yu Shih*

the lines. However, his reconnection with China is more on information gathering, analyzing, and explaining than bridging or engaging in Chinese affairs. After being a journalist for a long period, his scientific Chineseness emerges:

> It taught me to be a little skeptical. That you should never accept what's on the surface. You may know about it, but it is almost like the art of reading tea leaves. It is never easy. That is why China watching actually became part of my life. First is because I lived and worked there, and then I worked as a foreign journalist who had to explain what was going on in China to an international audience.
>
> (Santa Romana 2016:12)

### *Proposition II: sinological Chineseness is stable*

Richard Chu (2016), whose family came from Binondo, once been identified as an "Intsik," which he considers carrying derogatory undertones. He considers himself a Filipino for having a Catholic education. This dual identity led him to reflect on the historical conditions that have caused ethnic conflict. Free from much fixation on Binondo, he has initially acquired the intellectual faculty through scientific learning, with a purpose of bridging the distance between China and the Philippines. Then, he achieved the Sinological position in a scope much broader than a usual bilateral Sinologist. Considering his root in Minnan very early in his career, his

> ...motivation for going to China was partly personal, which was to seek my roots back in China and learn more about Chinese culture, the country, and its people, and about my own family's background. But it was professional as well, in the sense that I wanted to work in the field, where I could help bridge the people of China and the Philippines.
>
> (Chu 2016:6)

However, he had a strong wish to become a priest. Nevertheless, he was ready to transcend ethnic Chineseness. The training in Chinese history provided him intellectual tools to study China and Philippines simultaneously from an external perspective, thereby connecting him to a wide academic world; thus, he has cut across many different disciplines to make a new self-identity of being "transnational" (Chu 2016:12).

His scholarship is consciously marginal to China Studies in general but intertwined with Asian American, Chinese diaspora, and the Philippine Studies. Chu illustrates a journey from initially being an owner of ethnic Chineseness, through attaining scientific Chineseness, to practicing Sinological Chineseness, thereby exempting from "nation-based narratives,

## China watching and China watchers in the Philippines    121

where there's a thirst for either-or propositions" (Chu 2016:15) This Sinological Chineseness extends from not only a communicator between China and the Philippines but also epistemologically illuminating one for the United States and the Philippines, as he specifically wishes to "create research that will be applicable and relevant to both countries" (Chu 2016:12). Such a Sinological style of teaching and writing in between nearly resembles a priest determined to preach between communities, bridge new encounter, and proceed by

> always trying to figure out where I am in my life, personally and professionally. Professionally, this means in terms of how and where the field leads me, including which scholars I get to interact with, and whose work energized me. I think this is so important to me. That's why even if the Chinese Cemetery and Chinese hospital projects are not part of my next book project, I still want to undertake them; because they bring me again into contact, and into conversation with, all these other scholars.
>
> (Chu 2016:13)

Scholarship combined with activism has produced the Sinological Chineseness of Teresita Ang See (2015) in her preaching to both sides of the necessity and the routes of building an integrative nation in the Philippines. In her earlier career, See took a double learning path first in Binondo and then in the higher education among her Filipino classmates at the University of the Philippines. She found that the continuous loyalty to China is impractical for the Chinese who lives in the Philippines. In her endeavor to move beyond such cultural embedding, she embarked upon a journey to adopt ethnic Chineseness. Ethnic Chineseness that is usually focused on working for recognition than self-asserting immediately faces the challenge that the traditional Chinese identity turns hostile to such a strategy while the mainstream is unsure of how to even think of an integrative agenda, if not at all reacting suspiciously. See escalates her discursive power by engaging in activism where she benefited from her knowledge of both sides, such that she could enlist culturally sensitive communication in her attempt to enlighten the migrant and the hosting communities. Given such Sinological Chineseness, she has never ceased preaching.

Once integration has been considered achieved and Kaisa was established to reflect the benchmark of integration, See's perspective on China, without Binondo acting as China's vicarious enclave, is presumably from the vantage point of out-group. In fact, she has not considered herself being a China expert. In actuality, her style embedded in Sinological Chineseness triumph institutionally nonetheless as she not only heads the Philippine-China Development Resource Center to bridge mutually beneficial experiences between the Philippines and China but also in her leadership capacity in the Philippine Association for Chinese Studies. The Sinological

## 122   *Chih-yu Shih*

sensibility is clear in her design of a leadership training for students that ensures "the input is also how to be a bridge and then how to be proud of your being Tsinoy." Sinological Chineseness exists similarly in her bridging between China and the Philippines, aiding Xinqiao that arrived in the Philippines during the Cold War as the newest wave of the vicarious China and the PRC Chinese think tanks that know little about the Philippines. She recalls,

> China politics, geopolitics, China relations and everything. Um, we seem to have a better group of people who can really be the bridge. In fact, yeah I saw one of the questions, the advantage of this group of China experts is that they really focus on China studies, and they know a lot about China … It was the Chinese experts who were all surprised at the inputs of the Philippine experts. Uh, maybe it's very understandable because at that time the Philippines loomed very far from their consciousness. That's why they did not pay attention to Philippine studies and knowing the Philippines. They were surprised a lot by what the inputs of our China experts there.
>
> (Ang See 2015:15)

From being an out-group member fascinated about China, Eric Baculinao (2015) has lived in China for over 40 years to gain experiential Chineseness as an in-group watcher. He works both in China and the United States, thereby benefiting his own curiosity in acquiring views on China "from different perspectives and different scholars around the world" and focusing on "finding the intersection in common interests and decoding the intentions and apprehensions of China's bureaucracy and Western media for both sides." His practice of Sinological Chineseness thus began. His take on the Philippines-China dispute over the South China Sea is rather calm accordingly, emphasizing "more debates" in the Philippines to highlight "more different opinions" on China. He hopes that

> all these debates will lead us to the conclusion that being complacent or even narrow-minded about our understanding of China will not lead us to the correct strategy that would mean a victory for national interest that would be of benefit to the people. The conflict would only drag on, and that's not victory.
>
> (Baculinao 2015:9)

A Sinological type of warning is particularly powerful as he insists that a Filipino "distinguishes between advanced studies about China, and the influence of geopolitics that restricts [us from getting] a far more balanced, up to date, objective understanding of China" (Baculinao 2015:9).

Other than sharing his understanding of China whenever needed by the local Philippine communities, back home, and in Toronto, Baculinao

## China watching and China watchers in the Philippines    123

discovers that the legal knowledge among Chinese scholars is limited and that the Philippines may help by facilitating academic interactions. The Philippines is misunderstood as "the puppets of the Americans," such that appreciation for the history, in which "Philippine independence has developed so much and deserves to be understood," is much needed (Baculinao 2015:15). His goal is to "close that gap" of mutual understanding. His in-between position advises that the difficulty depends on nationalism and national interests:

> I think maybe it's because nationalism is an important factor. It's natural to encounter resistance, especially if you challenge conventional positions; you run the risk of being called anti-nationalist or unpatriotic, even if it's not the case. I think the main difficulty of breaking through our restricted understanding of China is the fact that we are so passionate about our national interest—which is a very positive thing—that sometimes we neglect to see the weaknesses of our own positions, of our own understanding, which then leads us to very weak strategies or tactics; weak in the sense that they cannot conceivably lead to a peaceful negotiated outcome of our disputes.
>
> (Baculinao 2015:15)

### Proposition III: ethnic Chineseness is unstable

Go Bon Juan (2015) reveals the pressure of remaining ethnic and argues that the study of China and Philippines should take an integrative approach by studying the Philippines in its entirety rather than the components of each of the nation separately. In addition, one should study the Philippines by comparing the country with other Southeast countries. He retrieves the historical paths, where the Chinese sacrificed during WWII, split after the Chinese Civil War, and became a policy problem. His thought is deeply ethnic in style to the extent that he is keen to a type of self-assessment that advises how the Chinese and Filipinos should learn and practice to integrate better. He is similarly conscious about how China as a perspective perceives, or misperceives, the integration as an example of the "overseas Chinese" problem. He appeals to *"utang na loob"* ("debt of gratitude") to oblige the Chinese to move beyond hometown nostalgia:

> in the hundreds of years since the Chinese arrived in the Philippines—and that this is not our place—but we were allowed to live here, live, develop, and have become so successful, there should definitely be some form of utang na loob. Doing good things for the country is not saying that you are just helping the people, it is utang na loob. It is time to pay back to the country.
>
> (Go 2015:6)

124    *Chih-yu Shih*

Go urges the Tsinoy community to simulate the national perspective but blames his people for being only concern of themselves. Instead, he promotes a "broad knowledge to solve Philippine problems, we need [to know about] the Philippine history, economy, [and] society" (Go 2015:16). Chinese Filipinos usually learn the Philippines through self-study. His methodology is historical and external in that he believes a deep historical research will show that the Tsinoy and Pinoy communities are already integrated. For example, his research showed that, in 1782, 50 mestizos were included among a list of 100 serving as Catholic priests under the Archdiocese of Manila. The distinction between local Chinese and Mainland Chinese is even political essential as he could not imagine "how many anti-Chinese racial riots there would have been" if they are not differentiated. He thus suggests,

> to let the Chinese and Filipino mainstream society discover that the relations are so tight. All in one. That we are in each other's lives and cannot be separated. Hundreds of years of history already show that. This helps very well in promoting integration. Why do we need to say/ differentiate you from us? There is no need to do that. We realize that we are close. We avoid the concept that the Chinese are no Filipinos, or that you are Filipinos [and] we are Chinese. If we cannot resolve this identity issue, then the two peoples' cannot become close, racial problems cannot be resolved.
>
> (Go 2015:17)

Florencio Mallare (2015) illustrates a shift from ethnic Chineseness to cultural Chineseness. He has been preoccupied with his early encounter with the Chinese Exclusion Act, which grants the authorities the power to deport Chinese and was practiced in history. He was by himself once under detention despite adopting a Filipino name. He anticipates the pressure from the indigenous society for him to defend his citizenship. His sensitivity toward the ethnic status and focus on the vulnerability of the Chinese communities attract his attention such that he has endeavored to answer the question, "What is my role now?" (Mallare 2015:3). He has not tried to bridge the gap between the Chinese and the indigenous communities as others do in the ethnic position. By contrast, his effort is to remind the Chinese Filipinos of the inferior legality incurred by their ethnicity. However, the rise of China seems to have provided sufficient boost to his morale as he finds that the claim of the Philippines in the South China Sea disputes has no ground and the Chinese expansion mimics the Monroe Doctrine or other Western practices, thereby legitimized by the Western standard. Such perspective-taking can engender a sense of duty to preach the Tsinoy community whereas may empower one to face the regime of Chinese exclusion.

## China watching and China watchers in the Philippines 125

A further return to the cultural Chineseness enables Mallare to speak with enhanced certainty of his identity. His suggestion to the younger generations of Tsinoy is contrary to the trending advocacy of indigenization. Specifically, he believes that the retrieval of one's own path that lead one's ancestors to migrate from China to the Philippines, which presumably reproduces one's Chinese in-group consciousness, is conducive to a comprehensive self-understanding for the Tsinoy community. He then detects a "lack of continuity" in the Chinese studies in the Philippines and suggests the adoption of a cultural approach:

> You have to know who are you … Identify yourself … Who are you … How did you come about here … Why are you in the Philippines? Why is your surname Mallare? and then you begin to think. The passion is so intense that I went back to China specifically to look at it.
>
> (Mallare 2015:29)

> Like the Chinese will exist; will still continue … just like encyclopedia … continuously … you go and understand the Zhou Dynasty, the ancient times in China … you know your history.
>
> (Mallare 2015:29)

In comparison, Charlson Ong's (2016) reliance on cultural Chineseness illustrates a different style, although similarly rejects the pressure of external examination imposed on ethnic Chineseness. Ong demonstrates a historical sensibility that tracks a life in its origin in China, but he uses cultural Chinese not to reconnect with an essentialized China but to trivialize and therefore broaden the scope of a collective identity. In other words, Chinese origins and their individualized contributions to the life of the Chinese Filipinos deserve recognition as a component of the Philippine nationality. Based on the ethnic identity of the Chinese Filipinos, Ong contrives the representation of the nuances of each life that renders any monotonous criterion irrelevant in assessing or transforming one's identity:

> the idea is to broaden or to deepen the idea of nation and community. I think that's the main work—to deepen and broaden the idea of community, of the nation, of ethnicity, to problematize it, and then to broaden and help people understand it. I think that's the work. As far as China is concerned, I think right now, a lot of the traffic is [happening in] both ways. There are many Filipinos working in China now, so I think it's going the other way. The labor movement is going the other way. Filipinos are working in China.
>
> (Ong 2016:16)

126  *Chih-yu Shih*

## In lieu of conclusion

I argue in the first half of the chapter that altercasting is not a psychological home in the long run for the people who only view themselves from certain in-group perspectives and impose self-role expectation in accordance with some imagined standards that define their group identity. People can be strategically reconnected with an imagined Chinese internal perspective in many ways to attain opportunities, dignity, or security. They may judge incorrect and suffer. They may also detect changes in historical conditions and adapt accordingly. In the long run, a lure to an out-group position is therefore expected to result in re-incurring of cultural resources to reconnect with China differently. Presumably, this condition leads to taking an out-group position. In the second half of the chapter, I use the interviews of the Philippines-China experts and scholars of Chinese Studies to illustrate these general trends toward an out-group position. An alternative exists in which one complicates cultural Chineseness by attending to practical nuances that render any definitive scope of cultural Chineseness unavailing.

The Philippines is a harbinger for what one may similarly discover elsewhere. Specifically, at the national level, shared Confucianism and other cultural Chineseness in Vietnam, Taiwan, and Hong Kong have prompted epistemological practices that can construct their out-group positions, as a sovereign state, a different nationality, a liberal democracy, an agent of containment, and a non-Chinese colony. At the individual level, discourses and knowledge produced along these lines of thinking creatively arise from the scholarship on China. Their politics of post-Chineseness uncovers the unnoticeable linkage elsewhere between those in the out-group position and their target of watching, for example, in the Southeast Asia where Chinese Southeast Asian scholars who watch China from the outside are actually each practicing a kind of reconnection with China. For another example, China experts in Europe or America who take the scientific or the civilizational approach similarly constitute their identities with scientific Chineseness, although with purposes different from those of the Southeast Asian Chinese. In fact, the relationships of Chinese European and American narrators with the mainstream in their societies immediately expose strategic choices of all, and they are aware as well as unaware of China being a constituting component of their identities. The case of the Philippines is only one of many cases that provide information on post-Chineseness as a process and a choice.

## Note

1  This chapter is derived from an article originally published in *Asian Ethnicity* (copyright Taylor & Francis) 13 December 2017 available on line http://www. tandfonline.com/ (Post-Chineseness as Epistemology: Identities and Scholarship on China in the Philippines, doi: 10.1080/14741369.2017.1515133).

## References

Ang See, Teresita. 2015. "Interview by Reynard Hing." *Department of Political Science, National Taiwan University: For China Studies and Cross Taiwan Strait Relations*, 6 November. Retrieved 23 February 2018 (http://www.china-studies.taipei/act02.php).

Baculinao, Eric. 2015. "Interview by Jose Mari Hall Lanuza". *Department of Political Science, National Taiwan University: For China Studies and Cross Taiwan Strait Relations*, 3 November. Retrieved 1 March 2018 (http://www.china-studies.taipei/act02.php).

Barbalet, Jack M. 2001. *Emotion, Social Theory, and Social Structure: A Macrosociological Approach*. Cambridge: Cambridge University Press.

Barbalet, Jack. 2014. "Greater Self, Lesser Self: Dimensions of Self-Interest in Chinese Filial Piety." *Journal for the Theory of Social Behaviour* 44(2):186–205.

Baviera, Aileen. 2016. "Interview by Lucio Pitlo III". *Department of Political Science, National Taiwan University: For China Studies and Cross Taiwan Strait Relations*, 29 February. Retrieved 23 February 2018 (http://www.china-studies.taipei/act02.php).

Brook, Timothy and Gregory Blue, eds. 2002. *China and Historical Capitalism: Genealogies of Sinological Knowledge*. Cambridge: Cambridge University Press.

Burke, Peter. 1991. "Identity Processes and Social Stress." *American Sociological Review* 56(6):836–849.

Callero, Peter. 1994. "From Role-Playing to Role-Using: Understanding Role as Resource." *Social Psychology Quarterly* 57(3):228–43.

Cariño, Theresa. 2015. "Interview by Dorcas Juliette Ramos-Caraig." *Department of Political Science, National Taiwan University: For China Studies and Cross Taiwan Strait Relations*, 7 December. Retrieved 23 February 2018 (http://www.china-studies.taipei/act02.php).

Cohen, Paul A. 2010. *Discovering History in China: American Historical Writing on the Recent Chinese Past*. New York: Columbia University Press.

Culp, Robert, Eddy U, and Wen-hsin Yeh. 2016. *Knowledge Acts in Modern China: Ideas, Institutions, and Identities*. Berkeley: Institute of East Asian Studies, University of California.

Dimen, P. Muriel. 2012. "Perversion Is Us? Eight Notes." In *Relational Psychoanalysis, Volume 2: Innovation and Expansion*, edited by Lewis Aro and Adrienne Harris. New York: Routledge.

Epstein, Charlotte. 2012. "Stop Telling Us How to Behave: Socialization or Infantilization." *International Studies Perspectives* 13(2):135–145.

FlorCruz, Jaime. 2015. "Interview by Robin Michael Garcia". *Department of Political Science, National Taiwan University: For China Studies and Cross Taiwan Strait Relations*, 8 October. Retrieved 23 February 2018 (http://www.china-studies.taipei/act02.php).

Go, Bon Juan. 2015. "Interview by Carmelea Ang See." *Department of Political Science, National Taiwan University: For China Studies and Cross Taiwan Strait Relations*, 18 November. Retrieved 23 February 2018 (http://www.china-studies.taipei/act02.php).

Hastings, Sally O. 2000. "Asian Indian 'Self-Suppression' and Self-Disclosure: Enactment and Adaptation of Cultural Identity." *Journal of Language and Social Psychology* 19(1):85–109.

128   *Chih-yu Shih*

Hau, Caroline. 2015. "Interview by Jose Mari Hall Lanuza." *Department of Political Science, National Taiwan University: For China Studies and Cross Taiwan Strait Relations*, 5 November. Retrieved 23 February 2018 (http://www.china-studies.taipei/act02.php).

He, Kai and Huiyun Feng. 2015. "Transcending Rationalism and Constructivism: Chinese Leaders' Operational Codes, Socialization Processes, and Multilateralism After the Cold War." *European Political Science Review* 7(3):401–426.

Higgins, Tory. 1987. "Self-Discrepancy: A Theory Relating Self and Affect." *Psychological Review* 94(3): 319–340.

Hillemann, Ulrike. 2009. *Asian Empire and British Knowledge: China and the Networks of British Imperial Expansion*. London: Palgrave Macmillan.

Ho, David Y. F. 1998. "Interpersonal Relationships and Relational Dominance: An analysis Based on Methodological Relationalism." *Asian Journal of Social Psychology* 1(1):1–16.

Ho, David Y. F. and Chi Yue Chiu. 1998. "Collective Representations as a Metaconstruct: An Analysis Based on Methodological Relationalism." *Culture and Psychology* 4(3):349–369.

Hsu, Francis L. K. 1971. "Psychosocial Homeostasis and Jen: Conceptual Tools for Advancing Psychological Anthropology." *American Anthropologist* 73(1):23–44.

Hsu, Jing. 1985. "The Chinese Family: Relations, Problems and Therapy." In *Chinese Culture and Mental Health,* edited by Wen-Shing Tseng and David Wu. Orlando: Academic Press, 95–112.

Hwang, Alvin, Francesco, Ann Marie, and Eric Kesslear. 2003. "The Relationship between Individualism–Collectivism, Face, and Feedback and Learning Processes in Hong Kong, Singapore, and the United States." *Journal of Cross-Cultural Psychology* 34(1):72–91.

Hwang, Kwang-Kuo, and Jeffrey Chang. 2009. "Self-Cultivation: Culturally Sensitive Psychotherapies in Confucian Societies." *The Counseling Psychologist* 37(7):1010–1032.

Hwang, Kwang-Kuo. 2012. *Foundations of Chinese Psychology: Confucian Social Relations*. New York: Springer SBM.

Katzenstein, Peter, ed. 2012. *Sinicization and the Rise of China*. Oxon: Routledge.

King, Ambrose Y. C. 1985. "The Individual and Group in Confucianism: A Relational perspective." In *Individualism and Holism: Studies in Confucian and Taoist Values*, edited by Donald Munro. Ann Arbor, MI: Center for Chinese Studies, The University of Michigan, pp. 57–70.

König, Lion and Bidisha Chaudhuri, eds. 2016. *Politics of the 'Other' in India and China: Western Concepts in Non-Western Contexts*. Oxon: Routledge.

Kwang, Peter. 1996. *The New Chinatown*. New York: Hill & Wang.

Lin, Tsung-Yi, Wen-Shing Tseng, and Eng-Kung Yeh, eds. 1995. *Chinese Societies and Mental Health*. New York: Oxford University Press.

Mallare, Florencio. 2015. "Interview by Sining Kotah." *Department of Political Science, National Taiwan University: For China Studies and Cross Taiwan Strait Relations*, 25 November. Retrieved 23 February 2018 (http://www.china-studies.taipei/act02.php).

Manomaivibool, Prapin and Chih-yu Shih, eds. 2016. *Understanding 21st Century China in Buddhist Asia: History, Modernity, and International Relations*. Bangkok: Asia Research Center, Chulalongkorn University.

## China watching and China watchers in the Philippines 129

Michalski, Anna and Zhongqi Pan. 2016. "Role Dynamics in a Structured Relationship: The EU-China Strategic Partnership." *Journal of Common Market Studies* 55(3):611–627.

Nyíri, Pál and Danielle Tan, eds. 2016. *Chinese Encounters in Southeast Asia: How People, Money, and Ideas from China are Changing a Region.* Seattle, WA: University of Washington Press.

Oldmeadow, Julian A. and Susan T. Fiske. 2010. "Social Status and the Pursuit of Positive Social Identity: Systematic Domains of Intergroup Differentiation and Discrimination for High- and Low- Status Groups." *Group Processes and Intergroup Relations* 13(4):425–444.

Ong, Charlson. 2016. "Interview by Yvan Ysmael Yonaha." *Department of Political Science, National Taiwan University: For China Studies and Cross Taiwan Strait Relations*, 18 January. Retrieved 23 February 2018 (http://www.china-studies.taipei/act02.php).

Qi, Xiaoying. 2011. "Face: A Chinese Concept in a Global Sociology." *Journal of Sociology* 47(3):279–96.

Renolds, Robert. 2007. "How Does Therapy Cure? The Relational Turn in Psychotherapy." *Counselling, Psychotherapy, and Health* 3(2):127–150.

Roseman, Ira J. 1984. "Cognitive Determinants of Emotion: A Structural Theory." *Review of Personality and Social Psychology* 5:11–36.

Santa Romana, Jose Santiago "Chito." 2016. "Interview by Lucio Pitlo III." *Department of Political Science, National Taiwan University: For China Studies and Cross Taiwan Strait Relations*, 14 April. Retrieved 29 March 2018 (http://www.china-studies.taipei/act02.php).

Shih, Chih-yu. 2013. *Sinicizing International Relations: Self, Civilization and Intellectual Politics of Subaltern East Asia.* London: Palgrave Macmillan.

Simon, Robin W. 1992. "Parental Role Strains, Salience of Parental Identity, and Gender Differences in Psychological Distress." *Journal of Health and Social Behavior* 33: 25–35.

Stephan, Walter G. and Cookie White Stephan. 1985. "Intergroup Anxiety." *Journal of Social Issues* 41(3):157–175.

Tagliacozzo, Eric and Wen-chin Chang, eds. 2011 *Chinese Circulations: Capital, Commodities, and Networks in Southeast Asia.* Durham, NC: Duke University Press.

Tanaka, Stefan. 1993. *Japan's Orient.* Durham, NC: Duke University Press.

Thies, Cameron G. 2015. "China's Rise and the Socialisation of Rising Powers." *Chinese Journal of International Politics* 8(3):281–300.

Thies, Camron. G. 2012. "International Socialization Processes vs. Israeli National Role Conceptions: Can Role Theory Integrate IR Theory and Foreign Policy Analysis?" *Foreign Policy Analysis* 8(1):25–46.

Turner, Jonathan H. and Jan E. Stets. 2006. "Sociological Theories of Human Emotions." *Annual Review of Sociology* 32:25–52.

Valenta, Marko. 2009. Immigrants' Identity Negotiations and Coping with Stigma in Different Relational Frames. *Symbolic Interaction* 32: 351–371.

Vukovich, Daniel. 2012. *China and Orientalism: Western Knowledge Production and the PRC.* Oxon: Routledge.

Wang, Gungwu, ed. 2014. *National Building: Five Southeast Asian Histories.* Singapore: Institute of Southeast Asian Studies Publications.

## 130  *Chih-yu Shih*

Wang, Gungwu. 2002. *The Chinese Overseas: From Earthbound China to the Quest for Autonomy.* Cambridge, MA: Harvard University Press.

Wasson, Leslie. 2015. "Identity Politics/Relational Politics." *The Wiley Blackwell Encyclopedia of Race, Ethnicity and Nationalism* 1–2, doi:10.1002/9781118663202. wberen446 Access July 20, 2018

Wehner, Leslie. E. 2015. "Role Expectations as Foreign Policy: South American Second.ary Powers' Expectations of Brazil as a Regional Power." *Foreign Policy Analysis* 11(4):435–455.

Wong, Meiling. 2010. "Guanxi Management as Complex Adaptive Systems: A Case Study of Taiwanese ODI in China." *Journal of Business Ethics* 91(3):419–432.

Yang, Kuo-shu. 1995. "Chinese Social Orientation: An Integrative Analysis." In *Chinese Societies and Mental Health,* edited by Tseng-yi Lin, Wen-shing Tseng, and Eng-kung Yeh Hong Kong: Oxford University Press, 19–39.

# Interview Transcripts

*Teresita Ang See*

**Expert: Teresita Ang See**
**Interviewer: Reynard Hing**
**Date of interview: November 6, 2015**

HING: Looking back at your childhood, would you say that being raised in a mixed-race marriage consciously or subconsciously made you more sensitive of things like the need for integration by immigrants and their descendants into mainstream Filipino society?

SEE: In my childhood, since I grew up in the suburb of Malabon, I probably never realized that my experiences were a problematic concern. I never encountered any experience of anti-Chinese*ness* which I learned much later on, when we moved on to Binondo. There I learned much later on that race could possibly be a problem. So, during childhood, it was never in our consciousness that there was a problem between Filipinos and Chinese; that's even when my eldest brother would always be teased because of his way of speaking Tagalog and his accent.

HING: I guess we could say that [the consciousness] was later than that, not because of being in a mixed racial marriage background. So the awareness of, you know, issues like integration, the inter-ethnic issues, that came later.

SEE: Yes, it was more of differences in upbringing, not race.

HING: That being said, that consciousness about issues like that came later in life, would you say that there was a seminal moment, like a trigger moment for you to say that "This is it"?

SEE: Yes, the culture shock, probably the consciousness that we may be different happened already in college because all throughout my youth, my childhood, my elementary school, and then high school, it's just all in the bastion of conservatism that's Binondo. So when I got to UP, probably that's the first shock in my life that my Filipino classmates are more intelligent, much more well off than me. I was a scholar all throughout, with very, very little allowance and everything. So, you'll look at the Filipinos in a vastly different way than when I looked at the Filipinos that I have encountered in my childhood. They were usually my uncle's

132 *Teresita Ang See*

workers in the factory, kargador, the drivers, the housemaids. Although in our household, probably because my mother is a Filipina, our housemaids are like our sisters.

HING: You took up AB Political Science in UP. Coming from a Tsinoy background, that's quite unconventional, even for the current times. Whose choice was it and why? What influenced it?

SEE: Probably because of my upbringing, I was very well read. In elementary school I already finished reading all the Perry Mason books. At first my dream was to be in Foreign Service but I thought maybe Political Science is a much broader course that will cover if I don't go into foreign service. But I was probably only two subjects less to finish double degrees. But frankly, my real love at the time was medicine. I really would have wanted to go to medical school, but I know that we could never afford it. And then the next love was being a lawyer, but having finished college in 1971, I needed to work because we still had sisters and brothers to support. My father died when he was only 44 and I was only turning 12 at that time and all of us, from the eldest up to me, we were all working students throughout our college.

In fact my mother was surprised on why I had to take Political Science. So Political Science can be considered probably an accident, more on because of the reading fare, reading all of the Perry Mason books and then the Ian Fleming James Bond books.

HING: It was also quite a fateful decision because in the social science sphere that's where you met your husband, Mr. Chinben See.

SEE: Yeah, because of the work that we do. Because I finished Political Science, my first job was with the Federation of Filipino-Chinese Chamber of Commerce, to fight for the *jus soli* citizenship. Maybe that was the second, really opening up. I wasn't aware of the lack of citizenship being a big impediment, except when I was in college, because I had to pay an additional foreign student's fee. I was still a Chinese citizen until I became eighteen.

HING: You mentioned a bit about that in your biographical notes that you were surprised that, you know, you were never aware of that official Chinese identity until UP, when you had to pay...

SEE: Yes, UP. And then, the Pagkakaisa sa Pag-unlad, where I met my late husband. I was with the Federation, we were "lobbying" for jus soli. He was the president at that time. We were doing research, being interviewed—radio, television, writing articles on supporting the *jus soli* that if you are born in the Philippines, you should be a Filipino citizen. I wasn't even aware at that time that what being a Chinese citizen entails, except for UP when I had to pay for that alien registration fee, but nowhere else. Because we were not in business, so you are not conscious that being a Chinese citizen will impede you from professional careers, from your businesses and many other things. So, helping to fight for the rightful place of those born in the Philippines—*jus soli* means born—that started me off.

*Interview Transcripts*   133

But my late husband and Bernard Go, another anthropologist from Cebu, they were already very conscious of that because they have done that for so many years; and I wouldn't be joining the Pagkakaisa sa Pag-unlad if not for my Political Science Background.

HING: The *jus soli*, that mission, was that the core mission of Pagkakaisa sa Pag-unlad? The very reason for its establishment?

SEE: Yes. It was established mainly to fight for the *jus soli* provision in the Constitution and side by side with that is the need to push for integration, that there's no other direction the Chinese-Filipino community would take except for integration. In fact, we were frowned upon; I mean we were really ostracized by many Chinese groups at the time. In fact, my late husband had a story that they were almost literally thrown out of Chiang Kai Shek College when they gave a lecture on the need to Filipinize the Chinese schools to make them loyal to the Philippines instead of China because that is the period of my miseducation because we were really being educated to not just to relate to our cultural heritage, but politically, the loyalty, the studies and the understanding are all towards China. So, Chinben See and Bernard Go were pushing for integration, that you cannot have double loyalty, and they were trying already to prove that you can be culturally Chinese but politically Filipino.

HING: What would you say is root of the disconnect between the reality that they are living here or they were born here, [yet] they seem to have the mentality that we are just itinerants and somehow there is that greater mission to, you know, if you are Kuomintang, it would be to "return and reclaim China", or vice-versa if you are pro-Communist that you know I will be physically here but *xin zai zhong guo* (心在中国; "your heart is in China"). What would you attribute that to?

SEE: I think the biggest disconnect lies in the school system, the way we were brought up. All the teachers were graduates of National Taiwan University, or if it's Cultural, the Q*iao Zhong* (桥中; abbreviated Chinese for Philippine Cultural College) maybe graduates from Jimei (集美) [University] in China. So, the sentiments are all towards China. I would say it's the upbringing and the education.

And then, many of the younger generations grew up... let's say if they have to go to business, they go to the businesses of their friends, of their father's friends. It was already much later on when you start seeing Tsinoys going into the professions. If you are in the professions, if you are an employee, then you encounter Filipino colleagues in work. The exposure of people to people started to change the mindset, but before 1975, before the diplomatic relations with People's Republic of China and the opening up of citizenship, most of the Chinese at that time, 90 percent, were still Chinese citizens. So your exposure would only be to the business because that's the only thing open to you. It would be much later on, [after naturalization, if they opted to be naturalized], when you can practice architecture, and other professions. All my contemporaries

134    *Teresita Ang See*

who finished medicine in college left for abroad immediately after graduation because they cannot even take the board exams.

HING: Being Chinese citizens.

SEE: Yes. So they all left for abroad immediately after graduation. So, your exposure, the disconnect is more because you don't have people-to-people experience. Your only experience is limited to the workers, the policemen, the congressmen who you encounter, and then all of these give negative impressions to the older generation. So, when you started going out let's say living in the subdivisions, going out of Binondo enclave, even if you stay in Greenhills, then you will have Filipino neighbors and you encountered them more.

HING: In that sense then, Chinatowns not only are a physical barrier for Chinese-Filipino contact, it also is some sort of a mental barrier, a cultural barrier. F. Sionil Jose argued against the presence of Tsinoy schools and although the realities have shifted, would you say that he had a point in saying that these should be struck down to pave the way for smoother integration?

SEE: In fact, Pagkakaisa, well the Chinese organizations were very unhappy about it because of the push to Filipinize the Chinese schools. But, our reasoning is that that's the only direction to take. The integration should start from the school where you teach a Filipinized curriculum, but you can retain Chinese. In fact, what they did not understand, if they had listened and see the vision of Pagkakaisa, things would have been different. Because if we Filipinize on our own terms, on what we want, then we would know better how to do it. I mean it (Chinese-language education) would not have deteriorated like what happened. I mean, we would have been able to craft a curriculum that is suitable to us. You Filipinize it, yes. You can teach Chinese history, focus on Chinese history, geography in English and that would have added to your knowledge about China. And then, the language courses will be purely taught as a language. That would have helped the curriculum so much, if they had listened on letting us work on the Filipinization of Chinese schools. It will definitely happen.

HING: So, we could now attribute the deterioration and let's say the Chinese language education here to the lack of input from the Tsinoy community during the Filipinization process...

SEE: Yes, it's one of them. It's one factor, although even during my time the Chinese language education was already going downwards. It's also a function of integration and the fact that we're only 1.2 percent of the population. So it's very hard for you to maintain a speech-speaking community in Hokkien, unless it starts from the family.

HING: Okay going back to the Filipinization process, would you say that because of the one-track minded nature of the Tsinoy leaders at that time that was due to ethnocentrism?

SEE: Yes, they were very conservative and probably it's also the lack of research, the lack of policy making among the Tsinoy organizations. They

*Interview Transcripts* 135

are not exposed on the successful experiences of other countries and how integration would have helped both sides, that it's a win-win solution for the Tsinoy community. There was so much resistance at the beginning. When Pagkakaisa was starting, [there was] a lot of resistance. It takes a lot of open-minded people to be supporting.

HING: Pagkakaisa sa Pag-unlad would be the predecessor organization to Kaisa para sa Kaunlaran. What prodded down the name change? Or was it a winding down of Pagkakaisa and establishing Kaisa? Because there was a gap between the establishment of Pagkakaisa and Kaisa.

SEE: Yes. A little bit nuance there. Pagkakaisa means you're not yet united. So Kaisa is already that you are, at that point, we were already feeling the integration has already happened. It's two-pronged. One is to wind down the old Pagkakaisa.

HING: The eventual winding down of Pagkakaisa, could you also attribute that partly to because Marcos after the 1975 opening of relations with China immediately sought to "solve" the problem of the Chinese citizens in the Philippines? So he opened the floodgates to naturalization that you have achieved more or less what you said...

SEE: Yeah, a big part of that was that one, although the integration and the citizenship was the core motive of Pagkakaisa, we were already doing also a lot of developmental work, very successful leadership training for instance for the young in Cebu, in Iloilo and Davao. We didn't do that in Manila but we did it in the provinces. We were very successful in getting these young people together. So, maybe like Kaisa, there were a lot of pioneering activities to build bridges during that time.

HING: One oft-cited incident that pushed the Kaisa pioneers to get on with starting Kaisa was the anti-Chinese demonstrations in Angeles in 1987.

SEE: It was Randy David, he's a sociologist who pointed out that the undercurrents of racism could always be exploited for political agenda. At the beginning we were not aware on why everything just erupted. The leader, the core group were the furniture association, and they were saying that the furniture business is going down, "sunset industry" because they cannot buy lumber anymore and they were blaming the Chinese although it was a national policy, the illegal logging and everything and they were blaming it on the Chinese. It was exploited and at the beginning, we couldn't believe that foreign powers would use that policy to divert attention away from them. And during that rally, that was the first time we realized that definitely the hand behind that anti-Chinese rally were foreign powers. It's the first time we encountered a public rally where the flyers were printed, not mimeographed, that was 1987. When we asked them how much the sound system cost, because it is in the public plaza and you could hear them very far off, they said it costs 20,000. It's a big amount at that time. So how could these people who said that furniture is a sunset industry afford that kind of budget. So now, if you relate it to now, that is probably one of the things that

# 136  *Teresita Ang See*

also scare the Tsinoys now, that foreign powers might exploit undercurrents of racism by raising the specter of the Tsinoy threat because of the China issue.

I would see it as really the lack of understanding of the foreign powers on what is the Tsinoy community. They were...the slogans were saying, it's not because what do they get or what benefit, it's more on creating another enemy; that they're telling the Filipinos, "We are not your enemies; your enemies should be the Chinese." That's why their slogan, instead of kicking out the foreign powers, you should kick out the Chinese in your midst. That is the underlying message of that rally at that time, but it's not because they want to curry favor; they do not need that, everything is favorable to them. It's more on diverting attention to another supposed specter of another enemy and at that time it showed how little they understood the Chinese-Filipino community. Also, because there's not much being written to support the cause of the Chinese-Filipino community at that time.

HING: So it was like, they viewed with suspicion the Tsinoy community as a fifth column for China.

SEE: Yeah. The Cold War mentality was...

HING: Through business links, through family links with China, you must be doing something for the government Beijing.

SEE: Yeah, and they could not even fathom that the last bastion of Kuomintang influence is the Federation of the Filipino-Chinese Chamber of Commerce. It was only in 1999, already late 1990s that they switched allegiance to China and that's something that none of them could understand, and none of them (foreign powers) knew about. How could the Chinese-Filipino community be a pawn of mainland China if they were very pro-Kuomintang? The lack of understanding surprisingly, they don't seem to go out of their way to really learn, possible also is it's also the fault of the Tsinoy community for not doing more on propagating, or information dissemination. Public Relations. Pushing what they are, who they are.

That's why Pagkakaisa would be seen as different. We did things that they did not think of doing, like producing the movie *Dragnet,* the first script written by Ricky Lee and with Erap as the actor and choosing his outfit. We had to study all the movies at that time which one had the consistent social theme, and it was Erap's production— that had the consistent social theme, and we asked him to produce *Dragnet* as a counterfoil to the successive movies with the Tsinoy as the villain.

HING: Kaisa's scope seems to be larger than Pagkakaisa's... would you say that this is inheriting the legacy of Pagkakaisa and at the same time evolving with the needs of the times? Like for example, there's no more need to work towards the naturalization issue but then there are other issues, Tsinoy community issues.

SEE: Yeah. Well when we started Kaisa, we had two or three brainstorming sessions on where we wanted to go. That is one thing that I wanted

*Interview Transcripts* 137

sana to happen to Kaisa kasi it's already 25 years. It's time to sit down and reevaluate. Not just yung SWOT analysis. It's more on really sitting down and we had three sessions, three full-day sessions doing that. 'What do we want to do?' and 'How do we do it?' I mean, getting down to the nitty-gritty of all your wishes and what you wanted to do. So we were all able to do it because maybe we had that group of people who had the vision and also the means to implement the vision.

HING: You are also one of the founding pioneers in the International Society for the Study of Chinese Overseas and the founding president of Philippine Association for Chinese Studies; and also, you've been active on the Philippine-China Development Resources Council. Because they have different thrusts, is there any synergy?

SEE: Well ISSCO is really very academic. I was not the founding president. Dr. Wang Gungwu was the founding President.

HING: Ah, Wang Gungwu

SEE: I was the second president. I inherited from him. It's all very academic and it's all on the Chinese overseas. The Philippine-China Development Resource Center, that one I was the founding president of that group and it's more again the role as a bridge, and there's a lot to learn from the development of China that the Third World countries like the Philippines could learn. We need those things. So, that was the...very successful exposure trips, bringing Filipino farmers, fisherfolks, teachers and health workers to China and vice versa, bringing them to the Philippines. The NGO movement in China was just starting, and they had so much to learn from the Philippines, and they benefited a lot from the PDRC work, opening their minds about the NGO community. One of the surprising comments that they had is that the NGOs who came to the Philippines to learn were all males and they encountered all the NGOs here were all run by females. So they were surprised about that.

And then, the Philippine Association for Chinese Studies, I was one of the founding board members, but I became president only in 2004. I have refused to be president of that because of the work in Kaisa, but PACS is more on the Chinese studies, promoting Chinese studies because also of the deterioration of the Chinese language in the Chinese language schools, not being able to fulfill their role. What we thought was that maybe you elevate Chinese studies to the college level, and that was how PACS was formed. Because we thought that Chinese studies will become very important. That was 1987 when we started the PACS. China was already opening up, it's no longer being seen as a threat, I mean the poor man's burden, [and] Asia has seen it now with a different eye. So we said, it will be very important and it's better that we are already ahead of everybody in having this group. But at least in the Philippines, we formed the group mainly for research, conferences and the first conference that we did as a post-Angeles rally was again because of the racial anti-Chinese issue. That's the tenth anniversary of

138 *Teresita Ang See*

Philippines-China diplomatic relations I think, because Dr. Bernardita Churchill heard in Veritas—it's a very supposed to be a very learned station; she heard it in Veritas, about very anti-Chinese sentiments and she convened that conference to focus on Philippines-China relation; and it was a big breakthrough for Kaisa because that was the time when I delivered that paper on the Chinese in the Philippines as assets or liabilities with Miriam Defensor-Santiago as the discussant of my paper. And that was the start of the helping the *xin qiao* (新僑 or "new immigrants"), the phenomenon of the...actually they are no longer *xin qiao* (新僑 or "new immigrants") because they arrived here in the Philippines in the 1960s. So, by 1988, '89, they had been already here 20, 30 years. So, that was my paper: Are they assets of the country? Or are they liabilities? If they are assets, how come the Americans, the Japanese, the Spaniards, they are wiser in knowing how to make use of the Chinese in the Philippines as their assets? How come it is still the Filipinos who cannot see it? And Miriam Defensor-Santiago picked it up very fast and then crafted the amnesty for the illegal aliens.

HING: Thank you very much Ms. Ang See for the rich material.

*Eric Baculinao*

**Expert: Eric Baculinao**
**Interviewer: Jose Mari H. Lanuza**
**Interview Date: November 3, 2015**

BACULINAO: [I began as a China watcher] in exile. It was by accident, a political accident. We came to China in 1971 together with a youth delegation, planning to visit China for 3 weeks, but a few days after we arrived in Beijing, there were bombings in Manila, and the writ of habeas corpus was suspended. Marcos was arresting lots of students and anyone in opposition, and then 1 year later, it went on to full Martial Law. I thought I would wait for 2 months, or a year or so; but in fact, we ended up waiting for 15 years, because had we gone home, we would have been arrested... At that point, I had already finished studying Chinese and I mentally became prepared for a long stay in China. I started working in media and China was becoming interesting intellectually, with all the reforms being launched by Deng. By 1986, the Marcos regime was toppled and I could go home, since I got my passport back. However, China was changing, and that kept me going. I wanted to know what would happen to the so-called opening up of China, and before I knew it, 44 years had gone by.

LANUZA: Can you tell us about the curriculum, the faculty and the institution, and your adviser during your period of education in China? I understand you studied there when you were in exile.

BACULINAO: In 1974–1975, after 4 or 5 years of being in China, they opened up the universities. Before that, most schools were basically closed for the so-called revolutionary reorientation of the educational system, the aftermath of the Cultural Revolution. When they reopened, we asked to go to school while waiting to go home to the Philippines. We went to a language school to learn Mandarin. Before that, we had interpreters and we couldn't read Chinese. To understand the Chinese and China better, we decided it would be good to learn the language while waiting to go home. I spent 3 years in a language school learning Mandarin.

As for the curriculum, it's basically language-oriented, but we had to take history, literature, and anything that would enhance our understanding of the language and the way the language is used especially in

140　*Eric Baculinao*

history, literature, and politics. We learned that all after graduation. We were able to read People's Daily, the Chinese Party paper, Red Flag, and theoretical journals.

There were very limited publications in China at that point in time, but by studying the language, we learned what political programs of the Communist Party of China [were there that] would help us understand where China was going, and what direction it was taking at that point in time...

I went to school in China to study language, and all the rest about learning and understanding China was on my own, with my acquired language facility. I learned to read all possible books about China that were available in Beijing. There weren't that many in the 1970s, early 1980s; not that many publications. Now of course, there are many books about China—but in those days, very limited.

LANUZA: Where did you get most of the material you used to learn about China, since you said that in the 70s and 80s these were limited?

BACULINAO: When China opened up to Western media in the early 1980s, many places were still off-limits to foreigners. In general, foreign media had to deal with lots of restrictions and other bureaucratic hurdles, especially if the stories involved travelling outside Beijing. Permissions had to be obtained in advance, and if the stories were deemed "sensitive" —politically, socially, militarily—permits would prove very difficult. China's open door policy meant that its media policies had to be reformed over time. Indeed, that Beijing now boasts of what probably is the biggest foreign press corps in Asia attests to the advances made, especially after the Beijing Olympics, although strict controls do remain.

LANUZA: Can you expound on your experiences when you were starting to work for the media in China?

BACULINAO: I started off as a researcher and translator for some media companies and a weekly columnist for a Hong Kong newspaper, but eventually settled down at NBC News. Reporting from China in the 1980s—when Deng's open door policies were beginning to take effect— had two characteristics: one, the world was hungry for information about China and curious about where post-Mao China was heading toward. China news had a huge market, so to speak. Two, China's bureaucracy and the Western media were like strangers to each other, and news coverage had to contend with many tough and exasperating Chinese rules and restrictions.

LANUZA: Last January 2016 you were a speaker in a forum on prospects of Asian development and peace. You said that the Philippines should be open to joint development ventures with China. Can you expound on your views on Philippine engagement with China? What is the nature of engagement would you like to see, working together towards resolving the maritime dispute?

BACULINAO: I basically wanted to ignite more debate on what new ideas or strategies could be explored to win our disputes with China on territorial and maritime issues, and to win them in a peaceful way. There

*Interview Transcripts* 141

is no alternative to a peaceful negotiated outcome for these disputes, because military conflict would be mutually destructive and not solve the problem.

As a neighbor and as the world's second largest economy, China is both a challenge and an opportunity. We should certainly fight for our sovereign and legitimate rights and interests, but we must also not neglect the potential areas for wider mutually beneficial cooperation, especially in the economic field. I want to argue that prioritizing economic diplomacy with China, or expanding the areas of cooperation that can immediately benefit our fishermen, our farmers, our workers, our businessmen, while not giving up at all on our sovereign rights and interests in the West Philippine Sea, might actually open the route to the eventual resolution of disputes with China. It's like hitting two birds with one stone.

Expanded economic cooperation builds up goodwill and mutual trust, which are indispensable for the resolution of our disputes. I could be wrong, but it is always good to provoke more debates for the common purpose of securing the peace and welfare of our people. The best foreign policy is friendship to all and enmity to none, which will prevent our country from becoming the battleground of great-power rivalries. With smart strategy, it is possible to transpose our weakness into a source of strength in our diplomacy with China; it is possible to win maximum favorable terms for the diplomatic resolution of our disputes with China over the long-term.

LANUZA: What are your views on the Maritime Silk Road initiative?

BACULINAO: It's the latest evolution of China's fundamental policy and strategy to seek a peaceful rise. I thought US Ambassador Chas Freeman put it quite well: that it was China's answer to America's Pivot to Asia strategy. While America is strong in conceptualizing military security responses to major threats, China's inclination is generally to set aside disputes and to seek win-win solutions, primarily in the field of economic cooperation, which is China's strong point.

Why a peaceful rise? Because to rise through military conquest or aggression—as was the road taken by great powers in the past—cannot be an option for China in the present-day world, bearing in mind the collapse of the Soviet Union. And so, the only choice for China, for its ruling Communist Party, is to rise peacefully, chiefly by expanding areas of mutual benefit.

The Maritime Silk Road initiative is part of China's grand vision to form a potential Eurasian world-island economy that will spur greater creation of wealth through increased connectivity and trade, a huge market of 4.4 billion people with about half of global GDP. China could invest as much as $1.4 trillion in this venture, twelve times more than the US Marshall Plan after World War II. We are an archipelagic country; we are in need of more infrastructure, more investments, more markets, and more trade, which could mean more jobs and better incomes for our people. Looking at the world, 20–30 years from now: we can only see

142  *Eric Baculinao*

vast changes, with China projected to become the world's largest economy. It would be a disservice to our people if we neglect to plan how this huge opportunity can be exploited to accelerate our own economic development and national renewal.

This is possible without giving up our sovereign rights and interests in the West Philippine Sea. In the long term, the mutual trust and goodwill developed in the course of expanded economic cooperation will eventually help the amicable resolution of our disputes.

LANUZA:  Can you describe your relationship with the Chinese government?

BACULINAO:  Officially, I'm a journalist, so we are hosted by the Chinese foreign ministry. That is the official relationship, a professional relationship whereby we are able to do our work, do interviews…but we have to follow the rules of China. It's a very professional relationship.

LANUZA:  What do you think is your prime contribution to views and theories on China, or Chinese studies in the Philippines?

BACULINAO:  I'd like to develop the idea that negotiations with China will have to involve exchanges of things that are valuable for both sides. I would even argue that our "weakness" is our source of strength, while China's "strength" is also its source of weakness; with the right diplomacy strategy, there is a way to bring that out, to inculcate the strategy and tactics of engaging the Chinese, in a long term complicated negotiations but which eventually will lead to a peaceful solution and better situation than what we face today under the current status.

That kind of thinking is not yet fully being exploited or being tapped. Right now, I would say that our current strategy is still wrapped in conventional thinking, and it will not lead us anywhere.

LANUZA:  What are any issues or problems that you have personally encountered in your past research on China or Chinese studies?

BACULINAO:  To be frank about it, I feel very strongly that up to this point Philippine scholarship on China and our policies—this includes our policy think tanks, even the thinking behind government decisions on China—is not open wide enough.

There is so much ideological baggage that constricts our views of what possible strategies can be used to engage the Chinese and to win our case with China on our maritime disputes, successfully and peacefully. Sometimes I'd like try to explore different approaches and ideas, but I can immediately sense a sense of resistance.

And I think maybe it's because nationalism is an important factor. It's natural to encounter resistance, especially if you challenge conventional positions; you run the risk of being called anti-nationalist or unpatriotic, even if it's not the case. I think the main difficulty of breaking through our restricted understanding of China is the fact that we are so passionate about our national interest—which is a very positive thing—that sometimes we neglect to see the weaknesses of our own positions, of our own understanding, which then leads us to very weak strategies

*Interview Transcripts* 143

or tactics; weak in the sense that they cannot conceivably lead to a peaceful negotiated outcome of our disputes.

LANUZA: Okay, Sir. What's your evaluation of China pedagogy in the Philippines and its future prospects?

BACULINAO: Chinese understanding of the Philippines is also limited. They have the legal system—a very new profession here, that for a long time was not taught in universities in China, so they are well behind us in terms of legal warfare, so to speak; years of law and legal strategy to win our case. Of course, world politics is not governed by law alone, not by legal strategy alone.

We can help in that regard by being more involved in promoting more frequent interactions between Chinese and Philippine scholars. They have very limited understanding, I think, partly because in the past, they thought that we were puppets of the Americans. So really, the most important thing for them is to understand us. They probably think Philippine actions are just based on American dictates and all that is reflected in foreign policy. That's probably a legacy of our colonial past or history, but that is a limited [view], because Philippine independence has developed so much and deserves to be understood.

There's a big gap between the Chinese understanding of the Philippines and the reality of the Philippines as a country, as a society, as a people; so we have to help close that gap. I would also say that this problem is mutual. We have a limited understanding of China, and the Chinese have a limited understanding of the Philippines.

LANUZA: What are your personal views on China's future?

BACULINAO: In the immediate 10–15 years, the Chinese will possibly become the number one economy, in aggregate terms, maybe. Of course, nothing is absolutely sure, but the fundamentals are there for China to become the biggest economy in the world in terms of population and economic growth, size of markets and overall place in the global market. They are trying to diversify their relationships and not just be dependent on America, but also to develop other relationships.

They are certainly on their track to almost approach American economic strength and eventually even exceed it, maybe in the next 15–20 years. But beyond that, it's really difficult to say, because that's when the Chinese Communist Party will be facing with a very different society, with large very wealthy middle class, a very prosperous society of consumers. It's [going to be] very, very different.

A Communist party that is ruling a nation of wealthy middle class: that has never been happened before. Imagine, the Communist Party was supposed to be a party of the working class, of the have-nots, people with nothing, the poor, the oppressed. It will be a challenge for the Communist Party, conceived by Marx and carried on by Mao, to be leading a nation of 1.5 billion, rich, middle class consumers who demand the best: climate, access to information, the best of everything.

144 *Eric Baculinao*

They will demand representation, their voices to be heard. How will the Communist Party deal with that? I mean, the rule is no taxation without representation. [The question is] how to give more representation in whatever flexible, creative way for these voices. There will be many voices. China will not be a nation of one monolithic opinion; it will be a nation of so many interest groups which will demand the facility to voice their opinions, their needs, and their expectations.

That is a challenge for the next 30 years, and I'm not so sure how the Communist Party can maintain its form of governance as we know today in trying to deal with that very mindboggling—unprecedented, I would say—challenge to governance. The Soviet Union also tried the socialist road, but again, what the Chinese have done is far beyond what the Soviet Union accomplished in its time.

The uniqueness of the challenges that the Communist Party of China is something that has never been encountered before. Maybe the Communist Party will change into something beyond our recognition; and that's probably not the Communist Party we see now. It will all depend on the security relationships at that point, maybe, when everybody is at ease; and then maybe China will loosen up, and give more representation [to its people], because there is no threat anyway.

Right now, they still perceive that they are being threatened by the Americans. There is a thinking here that the Americans want to contain China. So the threat factor influences governance. The vulnerability to threat influences the behavior of the Communist Party and its foreign policy situation. Ten to twenty years from now, a lot will depend on all these relationships between the big powers and the domestic situation in China.

I am very keenly optimistic that the next 10–15 years, they will still be on track to reach economic hierarchy with the US, although per capita, they will still be "backward." There's no way that with 1.5 billion at that point, in terms of economic strength, economic weight in the world, that they will equalize with the US. Strategically of course, they will improve their military modernization, so we will have a very "tall" China. But beyond that, the Chinese society will change also, such that it will force a different set of challenges to the Communist Party. How the Communist Party will react to satisfy the needs of that kind of society at that point in time is a big challenge. You know, China has always reinvented itself over time. I came here after the 70s, [with] this Mao model of governance and economy, and [have lived to witness] a present day Communist Party. How China can reinvent itself and maintain its rule, in a creative way—governing a nation of 1.5 billion middle class, rich consumers—will be quite a challenge.

LANUZA: Thank you, Sir for this interview. Can we contact you again if we have any further questions or clarifications?

BACULINAO: No problem.

LANUZA: Yes, Sir. Thank you, good day.

# Aileen Baviera

**Expert: Aileen Baviera**
**Interviewer: Lucio Pitlo III**
**Date: February 29, 2016**

PITLO: In what capacities did you pursue your growing interest in China Studies?

BAVIERA: After about 2 years at UP (1988–1989), I worked with the Philippine-China Development Resource Center (PDRC), a church-related non-government organization, which was setting up a China Program. I was asked to manage the research and the data bank. We had a great data bank with many acquisitions on China. Some books that you would not find in university libraries could be found in PDRC. We also had a newsletter, which came out once every 2 months called *China Currents*. I ran that for a time. We were only a small group then – never more than two or three researchers. My colleagues here include Theresa Cariño who was then teaching at De La Salle University and Elizabeth Te who would later work with the National Security Council, Department of Foreign Affairs, and who is now at the Philippine Embassy in Beijing.

Later on, I was also involved in the Philippine Association for China Studies (PACS), which was established in 1987. But plans for the creation of PACS began as early as 1986. The spirit of PACS then was inspired by Philippine democratization – that the country was in a social revolution and that we have to do better as a country and one way of doing that is by having better understanding of our neighborhood, including our big neighbor China. Teresa Cariño was also involved in PACS, along with Teresita Ang See, and sometimes PACS would hold their meetings in PDRC, so somehow I was looped into PACS. Both organizations have the same mission in mind – convinced that China is important but not many Filipinos know about it.

PITLO: How would you describe China Studies programs then in Philippine higher education? Was it taken seriously?

BAVIERA: At the UP Asian Center, yes. De La Salle University also had an active China Studies Program under Dr. Carino and Dr. Bernardita Churchill. Ateneo de Manila University then did not have a good program, but later on would develop its own as well.

146   *Aileen Baviera*

PITLO:  Would you say that there was an effort on the part of the Philippine government to make use of the academe to know more about China for strategic reasons, and how did the academe respond to this?

BAVIERA:  I had been in government at different times in the past and in different capacities. In the second time that I went back to FSI (1993–1998), I was appointed the Head of Research. In that position, I was well placed to focus on China and we did. I am proud to say that under my watch, FSI began publishing books and while we were doing more than China Studies, I made sure that China Studies was also taken care of. We published a book titled Philippine Perspectives on Greater China.

PITLO:  Back then, how would you describe the focus of interest of China Studies in the Philippines. Was it motivated more by trade or economics?

BAVIERA:  By the early 1990s, the South China Sea disputes emerged as an issue, and in 1992, PDRC came out with a book which I edited.That was my first publication on the South China Sea issue. It was essentially the proceedings of a round-table we had on the subject. There were other contributors in that book.

When I returned from PDRC to serve FSI for the second time, economic issues dominated interest in Greater China, including trade and investment linkages with Taiwan and Hong Kong. I also did research on the 1997 British handover of Hong Kong to China and I went to Hong Kong for fieldwork. Territorial issues were also heating up especially following the 1994 entry into force of UNCLOS, and the 1995 Mischief Reef incident. We had a database on Philippine interests in the South China Sea (we did not yet use the term West Philippine Sea) and I recall that we were the first to report to DFA that Scarborough Shoal was known as Bajo de Masinloc in old Philippine maps.

PITLO:  Would you describe Philippine interest on China as being more security-driven post 1995 Mischief Reef (Panganiban Reef) incident?

BAVIERA:  After Mischief Reef, yes. Before that, it was motivated more by the impact of the entry into force of the United Nations Convention on the Law of the Sea (UNCLOS) on Philippine territorial claims. And the concern was not just with China, but also with how to settle the disputes with other South China Sea claimants like Vietnam and Malaysia. Before the 1990s, these disputes were not much of an issue in Philippines-China relations, so the interest in China was broader, encompassing economics (trade and investments) and people-to-people relations.

PITLO:  Did you feel that too much focus on security prevents us from seeing our relations with China in a more comprehensive manner?

BAVIERA:  The South China Sea dispute was not the only security concern that involved China. There was also the brewing China-Japan contest over East China Sea and the Taiwan Strait Missile Crisis. These regional developments suggested that China was increasingly becoming a security player, thus the emphasis.

PITLO:  Would you say that your later interest in China would become more policy-oriented? How was China Studies received by people in government?

*Interview Transcripts* 147

BAVIERA: Yes, because of FSI. Back then, DFA, especially Undersecretary Rodolfo Severino, was very supportive of the important role being played by FSI. We were making assessments of the regional developments and coming up with strategies, for instance, on how to respond to a contingency arising from a cross-Strait incident in Taiwan – how to immediately evacuate overseas Filipino workers and the Philippine Representative Office in Taipei. On the occasion of the 1997 Hong Kong handover, we organized a conference aimed at assessing its implications and we invited Hong Kong scholars. We also helped in negotiating the bilateral principles for a Code of Conduct in 1995 (after the Mischief Reef incident). In the course of such work, another FSI colleague and I would join official Philippine delegations to meet our Chinese counterparts. We were given much leeway to work with other relevant government agencies, such as the Office of Strategic Studies of the Armed Forces of the Philippines. We would conduct meetings and consultations with concerned officials and organize simulation exercises. I would sometimes play the role of a Chinese delegate or official in such simulated negotiations and this was good training. I think these activities helped in cultivating appreciation of China Studies for people in the Philippine government. I remember one time in the past, the DFA China Desk received our paper and asked us how come we were able to prepare such work in short notice. In response, I told them that knowledge is cumulative, that we had closely been following the issues and actors over time and this made it easier for us to come up with recommended actions and proposals based on possible scenarios.

At around this time, I also met young PhD students, like Ian Storey and Zha Daojiong, who would later become established experts in maritime security studies, especially on the South China Sea. They would interview me on the subject to get Philippine or Southeast Asian views on the issue.

PITLO: If China Studies is increasingly being focused towards the security angle in government, would you say that the same treatment goes for the Philippine academe?

BAVIERA: It is hard for me to say. I think there is always interest in other dimensions, like culture and language. I may be a bit biased because I am exposed to the foreign service so my orientation has always been strongly on international relations, security and politics, more than anything else.

PITLO: Outside FSI and universities with China Studies Programs, are there other organizations that delve into China issues? Where do they get their funding?

BAVIERA: There are some. For instance, PDRC, the NGO where I also worked for, specializes on development issues of the Philippines and China, exploring parallels in the experiences of the two countries, and if there are avenues for bilateral developmental cooperation. In the course of my work with PDRC, I realized that no matter how big and powerful China may appear from the outside, it still had a lot of internal

148  *Aileen Baviera*

development issues that it needed to address. PDRC was church-related and received donations from Protestant churches. Another one is PACS which I mentioned to you before. Another is the Association for Philippines-China Understanding (APCU). APCU is actually an old organization and they contributed to establishing diplomatic relations between the two countries. Its head was Jose Joya, the painter who became a National Artist, so eventually most of APCU's activities would be largely drawn from the arts. APCU was focused on promoting people-to-people and cultural links and later on more and more Filipino-Chinese would join it.

PITLO:  The Filipino-Chinese business community was a major force in the Philippine economy. How would you assess their contribution in advancing China Studies in the Philippines then and now?

BAVIERA:  In general, the Filipino-Chinese business community was not really supportive in terms of promoting academic studies about China in the country. PACS, for instance, will get support from them only because it had interlocking memberships with Kaisa Heritage Center, an organization that preserves and promotes Chinese heritage. Even now, Filipino-Chinese enterprises rarely venture into supporting China Studies, although more involvement can be seen in recent times probably as a result of the realization that the challenges are growing. It appears that Filipino-Chinese businesses, while considering academics as worthy of being put in a pedestal, feel that academic pursuits would not help much in resolving the differences or disputes between Philippines and China because such approaches are not practical.

PITLO:  After your second stint with PDRC, you went back to the academe, this time, to specialize on teaching China Studies?

BAVIERA:  Yes, with the UP Asian Center. But I was also running a program at the Center for Integrative and Development Studies (CIDS). CIDS then had an Asia-Pacific Studies Program and a separate Maritime Affairs Program (where I was working) and we would collaborate with various research institutions. The China/Strategic Studies Program that CIDS is running now is very recent.

PITLO:  Seeing and being part of the evolution of China Studies in the Philippines, in the government, academe, and the NGO sector, what major reflections can you make of this area of study? Would you say that we Filipinos over time have matured in terms of appreciating China?

BAVIERA:  Yes, in a sense that there is greater realization that China matters to us. There is more public awareness. Universities are allocating more resources. Government is increasingly paying more attention. There is more compared to what we had before. However, these were not sufficiently institutionalized. You would imagine that with the importance of China to us, we would be having a lot of regular exchange programs with Chinese counterparts or even having interactions with China Studies programs of other universities like in Japan, or in the West or

*Interview Transcripts* 149

Southeast Asia. But we don't. Groups like PACS remained as informal as when they started.

PITLO: What are the challenges you see in terms of advancing China Studies in the Philippines? What happened to the organizations and programs promoting different aspects of China Studies that you mentioned before?

BAVIERA: There is the problem of continuity and institutionalization. PACS, for one, has some difficulty getting off because of its diverse membership representing a broad range of interests, and the fact that it is not formally linked to a university or academic institution. PDRC is no longer there. APCU is (as of this writing) a dying organization. DFA does not have formal arrangements with the academe to support policy work. There has long been a Council on Foreign Relations but nobody hears about them, much less about their impact or contribution. In the Asian Center, the creation of a research institute which will have China Studies as part of its agenda had long been proposed, but UP seems unable to support it. There is no continuity and no strategic vision.

PITLO: Even with the increased level of interest and importance we are attaching to understanding China, would you say that this is still inadequate compared to our information needs?

BAVIERA: Definitely.

PITLO: How would you compare China Studies in the Philippines with China Studies in the region? Is there a big gap? Are we being left out?

BAVIERA: Definitely Singapore does a lot in terms of its China Studies programs. Japan and Vietnam are also doing well. But compared to Malaysia, Thailand, and Indonesia, we are not worse off. We can even say that we have more active scholars in the field. This is because in our neighboring countries, emphasis is still on traditional Sinology. In Malaysia, for instance, China Studies still centers on Chinese language and culture but not on politics and security. So in comparison, we can say that our China Studies programs are somehow in the middle. However, we seem to have a dearth in terms of understanding China's economics and trade. We have very few active homegrown experts in this important area.

PITLO: There are forecasts saying that at some time in the future, China will overtake the US to become the world's largest economy and this would have tremendous geo-economic, as well as geopolitical implications. Considering the increasing role and influence of China in regional and global affairs, has there been any effort on the part of the Philippine government to raise the salience of China Studies? The level of importance we attach China does not seem to come close, for instance, to the level of importance we attach to the US despite the potential power shift that may take place in a few years. How do Filipino China scholars and specialists help raise the importance of China for Philippine foreign policy agenda?

BAVIERA: I think government is realizing the importance of China and this can be evidenced by proposals, every now and then, at Congress to set up a strategic studies institute or program, including the West

150    *Aileen Baviera*

Philippine Sea Center. However, the problem is that nothing concrete comes out from these proposals. In the academe, for instance, the National Defense College of the Philippines had substantial literature on China from a security perspective but, whether their findings and recommendations get to higher-ups or decision-makers is another matter. Technically, their studies should reach concerned officials for their appreciation, but it is uncertain whether that happens in reality.

PITLO: So you would say that we have a problem in terms of the linkage between academe, particularly those specializing in China Studies, and relevant government agencies which may find these useful in the fulfillment of their mandates and functions?

BAVIERA: I think there are existing linkages, only that they are more personal-based rather than being institutionalized.

PITLO: How many times have you visited China and how would you describe the nature of these visits?

BAVIERA: After I had exceeded 60 visits, I stopped counting and that must have been 10 years ago. Except from 1984 to 1987 when I never had a visit, I had been a frequent visitor to China. These include academic research and Track 2 conferences. While I was with PDRC, the visits were mostly development exchange programs so we would visit rural village hospitals or primary health care units in small towns. While I was doing a fellowship in Japan, for instance, my fieldwork was in China and I was able to interview resource persons from think tanks affiliated with China's People's Liberation Army. While with FSI, I was able to participate in the annual Asia-Pacific roundtables. Most of these visits occurred during the 1990s. Mostly, the Chinese host institution will arrange for my stay, although there are also visits where I have to make arrangements by myself.

PITLO: In the course of your visits to and conduct of research about China, how would you describe your interaction with Chinese scholars?

BAVIERA: There was always distance. The smaller the group, the lesser the distance. The more formal the setup, the more you would expect them to articulate the official line because people are listening. If you get them in small groups, then you would be more free to ask and you are most likely to receive answers, including those based on their personal views and assessments. If you get them one-on-one, it is easier. But trust is always important. That is why it is always important to build networks over time. The first meeting is always civil with both sides gauging one another. They have to know that you are not hostile and you have to know that they are open minded. Otherwise, there will be no point in furthering contact.

PITLO: Having interacted with Chinese scholars over the years, how would you compare them with other scholars in the region, such as from Japan and our neighboring countries in Southeast Asia? Are they less open to tackle sensitive issues like those relating to politics and security? Are they more reserved?

BAVIERA: I think some Chinese scholars in a way have blinders. They are not supposed to think too far from the official research agenda, which is largely defined, supported, and funded by the state. The end consumer

*Interview Transcripts* 151

and user of the research is the state. Those are the parameters that you have to work with. So one will get a sense that it is very directed, targeted, and strategic. When they ask you questions, you know that it is going to figure in a report that will reach the eyes of somebody. But when you have interactions with, say, Indonesian or Malaysian scholars, it is just frank talk and exchange of ideas. Hence, in a way, when interacting with Chinese scholars, you have a guarded sense.

PITLO: Seeing the close linkage between academe and government and strong state support for policy-relevant research in China, did you feel envious of your Chinese counterparts? Did you wish to see greater connection and coordination between Philippine government and academe as well?

BAVIERA: I think that is how it should be. But I do not regret that this is not the case in the Philippines. I think one can find ways. For instance, the West Philippine Sea Primer that we published (by the UP Asian Center and UP Institute for Maritime Affairs and Law of the Sea) was accomplished despite a meager budget. The same goes with the White Paper (Towards a Strategic Framework for Management of the West Philippine Sea: A White Paper by the WPS Informal Expert Group). With the right network and even with a shoestring budget, much can already be done. Besides, the lack of budget has not stopped me from studying China or sometimes giving unsolicited advice. Whether or not decision makers make use of it or whether or not they invite you to do the study, you just do what you think is important and needed, and then find a way to let them know about it. I worked with government, academe, and the NGO sector, and I do not feel constrained. The downside, of course, comes in terms of network-building. Most Filipino scholars do not get sponsored for travel abroad for research purposes or for cultivating contacts and engaging in networking. That is the big advantage Chinese scholars have over their Filipino counterparts. Chinese scholars can easily go abroad to interview foreign experts.

PITLO: As China's economic prosperity grows and as its desire to project a good image and its influence also increases, the Confucius Institute is one such component of promoting an appreciation of China abroad. Are there any other efforts to promote China Studies beyond promoting language and culture that China is undertaking and how are these efforts received?

BAVIERA: China has a lot of resources and they seem interested in knowing and understanding the world, including their neighbors in ASEAN. As such, ASEAN and Southeast Asian Studies programs have received considerable state-backing. Many of their scholars are traveling in and around the region, developing ties and linkages with ASEAN scholars. They also unveiled an ambitious plan to develop 100 think tanks that will come up with studies and recommendations for the consideration of the state.

PITLO: How can the Philippines better position China Studies to make it more relevant for government? What should be the future directions that China Studies in the country should tread?

152  *Aileen Baviera*

BAVIERA: In terms of recommendations, I think it is important to put more China content across different fields so that a broad range of stakeholders will come to appreciate the different aspects of China. For instance, increased attention can be given to the impact of China to regional and global economy, as well as business skills, techniques, and negotiation styles necessary in dealing with Chinese business people. It is not just simply the setting up of China Studies programs. Aside from that, there is also a need to strengthen China Studies program at the graduate level. Organizations promoting or advancing China Studies, like PACS, should have an institutional base for them to grow. The private sector should be mobilized to support the academe. The goal is to publish more original research and come up with research-based analyses and recommendations.

Relationships between those who produce research and its end users must be institutionalized. Right now, linkages between the bureaucracy and the academe are not institutionalized although there are instances when government agencies actively engage other stakeholders in the performance of their duties. For instance, legislators in Congress would regularly work with experts from the UP College of Law to improve or refine lawmaking. In relation to solid waste management, the Department of Environment and Natural Resources (DENR) would consult the scientific community and environmental experts in selecting the most appropriate approach to use. However, in relation to foreign affairs, the government seems to be protective and keeps information to themselves because involving outsiders may pose security risks. That is a concern. The absence of a strategic culture compounds this problem. But this may be changing. During the May 2016 elections, for instance, Philippine presidential candidates for the first time were asked about their foreign policy views particularly with respect to the West Philippine Sea disputes. As for the people, they just do not care, so foreign policy is not much of an issue. So if there is no public demand and government does not set expectations from the academe or from its advisers, academics would just pursue what they wish. As an academic, you can always do something that can be of value to government or civil society.

Another problem with the Philippine bureaucracy is that you tend to be ignored if you are an insider so sometimes you can even exert more influence as an outsider. This is quite ironic considering that they do not trust you enough to share information with an outsider, it seems that you sound more persuasive and convincing if you are an outsider.

PITLO: Thank you for sharing your rich story and experience. Aside from China Studies itself, you also shared very interesting insights in the dynamics between government and the academe in general and how this can be glimpsed in relation to China Studies.

# *Theresa Cariño*

**Expert: Theresa Cariño**
**Interviewer: Dorcas Juliette Ramos-Caraig**
**Interview Date: December 7, 2015**

## Family and educational background

RAMOS-CARAIG: Can you tell me about your family background?

CARIÑO: I'm Singaporean. I was born and raised in Singapore. My parents are ethnic Chinese who originally came from Fujian province in China. I am the fourth girl in the family, and I was given away at birth so that my parents could purchase a son. In those days, the traditional practice was that parents could betroth their female child to a male from another Chinese family. And when the child comes of age, she marries that man and bears his children. My adoptive mother thought that was a great pity.

My adoptive mother was the nurse who delivered me at birth. She adopted me with the help of another midwife. She was single at that time and she never got married. So I was raised by a single parent, a very strong, independent Hakka woman. She was originally from Sabah and was educated at the Anglican Mission School for girls so she spoke good English. That was my childhood.

RAMOS-CARAIG: Can you tell the details of your education?

CARIÑO: Originally, I was in the science stream in secondary school. I was in pre-med but I didn't like physics so much. I didn't have very good grades in the subject; I barely passed. So I decided that when I entered the university, I would switch to political science. It was a major change. I enrolled in the Social Sciences, majoring in Political Science at the University of Singapore, now known as the National University of Singapore. In the 1970s, political science was quite a new subject at the university. And I think I belonged to the second batch of students who took the discipline. Anyway, I finished my undergraduate degree in 1970.

I think the turning point for me was when I met my husband, a Filipino who was then working at the Presbyterian Church in New York. He was particularly interested in China and was very much aware of

154 *Theresa Cariño*

the Cold War. It was then the height of the Cultural Revolution, and the church where he was working had a project to study it. They wanted to understand what it was about, how it would affect China's future, and what its implications were for the rest of the world.

At that time, there were a lot of broadsheets about the Cultural Revolution, which projected it as a kind of utopia—that the Communist Party and the Red Guards were trying to achieve equality in China and that they would serve the people. Quite a few scholars in the West then thought that there was something politically significant about it. There was a lot of positive assessment. My husband was also in that category. When I met him, we were in a leadership training forum in Japan.

RAMOS-CARAIG: This is around what year?

CARIÑO: 1970. Japan was rising, and it hosted the first expo in Asia. So all of these events about China and Japan began to, sort of, affect me. I was suddenly aware of China. My husband was keen to see how a Maoist China would be able to help develop an Asia free from the colonization that had been taking place over the last 200 years. This was quite a post-colonial perspective and was also inspired by the role that Japan was playing. That was the beginning of my interest in China.

RAMOS-CARAIG: Is this one of the motivations why you decided to study Asian Studies?

CARIÑO: Yes, definitely. We spent 4 years in Switzerland (1973–1977) after my husband and I got married. I had also made a whirlwind visit to Saigon, now called Ho Chi Minh City, in 1970. At that time, Vietnam was divided into North and South, and I was able to visit some friends in South Vietnam. I saw the devastation to the south because of the war. The place was crawling with GIs or American soldiers. I met some Vietnamese Buddhist nuns who were very much opposed to the military dictatorship that was supported by the American government. This was my introduction to the Cold War and its negative consequences. I began to understand the nationalism of the Vietnamese. I also had some encounters with them. Back then, there were reports that some students were tortured and were kept in cages. That somewhat completely erased my hitherto very positive perspective of America. We all grew up thinking that America was the land of the brave and the land of the free, so I started asking why they were in Vietnam. It was a questioning of US presence in Asia.

There was also the issue regarding their bases in the Philippines. In the 1970s, the anti-American and anti-Marcos movements in the Philippines were well under way. I met UP students. All that led to the political questioning of an entire perspective and paradigm that we had been taught.

## Professional positions and experience in handling China Studies

RAMOS-CARAIG: So how did your professional career on China Studies begin?

CARIÑO: I thought that as an Asian, I should do something about the Asian situation. So, we came back to the Philippines. I could also have made

*Interview Transcripts* 155

my daughter Singaporean, but she was registered as a Filipino. There was some kind of commitment to being useful in Asia, and to try to help and participate in social issues.

So I took my masters at the Asian Center. And after I completed my degree, I was offered a job to teach at De La Salle University, where I taught at the History and Political Science Department. In the 1980s, the university was keen to start a China Studies Program. They were looking for a director, and I happened to be around. So it was perfect!

I was in La Salle for about 7 years doing the China Studies program. It was not easy to do since it didn't have scholars. We didn't have experts on China. At that time, there were a few at the University of the Philippines' Asian Center, such as Dr. Antonio Tan, who was a historian. And then we had Benito Lim and Cesar Majul. I think apart from Benito Lim, the others had not been teaching anymore. There was a dearth of Chinese scholars, so I used the China Studies program to invite scholars from overseas and we also had some scholars from other universities like University of Santo Tomas, such as Alfredo Co, who, for instance, taught Chinese Philosophy.

After 7 years, I decided to leave because I wanted to promote people-to-people relations.

RAMOS-CARAIG: So what did you do after leaving De La Salle?

CARIÑO: After De La Salle, I started an NGO, the Philippine-China Development Resource Center. When I started PDRC, one of the main foci was an exchange program with China. We would send representatives from Filipino NGOs to country each year, where they would look at how NGO work is being done there. It was also a study and exposure trip. At the same time, we received delegations from China, especially those engaged in NGO work. Our main partner was the Amity Foundation. Our exchanges covered themes like women, agriculture, health, renewable energy, and minorities.

The Philippines was quite advanced at that time, I think. The Chinese came here to undergo training in NGO capacity building.

We used to come up with a newsletter called "The Current Magazine," which talked about cross-straits relations between China and Taiwan, and China's foreign policy in Southeast Asia. We even had a booklet on the Spratlys published in 1994, which discussed joint development, which was a focus of some UP professors at that time. We were, in a sense, very much at the forefront of looking strategically at China. We wanted to know what was happening there and at the same time learn from and about the country. There's always this mutual learning process that I believe that we should undertake: to look at each other in a critical way.

We were able to send engineers to study biogas models in Chengdu, China. We were hoping to adopt and develop their own model for the Philippines. And there were also nurses and doctors who went to study acupuncture. They came back and set up clinics in the remote areas in the Philippines such as the Cordilleras and Mindanao, where they served the poor. Both projects were our concrete contributions.

156    *Theresa Cariño*

Back then, there was a whole debate about development. The question was "Where is China going?" This was in the 1980s and 1990s, when most observers felt that the Chinese were shifting towards capitalism. Did that mean that the socialist paradigm was lost? Up until 1989, almost everyone threw up their hands and said "yes."

RAMOS-CARAIG: You've written a number of books and papers, many of which were focused on the overseas Chinese. What makes it your interest?

CARIÑO:  I came from Singapore where the Chinese are a majority, so their identity was never very obvious. I never thought about it. But when I came to the Philippines, I suddenly realized that being a Chinese in the Philippines made a difference because we're a minority here. I became aware of some of the prejudices and biases against the Chinese. Some colleagues would make negative, absent-minded comments like, "Oh yeah the Chinese you know blah blah…" And then they would look at me and say, somewhat apologetically, "Oh but you're one of us so it's okay."

Anyway, it really makes a difference once you're part of the minority because you are more conscious of the questions: Who are you? Who am I?

I became interested in answering these questions and became involved with Tessy Ang-See, who is with KAISA, an organization which aims to integrate the Chinese in the Philippines. I started writing about them. But because materials from mainland China were scarce, it was difficult for me to write about China relying on primary sources. But I could interview the Chinese here, so I decided to look at the role of the Federation of Filipino-Chinese Chambers of Commerce. I did so not so much because it was a business community as because it was an umbrella organization that is supposed to represent the interests of the Chinese in the Philippines.

RAMOS-CARAIG: I also observed that your recent publications are about about religion.

CARIÑO:  It is because of my work with the Amity Foundation. In 1996, we moved to Hong Kong because of my husband's job. He worked in a church and was assigned to the Christian Conference of Asia, a regional body of protestant churches. The Amity Foundation, which was our partner before, has an office in Hong Kong. They wanted an editor for their newsletter, and I did it part-time. I loved the job because it allowed me to visit China four times a year to collect materials on Amity's development projects. In the 1990s, China was still very, very poor and Amity was doing a lot of rural development initiatives. It meant that I could go to really poor areas that were inaccessible to tourists. Because of that job, I became extremely interested in China's development.

I also began to take an interest in the situation of the churches. During the Cultural Revolution, the churches were all closed, and religion

*Interview Transcripts* 157

was suppressed. In the 1980s, when China opened up, there was an explosive flourishing of religion, especially Christianity, a process that continues to this day. I was a witness to the explosion of religion and Christianity. Amity has a religious connection. It was initiated by the last Anglican bishop of China, Bishop K. H Ting, in 1985.

## Reflections on conducting research on China Studies

RAMOS-CARAIG: What are your reflections on the methodology used on China or Chinese studies?

CARIÑO: Initially, until the late 1970s, those of us trying to study contemporary Chinese economics and politics had to rely entirely on secondary sources, which were usually written in English by Western scholars. This imposed tremendous limitations on China Studies in the Philippine context. The lack of fluency in Chinese of some of these early scholars (including myself), as well as the shortage of books and materials on China in university libraries, added to the difficulties. Travel to China was illegal during the Cold War, which strongly influenced perspectives on China and the Chinese. Much of the literature available then was highly critical of China and explicitly or implicitly anti-Communist. There were extreme views of China from both the left and the right among Wester scholars and in the Philippines.

In the past, the dominant approach or framework of analysis was to look at China in terms of authoritarianism and socialism. I must say that this Cold War legacy has lingered and remains powerful. There was a lack of appreciation for the cultural diversity and complexity of Chinese society and politics. Unless one has visited or lived in China, the enormity of the country and its population are not taken into consideration often.

After 1978, China's opening and reforms under Deng Xiaoping provided more opportunities for researchers and scholars to travel to the country. When I became the Director of the China Studies Program at De La Salle University in 1983, I began to organize workshops, seminars and conferences, in which scholars from mainland Chinese universities such as Zhongshan, Xiamen and Beijing, as well as the Chinese Academy of Social Sciences, were invited to participate. This provided a much welcome opportunity for scholars from China and Southeast Asia to enter into dialogue and have exchanges.

These encounters led to ties with the History Department of Peking University, the Institute of Southeast Asian Studies at Xiamen University, the History Departments at Zhongshan and Jinan universities in Guangzhou, and China scholars based in the National University of Singapore and Taiwan., including Leo Suryadinata and Wang Gungwu. Scholars from Hong Kong (like Prof. Wong Siulun, Director of the Asian Study Center of HKU and Prof. Tan Chee Beng at the Chinese

158 *Theresa Cariño*

University of Hong Kong) and Taiwan (such as Michael Hsiao of the Academia Sinica) were also invited to join these meetings and to lecture to students. One of our very first speakers from China was the late Prof. Zhao Fusan, the Vice-President of the Chinese Academy of Social Sciences (CASS). He was then the Director of the Institute of World Religions at CASS. He delivered a lecture series on Christianity in China in 1983.

The China Studies Program at DLSU was multidisciplinary and could have been more focused on Culture and Philosophy (closer to Sinology), but given my own background in Political Science, the program (from 1983 to 1991) concentrated on the socioeconomic and political transformation that was taking place in contemporary China and its relations with the rest of Asia.

The Program at DLSU did not offer an undergraduate course in China Studies, as you do now at Ateneo. Its aim was to generate interest in China among students and to encourage research and publications on China and the ethnic Chinese in the Philippines. Through international conferences and workshops, the DLSU program generated publications on a variety of topics with inputs by scholars from China and ASEAN countries, including the Philippines. Titles of books published by the program included China-ASEAN relations, China and Southeast Asia: Politics and Economics, Transnationals and Special Economic Zones: The Experience of China and Selected Countries, Literature on the Chinese in the Philippines, and Maritime Issues in the South China Sea.

The "Chinese in the Philippines" was very much an open field for research and investigation. In the 1980s, the literature on the Chinese in the Philippines was still quite limited compared to that of other ASEAN countries. Many of the published studies until the 1980s had mainly been historical and had relied heavily on Spanish, American colonial and traditional Chinese sources. During the 1980s and 1990s, more attention was paid to socioeconomic developments in China and the role of the ethnic Chinese in Asia. Stereotypes about the Chinese in Southeast Asia continued to prevail. Scholars in China and in Southeast Asia attempted to move away from the influence of the Cold War by the 1990s, but this was not always easy.

The establishment of diplomatic ties between China and the Philippines in June 1975 brought dramatic changes to intracommunity politics, which involved the rivalry between the pro-Beijing and pro-Taipei factions. My research into this matter eventually metamorphosed into a doctoral dissertation that Times Publishing published as "Chinese Big Business in the Philippines: Political Leadership and Change." (1998)

Given the small number of university faculty that specialized in China studies in the Philippines, and a shared passion for China studies, those of us from different universities (Ateneo, DLSU, University of the Philippines, University of Santo Tomas, and the University of Asia and the

*Interview Transcripts* 159

Pacific) decided to band together and form the Philippines Association for Chinese Studies (PACS). We also incorporated the help of KAISA headed by Teresita Ang See, and she became a staunch member and one of the presidents of PACS. Started in 1987, PACS has since grown in membership and reputation. Besides being a network, it has been a strong support group for China scholars and China Studies in the Philippines, nurturing and sustaining interest therein by sharing resources and scholars. I believe it has helped stimulate interest in China Studies among the younger generations. In recent years, it has been gratifying to see a rise in the number of younger scholars who specialize in the field. Many of them have spent time in China and received training and exposure in Chinese universities. They will be an asset to the Philippines because of the need to understand the implications of China's rise for the rest of the world. How the Philippines will navigate between the US and China in its international relations will be vital to the peace and security of this region. Having a pool of well-trained China scholars will surely benefit the policy-making process.

## Self-perceived contribution to views and theories on China or Chinese studies

RAMOS-CARAIG: What do you think is your prime contribution to views and theories on China or Chinese studies? What are the issues or problems you have encountered in your past researches on China or Chinese studies?

CARIÑO: In general, I still see a very wide gap in culture and perspectives between the Philippines and China. My interest has always been to try and close this gap by encouraging more exchanges among scholars and NGOs. I still believe that S-S exchanges are vital. While China's trade and economic exchanges with ASEAN countries have grown exponentially in the last 30 years, the mutual understanding, respect, and trust that is essential for lasting peace and security in the region is still sadly lacking. Some of the negative effects of the colonial era and the Cold War continue to haunt us, and the current competition for global and regional leadership between the US and China has been contributing to increasing tensions and instability in Asia.

Naturally, the factors that keep China and the Philippines apart have a long history. Language and culture continue to be barriers, and I hope that with the new generation of China scholars, these will not pose insurmountable obstacles towards better mutual understanding. I believe that scholars have a great responsibility to help keep the peace in the region. I see the same difficulties among Chinese scholars of Southeast Asia. So much of the relationship between China and the Philippines has been politicized and treated under the overarching framework of China-U.S. relations. And it has thus been difficult to reshape a new,

160　*Theresa Cariño*

creative and mutually productive relationship. How the problems are defined, described, and articulated often have a profound impact on how they are addressed and resolved. Conflict models and zero-sum games in our analyses do not help at all. Samuel Huntington's notion of civilizational clash seems to have rigidly framed the tensions between the U.S. and China. It should be pointed out that in fact, a growing number of political scientists are attempting to re-examine the idea or ideology of "sovereignty" and the notion of the "nation state," which has wreaked havoc on the histories of both countries. Today's Asian nation states were carved out of the colonial landscape by colonial rulers with little knowledge or sensitivity to local and indigenous expressions of faith, community, and state. In our history, decolonization and the building of new nation states have spawned resentment and violence, and included the crushing or marginalization of minority groups. It is time to rethink our notions of sovereignty and nation-states.

## Evaluation of future prospects of China Studies in the Philippines

RAMOS-CARAIG: What is your evaluation of pegadogy on China in the Philippines and its future prospects?

CARIÑO: My main hope is that Filipino scholars will develop a more multi-sourced, independent perspective on China and be less reliant on Western sources of scholarship (some of which is really good and critical). In this respect, the interaction with other ASEAN scholars is just as important as frequent interaction with Chinese academics. The more dialogue and exchange there is, the better off we will be. This had been difficult in the past, but I see more prospects for intensifying direct interaction and exchange as Asian countries become more affluent. We know more about Europe and the U.S. than we do about Indonesia, China, Brunei or Cambodia, all of whom are our closest neighbors. This also reflects our education and scholarship. The lack of literacy about Asia that surrounds us is inexcusable in this day and age.

The same ignorance and prejudice applies to Chinese scholars of ASEAN. Their areas of concern with regard to the Philippines have concentrated mainly on the strategic and economic. Very little has been done in the area of history and anthropology. There is a lack of knowledge and understanding of the sociocultural elements in other Asian countries. All these have to be corrected. Universities have to promote and mainstream Asian studies.

# Richard Chu

**Expert: Richard Chu**
**Interviewer: Carmelea Ang See**
**Date of interview: January 14, 2016**

ANG SEE: Dr. Chu, we will start with details of your family.

CHU: My family migrated from Jinjiang County, Fujian, China. My grandfather, Go Taco, came in using a *tua di mia* (大字名),[1] Chu Ongco. By using somebody else's papers he could stay legally in the Philippines. He helped in my great grandfather's lumber business and eventually brought over my grandmother, uncles and aunts in the 1930s.

My father was born in 1931, and brought over at seven. Family members would go back and forth until 1949.

My father was of one eight children who grew up in Binondo. He took Engineering at Mapua Institute of Technology.

My mother's parents came from a different village in Jinjiang, and migrated to Camiling, Tarlac, where my mother was born in 1939. She was sent to Manila for schooling and eventually studied at Far Eastern University to be a teacher.

CHU: When my parents got married, they lived with my paternal relatives in a compound on Soler Street, Binondo, where they also ran my grandfather's lumber business, Gotaco. With different families in the same compound, it was quite cramped.

A year after I was born, 1966, my parents moved out and worked for another business. In 1969, we moved to a bigger house in Pasay City and my father decided to start his own plywood business.

My four older sisters spent their younger years in Chinatown making them proficient in Hokkien. Compared to them, my two younger sisters and I had to consciously learn the language.

ANG SEE: Talk to us briefly about your Xavier experience, and then, Ateneo.

CHU: Xavier School was founded by foreign Jesuits on the China missions. After being expelled in 1949, they moved to the Philippines and opened in 1956 a school for children of Chinese immigrants. Many of these priests, from North America and some from Spain, were fluent in Mandarin.

162   *Richard Chu*

Xavier emphasized not only academic achievement, but also sports, music, etc. We had 2 hours of daily Chinese language instruction. Most of our teachers came from or trained in Taiwan.

I got a scholarship to Ateneo because all valedictorians of Jesuit high schools in the Philippines automatically get one.

I wanted to be in a nonbusiness course, but my mother wanted otherwise. I took Legal Management as a compromise; I could at least become a corporate lawyer. After only my first class in law, I switched to Interdisciplinary Studies, and focused on philosophy and education.

CHU:  After college, I became a Jesuit volunteer[2] in Cebu, where I taught the Old Testament and morality in high school, and was guidance counselor for first year high school students.

While there, Fathers [Ismael] Zuloaga and [Jose] Calle conducted a China mission workshop. They had been active in trying to spread Catholicism in China, once it started to open to the outside world. The workshop gave an overview of the history and state of China's Catholic Church, and what the challenges were for Catholics in China. It fired me up with a missionary zeal to participate in the propagation of Catholicism in China.

After my JVP year, I applied for the Xiamen University and Ateneo de Manila exchange program. In 1987, I went to Xiamen University (廈大) on scholarship. I brushed up on Mandarin, learned more about Fujian where my ancestors came from, visited my parents' ancestral homes in Jinjiang.

CHU:  When I came back and was not accepted into priesthood, I worked at the Chinese Studies Program as assistant to the director, Dr. Manuel Dy. I also taught basic and intermediate Chinese. Upon Dy's return from sabbatical, I became assistant director of the program.

Other faculty advised that I should not hold an administrative position while still young, and to pursue graduate studies. I thus went to Standford University for 2 years taking graduate courses in history and anthropology.

CHU:  My adviser was Harold Khan, a Qing Dynasty expert. I took other classes with Al Dean, ancient China historian, Lyman Van Slyke, modern China historian, and Hill Gates, a Chinese anthropologist.

When I finished my master's degree, I had to decide on a specific area for my Ph.D program. I was more interested in anthropology and ethnography, but my advisers said that it was easier to find a job as a historian.

I felt as an area of study, being a historian was more flexible in terms of using theoretical frameworks and methods. Anthropologists at that time were expected to study a particular society or community of people who were NOT of their own background. Since I already wanted to become an expert on the history of the Chinese in the Philippines, being an anthropologist would not allow me to do that.

Back then, anthropology heavily focused on subscribing to a particular theoretical framework. Instead, I wanted to decide on my theoretical framework, even combine frameworks, when conducting research.

My venture into the field of history was borne out of pragmatic reasons, and partly my own interests. Edgar Wickberg suggested the University of Southern California because he thought John Wills would be a good adviser. Wills is an expert on maritime Chinese history, and has done studies on the Dutch in Indonesia and Dutch relations with Chinese traders. I applied, got in; the rest is history.

ANG SEE: What made you decide to focus on mestizos?

CHU: During my coursework at USC, Charlotte Furth, an expert on modern China, introduced me to *Making Ethnic Choices* by Karen [Isaksen] Leonard, a historian and anthropologist. Leonard studied the Punjabi Mexican families in Imperial Valley, California. These families were formed during the early part of the 20th century, when Indian men from the Punjabi region in India came to work in the fields of California. They married Mexican women who were also laborers or farmers. The ethnographic study of these bicultural families fascinated me, because the fathers were Sikh, and mothers were Catholics with children growing up in this bicultural environment.

When I embarked on my research on the Chinese in the Philippines, I was interested in the intersection of nationalism and ethnicity—how nationalism leads to the construction or invention of national identities that are oftentimes rarified, homogeneous, and static. Having read works on nationalism and identity, I wanted to study how the ethnic identity of the Chinese in the Philippines, and Chinese mestizos, had been constructed and reconstructed over time.

I had experienced how ethnic categories applied to me affected my own self identity. For example, being called *"Intsik"* had some derogatory undertones when I was growing up.

Having "dual" or "conflicting" identities led me to study how we came up with this term for the Chinese, and how the Chinese had [equivalent] terms for Filipinos like *huana* and *chut si ah*—and why there is ethnic tension or racial division. I wanted to go into the historical roots of that phenomenon.

For me, the turn of the 20th century was crucial, because that's when many Chinese today trace their history of migration to the Philippines.

This was also the period when epithets—*Intsik, huana, chut si ah*—had become more popular, and acquired the connotations they have today.

Using Leonard's approach, I studied the lives of the Chinese and their mestizo children, and approached the study from a bottom-up perspective. Not only was I interested in the origins of these terms, I was also interested in how the Chinese and their children themselves understood these terms and used them.

164   *Richard Chu*

I focused on Chinese merchant families in Binondo during the end of the 19th century and the beginning of the 20th century. Many Chinese merchants intermarried with local women and produced mestizo offspring. Armed with those questions about ethnic identity, and using Leonard's model, I examined the lives of the Chinese and Chinese mestizos as a way to critique the use of nation-based ethnic identifications to exclude others.

The epithets we use against each other were all influenced by both Philippine and Chinese nationalisms. In their effort to create the "imagined community" that Benedict Anderson talks about, nation-states resort to exclusionary and inclusionary policies and help build stereotypes around certain groups of people. The "history" or "genealogy" of such ethnic constructions in the Philippines, as they pertain especially to Chinese and Chinese mestizos, is generally what I am interested in.

ANG SEE:  How has the journey treated you so far? Satisfied? Dissatisfied?

CHU:  The journey has been constantly evolving. At the beginning, it was very exciting. I never saw myself buried in old archival documents in dusty or dark-lit rooms. I realized later that I didn't have to isolate myself in order to do archival work. I trained myself to be proficient reading both Chinese and Spanish.

There were challenges while doing research on the Chinese in the Philippines, especially for the Spanish colonial period. It was an exciting journey; when trying to find answers in the archives, I would unexpectedly discover information about a particular person that would lead me to other information. It's like a mystery. I have always described doing archival work like detective work, because you have a hypothesis, and questions, but then you don't know exactly what the answers are, and you set out to investigate.

The research and writing for my dissertation took about 5 years. It was an exciting project that involved a lot of work. I derived a lot of pleasure reconstructing the histories of certain individuals and their families, which involved sometimes finding out juicy, interesting facts about their lives.

The pleasure came from seeing that my data was gradually *proving* my hypothesis: that the ethnic identities of Chinese and Chinese mestizos were more complex than what we had been reading about. Edgar Wickberg's analysis of Chinese and Chinese mestizo identities came from a macro-historical perspective; I wanted to demonstrate that, from a micro-historical point of view, things don't usually conform to norms or to societal ways of doing things. How people lived out and understood their identities did not usually conform to what the government or what other dominant groups would have liked to propagate.

My dissertation focused on the Chinese in the Philippines, even though I was trained as a Chinese historian. When I was preparing for my comprehensive exams, most of my fields covered China, except for the Chinese in Southeast Asia. Slowly, because of my research, I was

*Interview Transcripts* 165

veering towards more expertise on the Chinese *in* the Philippines, or Chinese diaspora.

The field of Chinese diasporic studies, which was previously called overseas Chinese or Chinese overseas studies, has been, and continues to be, a marginal part of China studies. China studies were formed out of the Cold war era, and all other area studies—Philippines, Russian, Latin American—were all created for the United States government to understand the "enemy's culture" better. People trained in their area had to be proficient in the language of the people they were studying, and to focus on the country's people, and not on the people in the diaspora.

When I started to focus on my research on the Chinese in the Philippines, I gradually veered away from becoming a China scholar. This can be seen in the conferences that I attended over the years. China studies scholars attend the Association for Asian Studies conferences. But starting in 1992, when Teresita Ang See, Wang Ling-chi and Wang Gungwu established the International Society for the Study of Chinese Overseas (ISSCO) I began to attend those instead. There was more overlap in my research interests with people in ISSCO. That is a reflection of how my identification as a scholar had begun to veer toward Chinese diasporic studies.

It also coincided with my first job in the United States. I applied to 30 jobs at the end of my Ph.D program. Twenty-nine were China-related or strictly East Asian studies positions. The UMass[3] position, which i took, was on the US Empire in the Pacific, with a sub-specialization on Asian American studies.

With the Philippines as the biggest colony of the US at the time, I started teaching this course on US Empire from the lens of Philippine colonial history.

My journey has become very interesting. It took me into directions that I did not plot. I find myself identified with three areas: Philippine studies, Asian American studies, Chinese diasporic studies. Last year, I was invited to a conference in Madrid with other scholars, especially Spaniards, interested in Spanish colonial Philippines. At Asian American studies conferences, I present my research about the "Chinaman question" in the Philippines and how it relates to the "Chinaman question" in the US. Finally, I attend conferences on the Chinese diaspora, like the ISSCO, as well as Philippine studies conferences.

My next book will make me more identified with Asian American studies as I compare the experiences of the Chinese in the Philippines with those in the US during the American colonial period. In that sense, my work is relevant to readers in the US.

Part of the satisfaction of being a scholar is to see your work appreciated by people you are directly in contact with day to day. My first book on the Chinese in the Philippines during the Spanish colonial era and then early American colonial era is appreciated by people in the Philippines, Spain, or those in China diaspora studies. But it has little direct relevance to Americans.

166    *Richard Chu*

My journey is also dictated by the question of relevance and application. Since I see myself more as a transnational person now, living part-time in the United States and the Philippines, I want to be relevant to both societies. The journey of my scholarship is pushing me to create research that will be applicable and relevant to both countries.

The journey has been interesting. It's not a dead end. It's always trying to figure out where I am in my life. Professionally, it is how and where the field leads me, including which scholars I get to interact with, and whose work energizes me. I think this is so important to me.

ANG SEE: Regarding this new juncture in your research on Chinese in the Philippines, Chinese in America, what's the prospect of followers? Are you grooming anyone?

CHU: The place where I teach has a five-college consortium: UMass, a state university, and four liberal arts colleges—Amherst, Smith, Mount Holyoke, and Hampshire. The five-college faculty position is when a person is hosted within one institution, but shared by the other four. My base is UMass, where I get my tenure, but the other four pay half my salary. Of the two classes I teach every semester, one is in UMass, and another at one of the four.

I have also sat on Ph.D committees of students from other universities. Philip Guingona from State University of New York is researching on Filipinos in Shanghai and the Chinese in the Philippines during the American colonial period. I was an adviser of his dissertation. Ethan Hawkley from Northeastern University wrote a dissertation on the Chinese in the Philippines in the 16th and 17th centuries. There are students elsewhere asking me for advice for their research, or to be in their Ph.D dissertation committee.

That's sort of my frustration because I do want more people to study the history of the Chinese in the Philippines, yet in my own university I do not have graduate students studying under me. That's kind of the irony there, that there are more people abroad doing research on the Chinese in the Philippines.

ANG SEE: You have exactly the same sentiments as Go Bon Juan. There is rarely new blood in the pool of those interested in this field.

CHU: Clark Alejandrino's first monograph was on the Chinese Exclusion Act of 1902. Now he is more of a China scholar. I think it would still be an asset to the Philippines if he decided to come back, but then his research is not focused on Chinese in the Philippines anymore. People like Ethan Hawkley, Josiah Que, Philip Guingona are people who work in Spain or elsewhere.

ANG SEE: You have seen the swirling changes in the community, especially among young Tsinoys. How do these changes feed into your study of the Chinese diaspora? And if you're going to continue on diasporic studies, will research extend to the *Xinqiao*, the new arrivals?

CHU: From what I see, Tsinoys are very involved in sociopolitical and civic activities. I laud them for that, but very few want to do in-depth research about their history or contemporary issues. This might be because they

*Interview Transcripts* 167

don't feel the need for it; they feel that we are very integrated in Philippine society, so there is no need to understand us or our history more. However, I think that there is an interest to learn about their history and culture, as can be seen in the Binondo Heritage [FaceBook] Group numbering around 2,500 members, except that to engage in research themselves is not their cup of tea.

I sense that their way of thinking about their ethnic identifications is still influenced by nation-based narratives, where there's a thirst for either-or propositions—an attempt to create clear markers of identification. Even though "Tsinoy" serves as an alternative to *Intsik* and also as a challenge to the monolithic, either-or *Intsik* vs. Filipino/*huana* binary, because to be Tsinoy is to be both "Chinese" and "Filipino."

Even though "Tsinoy" tries to blur those lines, the movement is still fueled by questions of nationalism, which is not bad at all. In fact, I think that can go hand in hand with a more critical understanding of how ethnic categories are constructed. The only danger lies in constructing a Tsinoy identity that is "palatable" to the majority—where Tsinoy history or identity is "positive," so that any kind of incursion of another group that may smear that kind of "positive" identity is rejected.

It doesn't mean that we should stop building consensus, building harmony. We have to be careful that the Tsinoy and the Pinoy communities not pit the Tsinoy against the *Xinqiao*. To do so may lead to an exclusion of other kinds of people. We might just repeat everything that we are fighting against—this sort of discrimination against others.

ANG SEE: I'm also asking because the children of the Xinqiao of the 1990s have already graduated from college, in their mid-twenties, thinking of marriage. Many of them have integrated and this is only second-generation.

CHU: It's interesting from a historical point of view. I'd like to see whether history repeats itself.

When that changes, what happens? For instance, in the 1850s, when immigration policies of both Spain and China were more relaxed, a new infusion of Chinese came here. How did the old-timers, or Chinese mestizos, view these newcomers? After World War II, a similar phenomenon occurred, when China became Communist and Chinese immigration to the Philippines trickled down.[4]

CHU: I grew up in a generation where there were no *Xinqiao*. It would be interesting to study how the *Xinqiao* affect us and how we [the "locals"] view them. We're like the Chinese mestizos of the 1860s and 1870s, looking at newcomers. These newcomers now have their own children who are more integrated than their parents. How do older generation Tsinoys look at this new generation?

ANG SEE: The most difficult time was in the 1960s, where someone could and would extort money from you. That level of discrimination is not present. Their children are "embedded" in school with Tsinoys. They navigate both Philippine mainstream, Tsinoy communities, their parents' communities.

168  *Richard Chu*

CHU: That's interesting because, even there, there is a generation gap between those who are doing [research on] the Chinese overseas and the Chinese diaspora. Scholars of Chinese overseas studies like Wang, Ang See, Tan Chee-Beng, Suryadinata, are of the earlier generation.

They approach the study of the Chinese with different theoretical perspectives, mostly concerned with issues of national integration, which younger scholars aren't. Some prefer to use the term "Chinese diaspora" in order to focus on the flows of capital, information, technology, and bodies—processes that are part of what affect, influence, or shape of what it means to be "Chinese" today, while at the same de-centering "China" as the foundation of what constitutes "Chineseness."

Despite the difference between the older and younger generation of scholars, the field is growing. Years back, Brill [Publishing] started a series on the Chinese overseas. My book [*Chinese and Chinese mestizos in Manila, Family, Identity, and Culture, 1860s–1930s*] was the first, followed by several others. The National University of Singapore, and Brill, has established the *Journal of the Chinese Overseas*.

The direction of where the field is going depends on whether there is a changing of the guard. The new generation of Chinese scholars in China or Taiwan interested in studying the Chinese overseas have different perspectives. I see them beginning to interact with more established scholars and younger scholars in other parts of the world.

Going back to the Chinese in the Philippines field, I certainly hope that the younger generation Chinese Filipinos, as well as the universities, will continue to encourage people to do more scholarship.

## Notes

1 The *Tua Di Mia* 大字名 was a 30×40 cm piece of paper entitled Landing Certificate of Residence. This certificate indicated the name of the migrant, his origins in China, and his relatives (usually the father) in Manila. More often than not, the certificate also showed the Chinese characters of the migrant's name. The Chinese Exclusion Act of 1902 only allowed Chinese migrants who were merchants or sons of merchants to enter the Philippines. As such, any Chinese who desired to come into the Philippines, but had no relatives living there, found neighbors or friends or uncles to stand in as a father on paper. Hence, the legal English name is often not the migrant's real family name. Dr. Chu's ancestors are from the Go clan.

2 JVP, or Jesuit Volunteers of the Philippines, the volunteer program of Ateneo de Manila University. Students volunteer for 1–2 years after graduation and are sent to Jesuit communities around the country to serve.

3 University of Massachusetts, Amherst

4 Note: Immigration patterns to the Philippines could be described as "stop and go." Before China closed its doors in 1949, there was a steady influx of migrants during the transition from Spanish to American colonization (1850s–1930s). The next so-called wave of migration happened from the 1950s to the 1960s. The latest wave of migration took place over a 10–15 year period, beginning in the mid 1990s.

# Jaime FlorCruz

**Expert: Jaime FlorCruz**
**Interviewer: Robin Michael Garcia**
**Date of interview: October 8, 2015**

GARCIA: How did you come to decide to stay in China? Why decide to go there in the first place? When did you go?

FLORCRUZ: The first time I really got interested in China was in college. I went to a forum in the University of the Philippines (UP) in Diliman featuring Orly Mercado and Charito Planas, who had travelled to China. That must have been 1970 or 1971. They travelled there and talked about their experiences so that kind of further ignited my interest. But it was not until 1971, specifically in August, when I went with Chito, Eric and a group of fifteen student leaders for a 3-week tour in China. But at that time, going to China was technically illegal. Philippine passports were typically stamped with a note saying *"Not valid in Communist controlled areas/regions of the Soviet Union, Romania, Korea, China."* However, many groups had already gone and came back, and they talked about it publicly. So we thought, even though it was still technically illegal, it was becoming more possible to go.

When we received an invitation from the China Friendship Association, the letter invited us to form a fifteen-member Philippine youth delegation for a 3-week tour, all expenses paid, hosted by the China Friendship Association. The group was mostly a section of student leaders from UP and the Polytechnic University of the Philippines (PUP). The group was also comprised of a professional young journalist, some women activists, a Muslim, and a young priest. So we went to Hong Kong. A group of us went there on the 20th, and then the next day, we met up with the China Travel Service, who gave us our tickets. We took a train from Hong Kong to Shenzhen.. We went to Guangzhou next. From Guangzhou, we flew to Beijing to start our 3-week tour. That's how I ended up in China, initially, for just 3 weeks.

170  *Jaime FlorCruz*

GARCIA:  Did the China Friendship Association decide who were going? Are they a genuine civil society organization?

FLORCRUZ:  It was the Chinese government itself who invited us and the China Friendship Association was a quasi-government agency based in Beijing. Because China at that time did not have diplomatic relationships with many countries, they used an association like that to reach out and bring in foreign visitors. As you would expect, most of the visitors they invited were activists or leftists who, they think, are maybe interested in China.

GARCIA:  How did you come to be sympathetic to the leftist movement?

FLORCRUZ:  There was the influence of Mao Zedong's ideas among student groups like ours; we were looking for alternative models in terms of how we could change the country. We were influenced by Mao's ideas on land reform; we opposed the Vietnam War and called for freedom of expression and assembly. For that, some people branded us Maoists. But apparently, I hardly understood what Mao said. Before I went to Peking, I was attending PUP, where I was editor in chief of our college paper. And I was concurrently the President of the League of Editors for a Democratic Society, which was one of the national college editors associations. I was also active in a nationalist theatre group.

GARCIA:  After the 3-week tour in China, did you immediately go back to the Philippines?

FLORCRUZ:  No. What happened was, five of us became accidental tourists. There was a bombing incident in the Philippines – the Plaza Miranda bombing on August 21. That was the day when we arrived in China. It was exactly that day. We didn't know of course what was going on in Manila. Three days later, our Chinese hosts called a meeting and said, "something happened in your country, we heard. We have no details and we do not know what it means to you" because they knew we were against the government. So it turned out there had been a bombing incident that night. Marcos, the president, suspended the *writ of habeas corpus*, an act that allowed him to arrest anybody without court warrants and to detain them indefinitely. We didn't know what it meant for us. In the meantime, our parents, our relatives, and our friends were meeting also to discuss what happened and what it meant. They talked with lawyers. And the advice that later came to us was to stay put until further advice. Then what happened was that of the 15 in China, five of us turned out to be in a blacklist in Manila. The ten who were not blacklisted decided to go home. Five of us – Chito, Eric, I and two others – stayed.

When it turned out that the five of us – Chito Sta. Romana, Eric Baculinao, Rey Tiquia, and Grace Punongbayan, also of UP, and I – couldn't go home yet, we asked our Chinese hosts if we could stay. Then

*Interview Transcripts* 171

they said, "Yes, you may stay if you have to and you may leave anytime you wish. We promise to help with the logistics."

We asked to earn our keep. The Chinese had asked us to wait patiently in our hotel until we could go home. But we wanted to do something. So we asked repeatedly to earn our keep and to work. Finally, they gave us permission to do so. The trend at that time was to go the farms. So we worked on a farm in Hunan province for about 7 months.

GARCIA: How was the routine there? Did you earn a living?

FLORCRUZ: We woke up early at five in the morning. But we were not required to work the whole day. The initial deal was to work in the mornings through noon or until early in the afternoon. After working, we studied to learn Chinese – elementary Chinese – from an interpreter who went with us. He doubled as our Mandarin teacher. And we did that for, like, 3 months, until we were conversant in Chinese. After the interpreter went back to Beijing, we began working almost the whole day. It was very difficult because we had not done any farming in our lives. It was very romantic in the beginning. We were not really paid; we got a monthly stipend, 40 yuans, which was a lot of money at that time. We also had free board and lodging at the farm.

GARCIA: What was studying at a Chinese university like at that time? What was it like to attend Peking University?

FLORCRUZ: It was a very interesting and exciting period to be in *Beida* (Peking University), and to know those people who were very passionate about studying because for them it was the last chance to change their futures and recoup their careers. But also it was a time of reflection – a time when students and teachers were debating about what happened in the Cultural Revolution; where China should go; and what it meant to reform China. It was just the beginning of that period. There was this intellectual ferment and they called it, "the liberation of the mind" – wherein people were really starting to break away from the dogmas of the recent eras, and to think out of the box and just debate about where we should go from here.

The classroom lectures were interesting, but many of them were constrained by lingering ideological and political lines.

But outside the classrooms, in the dormitory, there was a lot of free flow of information and robust debates, which for me was the best part of my time there

GARCIA: Were there any professors or ideas that were remarkable to you during those times?

FLORCRUZ: One professor I remember among the younger ones was Wang Xiaoqiu, who taught modern contemporary Chinese history. He was good at explaining historical issues, including debatable, controversial

172 *Jaime FlorCruz*

periods, in a very acceptable and compelling way. Of course, in my experience, after 4 years of studying history at Peking University, I seemed to have learned more than one version of the stories. China at that time was still going through a transition. Some historical interpretations were still contested and changing, and we were discussing or discovering new perspectives and if not, new facts about what actually happened in recent years.

GARCIA: Were you able to share all these experiences in China, for instance, with your family, friends, or a bigger audience in Manila? How were you able to do it? Did you come home?

FLORCRUZ: Only after I returned home could I engage a bigger audience, for example, through forums that I have been invited to speak at. I have given lectures, speeches, or presentations at the Ateneo de Manila University and at the University of the Philippines. KAISA invited me as well, as did the Federation of the Filipino-Chinese. I have also been frequently consulted on various topics by various organizations. Moreover, I have spoken in forums organized in Philippine universities, including the Polytechnic University of the Philippines, Ateneo de Manila

University, and University of the Philippines, as well as in forums organized by the FilipinoChinese business communityI never miss an appropriate chance to say that I am a Filipino who happened to be working in an American company in China. They like the fact that I am a third country observer. In other words, for them, I am neither a Chinese nor an American. Even though I work for an American media outfit, I think they appreciate the fact that not being an American, I look at them from a unique and different perspective. I compare China now and China 30 years earlier because I have seen what China was like 30–40 years ago. I can appreciate the changes – big and small – whenever I compare China now and China then. I will say that the situation is a glass half-full, not half-empty, because I have seen it empty. I think Chinese appreciate it whenever I say that.

I have always encouraged Filipinos to go and visit China even though for a short time because I experienced myself what a big difference it made to see it, to feel it, to smell it, and to personalize China, instead of just second-guessing it from the outside and from a long distance. I think that is one source of misunderstanding. It is so easy to fall into the trap of racism. You know, stereotype the other side when you did not have a first-hand experience of the place. Whenever I share my personal experiences, I think it helps Filipinos, for me anyway, get some sense of the texture of the country – the nature, the friends that I have met. In the end, I always tell them, you know, strip away the ideology or the color of the skin, or the shape of our

*Interview Transcripts* 173

eyes, we Filipinos and Chinese are all the same. We are human beings who care a lot about our family and our country. We all want a good, secure, and stable life. I think if we stick to that, we can understand each other better and maybe live in accord. My experience has been generally positive, amidst all the ups and downs. We went through a difficult period, especially in the first few years in China, which were marked by uncertainty, homesickness, and monotony. We were cut off from information and entertainment, and especially from our loved ones. In a way, looking back, it was a blessing because it made us mentally tough as people. It forced us to be self-reliant; to be mature and patient; and to be optimistic that things would turn out okay in the end.

GARCIA: From Newsweek, how did you become a journalist for *CNN*?

FLORCLUZ: Right after Peking University, I worked for *Newsweek* and then, for *Time*

Magazine. For *Newsweek*, I think it was about a year and a half. In 1982, I joined TIME

Magazine as a reporter and subsequently served as TIME's Beijing bureau chief for 10 years (1990–2000). My big break came months later when I reported on the trial of Chairman Mao's widow, Jiang Qing, and her "Gang of Four," from December 1981 to January 1982. Years later, I was part of the team which broke for TIME Magazine the news of the suicide of Jiang Qing, who was then on house arrest. We broke it days before the Chinese official media reported it.

The only year I was out of China for a long time was in 2000. I had a fellowship at the *Council of Foreign Relations* (CFR) in New York for the *Edward Murrow Press Fellowship*. Each year, they choose one journalist for a year-long stay in CFR to do whatever he or she wishes to do: research, write a book, essay, and join activities.

GARCIA: Largely, people working in the media, whether or not they are international media bureaus, were Chinese? Or were there a lot of foreigners like you?

FLORCRUZ: Mostly foreigners. Those who are accredited in China were foreigners. The company or a media group has to nominate you, and then the Chinese foreign ministry will vet and approve your accreditation. At that time, it was hard; most of the time, they send people from the US or Europe to be based in China. But in my case, they found me there.

GARCIA: How is it like to be an international correspondent based in China?

FLORCRUZ: Working as an international correspondent may sound romantic and glamorous, but in fact it entails a lot of hard work and hassle. After all, only three decades ago, weather forecast in China was virtually considered a state secret. Phone numbers of officials and government agencies were also difficult, often impossible, to obtain.

Twenty five years ago, reporters were permitted nothing more than carefully guided visits and predictable interviews. Until 2007, on the eve of the 2008 Olympics hosted by Beijing, foreign reporters in China were not allowed to travel and conduct interviews outside Beijing unless they secured permission from local foreign affairs offices 10 days in advance. Of course, we had to defy that rule to do our usual job as reporters. That "10-day rule," ridiculous as it was, was not rescinded until 2007.

Now, as China evolves into a freer, more pluralistic society, getting timely information, conducting interviews, and going on reporting trips have become relatively easier. Some restrictions and constraints remain but covering China has become relatively easier, if one is hard-working, resourceful, patient, and intrepid.

Working as an international correspondent is like getting on a roller-coaster ride. It's a thrill, with twists and turns, ups and downs. We cover landmark events, interview fascinating personalities and travel to exotic places. But it's also are frustrating as we frequently encounter bureaucratic foot-dragging, harassment, and interference. You know, the "hand in front of the camera."

We often encounter that when we travel in towns and cities to do unpalatable stories— fatal accidents, corruption cases, street protests or labor unrest, etc. Local officials do not want the media there because they know that we are sniffing at unpalatable issues that, in their mind, will embarrass them, or will tarnish the image of their place, thus possibly turning off tourists or investors, or will simply get them into trouble with their higher supervisors. So sometimes, they employ local police or thugs to shadow, confront, or intimidate us ostensibly because we had no official permit. Or they come up with other excuses.

In 2001, when we tried to do a story on the AIDS epidemic spreading in Henan villages because of the sale of blood for money, we had to sneak into a village with the help of Chinese NGOs. To get our stories, we had to play hide and seek with local officials and police so we could interview victims' families, shoot in the villages, and get out safely to tell our stories.

In rare cases, harassment involved brief detention and questioning by local police whenever we got busted. That happened to our crew when we tried to cover labor unrest in Guangzhou, a sad story which involved cases of overworked and disturbed migrant workers committing suicide by jumping off buildings.

*Interview Transcripts*   175

GARCIA: How would you describe today's China with that of 43 years ago when you first arrived? China has become one of the fastest growing economies in the world. How would you describe the changes in the society?

FLORCRUZ: China in 1971 and China now are as different as night and day. There is a huge billboard in a Beijing intersection which advertises Nokia phones or some commercial product. When I first saw that signboard over 40 years ago, it carried the slogan "NEVER FORGET CLASS STRUGGLE." That shows how much China has changed over the years.

When I first saw China, it was poor, backward, and dull. It was in the throes of the tumultuous Cultural Revolution. After years of chaos and isolation, China is now firmly locked into the global community through diplomacy, tourism and trade and, yes, through the news media and the Internet. After years of stagnation, China now is now bursting at the seams with explosive energy along the road to modernization. Having seen what China was like in 1971 makes me appreciate even the most incremental changes. Just about any change has been an improvement from where I started.

Today, I see an enormously complex China. Great achievements stand alongside daunting challenges. The country's economic growth the past 20 years has been phenomenal, but it has also triggered inevitable and often unintended consequences: rising unemployment, yawning income gaps, regionalism, rampant corruption, rising criminality, and social malaise. Millions of Chinese still live on $1 a day, and large income disparities persist. Yet the Chinese cannot be blamed too much for optimism after decades of rapid socioeconomic transformation on the back of a historical calamity. Compared with the past, the future for them beckons not as an inevitable crisis but as an extraordinary opportunity. For better or worse, the changes taking place here are simply breathtaking. More changes can be expected now that China is closely linked with the global ecosystem.

GARCIA: What do you think we can do to overcome the "china problem"?

FLORCRUZ: I think understanding China is one of the pressing needs. We all agree that China will be important as a neighbour and as a global player. So obviously, we should know how to coexist amicably with China, and the first step is to understand it. Hopefully China will seek to understand the Philippines as well. But on our part, I really hope that we can boost our knowledge about the country by developing more China watchers, people who really focus on the task of learning about it and then imparting the knowledge to the general population and sharing it to the policymakers. It is about time to do that, and one step to do that is through collective wisdom of our China watchers, who are too few.

But hopefully, this is a good beginning, a kind of spur and process to encourage more Filipinos especially university students. Learn Mandarin – learn it well. Spend time in understanding China. And then, share it with the population. Finally, let me say that when China sneezes, we should expect the rest of the world to catch a cold.

# GO Bon Juan

**Expert: Go Bon Juan**
**Interviewer: Carmelea Ang See**
**Date of interview: November 18, 2015**

ANG SEE: We're here to record the history of Mr. Go Bon Juan as a scholar. Please tell us your family's path to the Philippines.

GO: When we arrived in the Philippines, I entered Grade 3 instead of 4 because the standard of English language classes in Hong Kong is lower than the Philippines. I studied in Northern Rizal Yorklin School for elementary and then Kiaotiong (僑中)[1] until I finished Grade 12 in Chinese class and Grade 10 in English class.[2] My formal education is basically up to that point only.

GO: I took up Education at National University for one semester, then went to University of the East for another semester taking up commerce. Everything else is self-learned.

The most important learning was in 僑中. When I entered high school, I was immediately involved in the student council. By Grade 11, I became student council chairman for 2 years.

僑中's student council was very famous for its student journal, because 僑中 was very liberal. That was a very important exercise. This was when I started to write, edit, and it led me to love reading as well.

I was born in China in 1949. We moved to Hong Kong in 1954 for about a year and then returned to Chimho, China where the people were mostly fishermen. We returned to Hong Kong for around 6 years before going to the Philippines. I have been here since 1960.

I have more social consciousness. I sympathize with poor people in the Philippines. When we arrived, my father's workers were poor and I sympathized with their conditions. I also have an interest in social problems so I want to know why. I read those kinds of books, especially if related to the Chinese in the Philippines.

Sometime in the 1980s, Chinben See 施振民, Teresita Ang See 洪玉華, Lily Chua, Victor Go 吳勝利 wrote Crossroads for Orient News[3]. I felt that the overseas Chinese problem[4] could be solved but there are two very different viewponts on the issue.

178　*GO Bon Juan*

One viewpoint is from mainland China that sees the overseas Chinese belonging to China's. The Chinese in the Philippines, meanwhile, see that to solve their problems, they have to depend on China.

For Crossroads, the significant and unique viewpoint is from the Chinese in the Philippines. The writers were all born here. So, I sought out Victor Go, who introduced me to Chinben See.

The way I view the overseas Chinese started from discussions with Chinben, who introduced me to this field of study. The more I read, the more I learned. It is not enough to only look at the Philippine ethnic Chinese problem. It has to be the entire Southeast Asia. You should compare what happens in the rest of the world. If you do a comparative study, then you will discover more about the Philippines.

If you want to know about the sojourners (華僑) and Chinese Filipinos, the you should learn about history, the Chinese community's situation: economic, social, cultural, etc. You cannot finish learning them all. By then, I realized that I have to depend on myself, because there are very few people who have done studies in this field. For Chinese Filipinos, there are only a handful.

Tan Taybin (Chen Tai Min 陳臺民), Tan Diathu (Chen Lieh Fu 陳烈甫), Tan Siukok (Antonio Tan 陳守國), Lao Chi Thian (劉芝田)—are the very few who wrote about the Chinese quite well, mostly about history. As well, they had different political backgrounds. Lao Chi Thian and Tan Diathu leaned towards the Kuomintang 國民黨.

Tan Taybin is a little pro-China. He wanted to write ten volumes of the history of the Chinese in the Philippines, but came out with only two. At that time, he was working at Chinese Commercial News which abruptly stopped operations.

GO: Siong Po closed down twice – first during the Second World War when it refused to be used as Japanese Propaganda. The editor, Yu Yi Tung, was executed and the newspaper shut down. The second time was when President Ferdinand Marcos declared Martial Law in 1972 and shut down all media outlets. Tan Taybin's two volumes on the early Spanish period came out in the 1960s.

Antonio Tan concentrated on the American period and the Chinese political awakening, plus one book on the Japanese occupation.

Many other topics have not been written about. Very few people have touched on how to solve the huaqiao/huaren problem (Chinese migrant issues and Chinese Filipino integration). Although, Pagkakaisa[5] gave a particular direction to the problem. It was a different argument altogether.

Another problem on the Chinese in the Philippines is that the emergence of intellectuals is quite late, only in the 1950s and 1960s. Tan Taybin talked about the huaqiao's path in his writings.

GO: In the Philippines, the Chinese are mostly businessmen. As a group, how can they point out a direction to take on how to solve the huaqiao

*Interview Transcripts* 179

problem? The Federation of Filipino-Chinese Chambers of Commerce and Industry (Siong Chong 商總)was formed in 1954, but it was a Taiwanese instrument that was supposed to control the Chinese community. They didn't think about integration as a solution to the Chinese problem. Antonio Tan was mainly a historian and did not consider integration of the ethnic Chinese to Philippine mainstream. Pagkakaisa was concerned but they had to close shop because of Martial Law. So now, we want to continue the work. Pagkakaisa's task was to study how to influence the society. On one hand, it has not happened yet. It takes time.

The Chinese in the Philippines were divided into two groups. Those who are pro-Kuomintang will not think of integration. Those promainland China perceive that China will protect the overseas Chinese. In the early 1970s, many of them thought that when diplomatic relations were established, the Chinese problem would get solved.

That did not happen, instead, we had kidnapping[6] in the 1990s. When the new Kaisa was formed,[7] the timing was good. The kidnapping problem made the local Chinese realize that they have to depend on themselves in cooperation with Filipinos to figure out how to solve problems in the community.

The first time I joined a conference was in Australia in 1986. It was the first time I was exposed to an international conference. After that, I joined a number of conferences for more than 10 years, like ISSCO[8]. I heard a lot and learned a lot. But at the same time, I feel that there are many aspects that are not touched upon (做不了). I find that scholars' circles are too small to truly resolve issues or to exert influence. In every country, there are just those two to three people devoted to Chinese studies. What we need is local Chinese who conduct Chinese studies so they know the problems of their own country. Also, they should have enough intellectual capability to discover the issues, analyze them, offer solutions, and do things (做事情), influence policy or take action.

Furthermore, overseas Chinese Studies is very comprehensive. There is a need to compare with other countries to find out more about the Philippine Chinese. Those who can do research have a certain passion. This is very lonely work, but necessary.

In the Chinese community, new organizations are still cropping up. If the existing organizations could already solve community issues, then we don't need new groups. So much resources are expended, but not much spent on results or processes to help solve problems, which is what we need. They are often more concerned with themselves, not other people.

What we want is that the Philippine Chinese should also have *utang na loob*[9]. In the hundreds of years since the Chinese arrived, we should think that we were allowed to live here, become successful. Do good things for the country to help people, and pay back to the country.

180  *GO Bon Juan*

ANG SEE:  Is this your reason to be one of the founders of Kaisa?

GO:  I gathered different people from different groups – the Pagkakaisa group[10], people from 僑中, Xavier School (光啓學校), Chiang Kai Shek College (中正學院). I did the legwork. If you look at the Chinese community organizations, most are in business and cultural work is very weak. They always just use sampo (三寶)[11]. It is not enough.

ANG SEE:  Let's talk about Hua Ching華清, your pen name in World News (世界日報). You write about Philippine affairs and about the Chinese in the Philippines. Are the organizations your target audience?

GO:  Kaisa's cultural work has two aspects: one toward the local Chinese and the other toward the Filipinos. Kaisa's weekly publication, Yong Hap (Integration 融合), has been in the newspaper for 28 years with thousands of issues. The target for the local Chinese to realize and accept the concept of integration.

The objective of my writings as Hua Ching華清is slightly different. It is meant to help the local Chinese discover and learn about the Philippines. There were times when I also wrote editorials for World News, which discussed complicated Philippine issues. I wanted to help the Chinese understand and analyze the country's economy, politics, elections.

GO:  One shortcoming of researchers is that some want to find ready materials, but there is nowhere to find that. There are materials that you find by accident in another book. We have not fully mined material from Archivo General de Indias in Seville, Spain, University of Santo Tomas Archives, Mexico's general archives.

What we lack with Philippine Chinese studies is data. We always say that the Chinese are very good in business, the economy so and so[12]. But reliable data is very limited.

If you want to study the economy, look at the percentage of car buyers. Look at the builders of high-rise condominiums and gated subdivisions.. You can also look at who went to China to buy property or those with bank accounts in Hong Kong. Those are confidential, of course, but they are good sources of accurate information.

GO:  I attempted it once before when I worked in a bank, because bank records are more accurate. But I discovered It is very difficult to differentiate Chinese-owned from those that aren't. For example, the current largest bank in the country is BDO owned by Henry Sy, a local taipan. How do you identify the depositors? You cannot say Henry Sy or BDO dominates such percent of the banking industry, because the depositors are not all Chinese.

However, in a lot of research, this is the basis. Researchers look at the Philippines, at the taipans, and add together what they own.

ANG SEE:  Two weeks ago, I heard again that the Chinese control 60 percent of the economy.

*Interview Transcripts*   181

GO: The earlier data is more reliable like the Philippine surveys from 1903, 1918, 1939, 1948. The data that says Chinese control 56.2 percent of the Philippine economy came from misinterpreting a study by [Kunio] Yoshihara.

Yoshihara studied the Philippine manufacturing industry in the 1970s. He got [data about] the top 1,000 corporations and extracted around 250 manufacturing firms and analyzed these. These were further divided into three categories of ownership each making comprising a third – Philippine domestic, Chinese, foreign. If only Chinese and domestic firms are considered, then the Chinese-owned firms comprise 56.2 percent of the shares. That is the source of that data. And yet, when people saw the study, they started erroneously citing it – that the Chinese control 56.2 percent of the Philippine economy.

ANG SEE: How does your scholarly output combat the lack of data?

GO: The most important is that Tsinoys are Filipinos. Their wealth is the wealth of the Pinoy, not the Chinese. There is no need to separate. If you keep wanting to separate, it will be detrimental to the Chinese Filipinos. The Chinese will just become more and more scared. The more they develop, the worse it becomes because [people will see that] there are so few Chinese, but so much wealth. If the Philippine public does not see this as the wealth of the country, you're in trouble.

ANG SEE: When you write of history, or Philippine situationers in World News, would you say you have influenced the mindsets of people from different Chinese organizations?

GO: Yes, through word of mouth. In the past, no one will talk of integration, they were against it. They now accept the idea with a lot of people mentioning integration. It means, in a way, that they are paying attention, and some do accept. We cannot claim that everyone agrees. But one thing, regarding care for the Philippines, this is something everyone accepts.

When World News started in 1981, it only had foreign news on the front page. During the 1986 EDSA Revolution, I was editing domestic news, but publishers did not allow the EDSA revolution to be out on the front page. On the last day, February 25, I stayed at World News until midnight. The only thing I did was to put Cory Aquino's photograph on the front page—no news—but just to show that she is the new president. They got angry at me.

GO: But now, local news is in the front page. It was one change; the publishers are now paying attention. That's where World News is winning over other Chinese language newspapers. Their local news often fills up three sections, sometimes four sections, while others only have the front section. This is important because the concentration is now local. They now realize it: that even if there are global affairs/events, we are first affected by Philippine affairs.

182  *GO Bon Juan*

ANG SEE:  Let's go back to your work with Kaisa and the work of integration. As you said, we are all local-born. So in your observation of the young local-born Tsinoys, a lot of the parents are now local-born, natural born as well. Do you see a relevance to the organization that you helped start?

GO:  Yes there is still relevance. Nation-building is not just about donating money, a barrio school, or fighting fire (as volunteer fire brigades). The biggest problem in the Philippines is poverty. So much is lacking: health, education, infrastructure... efforts should be towards that. While the Chinese contributions are large, they could offer so much more. What if they build one entire infrastructure? Or develop one industrial park? That has purpose, direction and impact. It is a different point of view, a different level of awareness. No one has thought of how to organize these resources.

This should be the concern of the community, of society, the nation. We should have this kind of awareness to feel that we should be doing something.

[Regarding conferences] International organizational methods are often poor. A conference has a theme, but many submitted papers do not adhere to the theme so they are divided into panels, sometimes with three or four papers that do not match. Many attendees come for the opening and then disappear. Everyone selects topics they are interested in. So much time and effort spent on preparing but only a few people are there.

Dr. Ellen Palanca has written about the top 1,000 corporations, Theresa Chiong Cariño wrote about Siong Chong. We know their backgrounds, and much of the information they gathered they asked from us (GBJ personally and Kaisa). John Omohundro of University of Oregon, lived in Iloilo for 1 year, so he could write authoritatively about the topic.

In every country, there are only a few experts in Chinese Studies. Take Dr Richard Chu, for example. His defense panel do not necessarily know the field of Chinese Studies in the Philippines.

GO:  Based on what I have read, I have thought of many areas for research, but who is going to do it?

ANG SEE:  I would like to ask you about any involvement in transnational research projects.

GO:  The Encyclopedia of the Chinese Overseas. In a way, it was transnational— but more because I found funding for the researchers. I joined and contributed articles into the encyclopedia. The other one is with Taiwan's Academia Sinica.

The field is interdisciplinary. Many fields interconnect. You cannot be limited to the social sciences, or culture, economics, politics.

I want to add [that] the research orientation of Kaisa Para Sa Kaunlaran is more for social activism and impact. It is not research for the

## Interview Transcripts    183

sake of research. This is how it is different from the academe: we want to solve the issues that challenge the Chinese community and be a guide, to influence community members to contribute to the development of the Philippines.

There are truly only very few Chinese in the Philippines who are interested in researching. The Philippines is a poor country but with so many worthy things to learn about. Without them, you cannot discover the problems besetting the Chinese in the Philippines. People today talk about globalization. In fact, the globalization started more than a hundred years ago. In the world, events that occurred in Spain, the United States. Everything is interrelated.

I write to let people know the information. Another is to let the Chinese and Filipino mainstream society discover that the relations are so tight – that we are in each other's lives and cannot be separated. Hundreds of years of history show that. This helps very well in promoting integration. Why do we need to say/differentiate you from us? If we cannot resolve this identity issue, then the two peoples cannot become close, racial problems cannot be resolved.

Chinese Filipinos call themselves Tsinoy. The younger generation Chinese Filipinos refer to themselves as Filipinos.

ANG SEE:  In the past few years, we have been dealing with the West Philippine Sea (South China Sea) issue. Researchers, academics, media all ask the Chinese who they side with. What's your opinion on that?

GO:  The best method is still negotiation.

If we say that we side with China, people will be angry. If we say we side with the Philippines, we cannot avoid the comments, especially from the old generation. They have a sentimental attachment to China. We cannot force them to change their minds. This kind of problem cannot be generalized. Of course, the younger generation sides with the Philippines.

If we really want to understand and analyze these problems, there are conflicts of interest regarding petroleum, natural gas, regarding sovereignty, territory, politics. It is very complicated. We cannot just say who is right or wrong and side with that. But because we [China and the Philippines] are both in Asia, this kind of problem should be negotiated on—not to be taken advantage of—to resolve conflicts.

The academe is very important. We need the expertise and the efforts. But one important thing/a very big challenge is about the results. How can the results from the academe influence government policies/promote and develop this society?

## Notes

1  Interviewer's Note: *Popularly known in the Chinese-Filipino community as Kiao-tiong* 僑中, *the formal legal name was Philippine Chinese High School (*華僑中學*),*

184   GO Bon Juan

*established in 1923. The name changed to Philippine Cultural High School in 1976, and is now the Philippine Cultural College (*菲律濱僑中學院*).*

2  Interviewer's Note: *Elementary school in the Philippines is from Grades 1–6. High school used to be only from Grades 7–10. The educational system changed in 2012, and the year 2016 saw the first batch of Grade 11 students. However, Chinese language education up until the early 1970s was still up to Grade 12. This was reduced to 10 grade levels so students proceeding to university would also have "graduated" from their Chinese language classes.*

3  Interviewer's Note: *GBJ is referring to a series of articles that appeared as a column from 1979 to 1980 in Orient News* 東方日報.

4  Interviewer's Note: *Problem of integration and racial tension with the mainstream Philippine population, which was quite heightened in the 1960s to early 1970s.*

5  Interviewer's Note: *Pagkakaisa sa Pag-unlad (Unity for Progress) was formed in 1970 to encourage and promote assimilation and integration of alien minority groups into mainstream Philippine society; promote the belief that integration of minority groups shall benefit the Philippines; cooperate with other organizations to serve directly in worthy social charitable and civic projects which develop communication and collaboration between Filipinos and members of other ethnic groups.*

6  Interviewer's Note: *Beginning in the 1990s up to the present, Chinese Filipinos became favorite targets of kidnaping syndicates in the Philippines. They were "easy" targets because they paid monetary ransom quite quickly and never reported to the police. The kidnapping problem has not yet been solved. At its height, there was one kidnapping incident every other day, between 1996 and 2000. The statistics now are just a handful of incidents per month. See Kidnap 199).*

7  Interviewer's Note: *Kaisa Para Sa Kaunlaran (Unity for Progress)* 菲律濱華裔青年聯合會 *was formed by the former members of Pagkakaisa sa Pag-Unlad in 1987 after the restoration of democracy in the Philippines after 20 years during Martial Law rule.*

8  Interviewer's Note: *International Society for the Study of Chinese Overseas. Go Bon Juan was among the founding members that included Teresita Ang See, Dr. Wang Gungwu, Dr. Wang Lingchi, Dr. Zhou Nanjing, Emmanuel Ma Mung, and many other internationally prominent scholars in overseas Chinese Studies in the world.*

9  The Filipino concept of owing a favor.

10  Interviewer's Note:x *The former members of Pagkakaisa were already forming themselves together to become a new group when GBJ approached them.*

11  Interviewer's Note: *The local Chinese community has three treasures, all under the auspices of business organizations around the country: the volunteer fire brigades, free medical clinics/medical missions, and barrio schools where local business organizations donate funds to build school rooms for the local public schools around the country.*

12  Interviewer's Note: *There is a misconception in the Philippines that all Chinese are good in business, and that the ethnic Chinese minority controls the economy. The reality is that the Chinese are not major players even in the retail economy, as people perceive.*

## Reference

"Kidnap fever intensifies in Manila." 1992, January 12. *Tulay, Chinese-Filipino Digest* 4(7): 6–7.

*Caroline Hau*

**Expert: Caroline Hau**
**Interviewer: Jose Mari Hall Lanuza**
**Date of interview: November 5, 2015**

JM LANUZA: Please start by telling us about your family background.

CAROL HAU: I was born on August 30, 1969, in Manila and I grew up in Chinatown, the second of five children and the eldest of four daughters. My parents are professional painters who belong to the Linang School of Chinese Painting, and they teach traditional Chinese painting.

I actually went to a "Chinese" school—to St. Stephen's High School—from 1976 to1986. I graduated from high school in 1986 and then entered the University of the Philippines at Diliman as an English major, graduating in 1990. Then I went on to Cornell University where I obtained my MA and Ph.D in 1998.

My father was in the flour retail business before he and my mother decided to become full-time painters and founded the Philippine Chinese Art Center in 1975. I have childhood memories of my parents teaching me to paint bamboo, and of hanging out where my parents conducted Sunday afternoon classes in the early seventies, before they decided to do full-time teaching.

LANUZA: How did you begin as a China scholar or a China "watcher"?

HAU: In a sense, it came naturally to me because of my parents. My father liked to regale us children with stories of his childhood in China. At university, I took up courses on Asian history, on Chinese literature and language, and Chinese art. When I was doing my Ph.D, I started reading a lot of books on ethnic Chinese and Southeast Asia, so that's how I learned about the Chinese, not just in the Philippines and China, but also the Chinese in Greater China and Southeast Asia.

LANUZA: How did your parents influence you earlier in your life, with regards to your interest in "Chineseness"?

HAU: I grew up surrounded by my parents' paintings and the books and other materials on Chinese art that they collected, so I basically learned about Chinese history and civilization through Chinese visual culture.

186 *Caroline Hau*

As a child, I remember my parents bringing me to a museum to see a Han Dynasty jade burial suit. My parents liked bringing us children to museums and galleries.

We spoke Hokkien at home, and my father enrolled me in Chinese calligraphy classes one summer when I was in high school, and assigned me to do calligraphy every day. My parents encouraged me to read, paint, and write.

LANUZA: Can you recall your first experiences when you were first beginning as a China scholar?

HAU: It was really tough. Even though I went to a Chinese, I never felt that I had achieved enough proficiency to be able to do the kind of research that would qualify me as a Chinese scholar. So in a sense, I don't really consider myself a China scholar, but I am interested in the Chinese and Southeast Asia, particularly the Chinese in the Philippines.

At home, we spoke Hokkien rather than Mandarin. I learned Putonghua in school, but my native mother tongue is Hokkien, code-switched with Tagalog and English. My interest in things Chinese was a way to understand myself, my family, what sort of community I grew up in, and also to understand ethnic Chinese relations in Southeast Asia. It was less about China, and more about Chinese in the Philippines and Southeast Asia.

LANUZA: From your undergraduate to your postgraduate, what was your usual choice of research subjects that pertained to China or Chinese studies?

HAU: My training was in literary studies, so the main framework for analysis for me concerns

Philippine nationalism and its implications for Philippine literature. I have looked at ethnic Chinese issues in relation to Philippine nationalism. Secondly, I also am interested not just in literature but also in cinema and popular culture, so part of my research focuses on how literary or cinematic works help us understand issues pertaining to ethnic Chinese in the Philippines and Southeast Asia.

LANUZA: How did you begin your professional career as a China Studies scholar or "watcher"?

HAU: My first love is fiction. In fact, I loved to write short stories and wanted to be a writer, not an academic. A lot of the early stories I wrote obviously drew inspiration from the stories I heard from my parents. During the Second World War, my paternal grandfather was a guerrilla who was active in Laguna and in Quezon, so I drew on his experiences. Some of my earliest stories were published, when I was still an undergraduate student, in *Tulay,* a Chinese-Filipino digest, and a lot of these stories in fact were stories about Chinese in the Philippines. Fiction was one way by which I started to make sense of the issues pertaining to Chineseness. Later on, I started to do academic work on the Chinese, again in

## Interview Transcripts   187

snatches, and it was never a sustained effort. But over the years, I worked on issues that I thought were interesting,and then I wrote them out.

LANUZA: How was your professional track and intellectual growth after graduate studies [in relation to the subject]?

HAU: Graduate school exposed me to historical and comparative approaches to the study of the Chinese and Southeast Asia. What I got from grad school was a much broader perspective that allowed me to look at Chinese in the Philippines in relation to "Chinese" in Southeast Asia and the "Chinese" in Taiwan, China and Hong Kong.

Grad school prepared me, but there were a number of important changes that were going on in Philippine society. I was lucky enough to live through a time when you could track the evolution of changing meanings and significance of the Chinese. For example, maybe 50 years ago, anti-Chinese sentiments would be very ordinary and casual; now, we can't really vent these sentiments anymore without being criticized.

This kind of shift in understanding of how Filipinos regard their own ethnic Chinese Filipinos has changed dramatically. Some of this has to do with the rise of East Asia, like Taiwan and Hong Kong, and of course later on, mainland China. But others have to do with the transformation that our Philippine society is undergoing, as more and more of our Filipinos go abroad. The kind of experience they are having abroad is parallel to the kind of experience that Chinese migrants had in the Philippines. These changing social mores and a popular understanding and acceptance of the Chinese was something that I was interested in tracking and seeking historical explanations for.

LANUZA: Can you tell us about your experience or involvement in terms of professional societies, associations, and research teams that deal with China or Chinese studies—including Kaisa.

HAU: My parents, as professional Chinese painters, were very active in promoting cultural exchanges between the Philippines and China. Some of my first exposure had to do with my parents inviting Chinese artists over to the Philippines to exhibit their works, and my parents going to China to exhibit their works. Then I became interested in issues of Chinese identity because of the kind of fiction I was working on in the mid-1980s, and that was when I was introduced to Teresita Ang See, Go Bon Juan, Joaquin Sy; that was how I ended up joining some of the activities for Kaisa.

Many of these activities had to do with, for example, writing for *Tulay*. My first book publication experience was co-editing an anthology of short stories and poems in English and Filipino with Teresita Ang See and Joaquin Sy. It was mainly in the publication arm that I was active. But at the same time, Kaisa allowed me to think about issues of integration, because one of the missions of Kaisa is to promote the integration of the Chinese into Philippine society.

188  *Caroline Hau*

My involvement in Kaisa has a lot to do with learning to speak out as a Filipino while remaining aware of one's Chinese ancestry and heritage.

LANUZA: What were the national events or experiences that you think affected your China research?

HAU: Definitely the kidnappings [of Chinese in the Philippines]—because they were a very hot issue in the 1990s. Second, is the [Chinese] integration effort… Under Cory Aquino, there was a kind of explicit acknowledgment by some Filipino elites of their Chinese ancestry. The question of Chinese *mestizos* and their complicated relationship with Chineseness was something that got me thinking about what kind of history this relationship has—which is actually quite problematic, because some of the most anti-Chinese Filipinos at that time were actually *mestizos*.

This kind of question got me thinking: What is the history? Why is it that even though a substantial portion of our elite has some form of Chinese ancestry, these elites were at the forefront of developing a political ideology that was quite anti-Chinese? I was also bothered when I first came across the foundational documents of the Katipunan and found a very important passage where they basically said, you can't learn anything from the Chinese because they know only trickery, thievery and misery, the Chinese are not capable of imparting anything enlightening that you can learn from…

The kind of anti-Chinese sentiment that shaped the Katipunan's foundational documents bothered me greatly, because I always thought of myself as Filipino. The desire to try to understand the evolution of anti-Chinese thinking, and the kind of cultural differences and similarities that this history has shaped, as well as how this impacted the lives of both Chinese and Filipinos, got me started.

LANUZA: What about your own personal experiences that you think have affected your China studies and China research?

HAU: When I went to UP, I was exposed to a wider variety of students from different provinces. That got me to start asking questions about the history of the Chinese in the Philippines and the current trajectory, as well as changing meanings of Chineseness in the Philippines. And as I read more books, I then understood that the history was quite complicated, and that the kind of things we understand about the Chinese were not only *there* but historically shaped, and are also changing.

LANUZA: What can you say about the pedagogical materials on China or Chinese studies?

HAU: In the Philippines, the infrastructure for training people in Chinese studies was practically non-existent, at least in my time. Maybe it's changing now. For one thing—and I don't mean this as a criticism of the schools I went to, I think this was a more general phenomenon— many people who went to Chinese schools actually did not acquire any fluency or proficiency in Putonghua. Many of them were proficient in Hokkien because that was the language they spoke in their family, but

*Interview Transcripts*  189

the school system at that time wasn't good enough to teach people to read newspapers, and you couldn't really do the kind of scholarly work that would qualify you as a China scholar.

In the Philippines, we still need to improve our China studies programs. This is a symptom of a larger sort of intellectual failing. For a long time, the Philippines' intellectual sphere was very much oriented towards Americans, and to a lesser extent, Europe, —specifically Spain. The intellectual orientation towards Western, particularly American, academia and American discourses in a way hobbled Philippine studies and prevented it from expanding its horizons to include its Asian neighbors.

LANUZA:  Can you tell us about the development and evolution of your own research on the subject?

HAU:  As I've mentioned before, one of my first academic publications was on the kidnapping of the ethnic Chinese in the 1980s and early 1990s. Since that time, I have actually gone into history more and more just to understand the origins of the Chinese Question in the

Philippines. For example, I spent some time thinking about where the word "*Intsik*" came from, what kind of terminology was used to call the Chinese, because the changing terminology tells us something about changing attitudes towards the Chinese

In later years, I also tried to look at topics that are beyond the humanities, meaning topics that have broader implications, such as China's rise, for example, and its cultural implications. I have collaborated with my husband to publish a book called *How is China Changing East Asia*. It's a collection of essays that look at economy and politics, and my part in that book consists of trying to understand what is Chineseness and how modern China has been shaped by the 19th and 20th-century Anglo-Pacific regional system, how the Chinese in China are as culturally "hybrid" as the Chinese in Southeast Asia. I am using Chinese in the Philippines and Chinese in Southeast Asia as a kind of ground or framework to understand the Chinese in China, rather than the other way around.

Most of the time, when you study ethnic Chinese, we think about China as the origin. First of all, it is the home country where migrants and ancestors come from, and therefore it is always about how China shapes Chinese identity outside China. But I try to reverse this by looking at how China itself may be shaped by the kind of historical interaction between China and Southeast Asia, Japan, and the Anglo-Pacific regional system. I look at China from outside China.

LANUZA:  Have you involved yourself in academic debates on the subject?

HAU:  Definitely for Chinese in the Philippines. I see myself as continuing the work of Edgar Wickberg, and in dialogue with colleagues like Richard Chu and Teresita Ang See and other people. As far as the study of Chinese in Southeast Asia is concerned, I join the debates insofar as I

190  *Caroline Hau*

can use the Philippine case to think about some of the issues that are also relevant for the study of Chinese in other parts of southeast Asia.

I have also been part of public debates pertaining to the Chinese in the Philippines, the most recent one being a series of articles I wrote in response to F. Sionil José's series of column articles on the South China territorial issue, the ensuing tensions between China and the Philippines, and the Philippine Chinese.

LANUZA: Have you had experience or any experiences collaborating in transnational research projects on China or Chinese studies?

HAU: Yes, I was part of a book project edited by Peter Katzenstein called *Sinicization and the Rise of China*, a few years ago; I think the book came out in 2012. That book brought together a number of scholars working on China.

The contribution I made was an attempt to understand the historical patterns of hybridization of the Chinese in Southeast Asia and how this might help us understand the rise of China. I came to a very different conclusion at odds with popular understandings of China's rise, the popular understanding being that there is a Beijing consensus in the making and that China will be unilaterally shaping the way business and politics are conducted in this region. My work on Southeast Asia complicates this argument, showing that in fact modern China itself is quite hybridized, and that this hybridization in part has to do with its interactions with Japan, Southeast Asia, including Chinese Southeast Asians, and the Anglo-Pacific world. One way for people to understand the complexity of China is to realize that the perspective cannot just be China-centered. Any study of China should not only be focused on China; it should also understand that China is nested in a larger region, and more so in a larger world. That kind of region- and world-making has contributed greatly to the shaping of the Chinese nation as well as civilization in the present era.

LANUZA: Can you tell us more about your other overseas experiences, such as visits, speeches, conferences about China or Chinese studies?

HAU: I was involved in this Katzenstein book project. I have presented papers on the Chinese in the Philippines at the Association of Asian Studies conferences in Hawaii and at ICAS in Macau. After "The Chinese Question" came out in 2014, my focus has shifted more towards Philippine studies again, so the next book I'm working on is on Filipino elites. It's called *Elites and Ilustrados*, and there will be a chapter on the ZTE scandal and its aftermath.

Kyoto has also good relations with the Asian Center at UP and we have also forged relations with San Carlos University and Mindanao State University. These networks are important for promoting Southeast Asian Studies. But these networks are also friendships which I have forged over the years and which have actually shaped my own thinking.

*Interview Transcripts* 191

LANUZA: What is the main focus of your academic publications?

HAU: In terms of the Chinese studies, I have edited an anthology of plays, short stories and poetry in English and in Filipino called *Intsik: An Anthology of Chinese-Filipino writing.* I [also] mostly focus on cinematic and literary works, for example, like the *Mano Po* movie series by Regal Entertainment, and on well-known literary works by Charlson Ong, who writes in English, by Bai Ren and Du Ai, who write in Chinese, but also on little-known works by people like Jose Angliongto, who actually has the distinction of being the first person to publish a novel on the Chinese-Filipinos which came out in the late 1960s.

I see my research as partly a work of retrieval, but also as work that tracks the changes in popular understandings of, and sentiments toward, the Chinese. But the focus has been mainly on literary and cinematic works, and to a lesser extent, on history and politics.

LANUZA: What do you think is your prime contribution to views and theories on China or Chinese studies?

HAU: I think the Philippines can offer ways of thinking about Chineseness and about the history of the Chinese in Southeast Asia that can enrich Chinese studies. Given that for most of the past 300–400 years, Southeast Asia was the main receiving region of Chinese migration, Southeast Asian Chinese played an important role in the development of China, not just economically, but (arguably) culturally, in ways that haven't really been studied very deeply or understood so well. I think that what Liu Hong calls "Sino-Southeast Asian studies", which are studies of interactions between China and Southeast Asia, is a fruitful area of research where I can make my contribution, and it's always a contribution from a Philippine perspective.

Our case is quite distinct from Thailand, Indonesia and Malaysia, and I think anyone who wishes to understand the trajectory of Chineseness in Southeast Asia should factor in the Philippine experience. It is an important case study that might be able to help us rethink some of the fundamental assumptions we have about what is Chinese.

LANUZA: What are the issues or problems that you have encountered in your past research on China or Chinese studies?

HAU: I think that from the beginning the main problem is China itself. We take too much for granted when we say that Chineseness is what China has, and that Chineseness comes from China, and we tend to take these issues for granted because we think there's something out there, and it's Chinese. The issues we need to grapple with as China scholars always concern the signifier "China", and to some extent the signifier "Chineseness"—and it always starts with questioning what China is. Many scholars have debated China or what China is. There's no consensus on what China is: Is it the current government? Is it the nation-state? Is it the civilizational process? Is it Cultural China? "What is China?" has been one the biggest questions.

192    *Caroline Hau*

LANUZA:  What is your evaluation of China pedagogy in the Philippines and its future prospects?

HAU:  I really hope we can improve the teaching of, and the pedagogical base for, China studies. I hope we can train our Filipino scholars who work very well and are able to produce good work, because I think there's a lot still that needs to be done to understand the Chinese in the Philippines. There's a lot of archival research that can be done. Every era demands a different view, a different thinking. All the more reason and urgency for us to train good Filipino scholars who can work not just on this topic, but can also contribute more generally to China studies.

I think the fundamental trend in recent years has been the shift toward area studies, particularly Asian Studies, from its original grounding in Europe and America, back to the region.

LANUZA:  Can you evaluate and compare the different China studies communities across the globe?

HAU:  Chinese studies is very strong in Japan, they have done excellent work in that field. It's far less so in the Philippines. Most Southeast Asian institutions still struggle to set the groundwork, to promote Chinese studies in Southeast Asia. I see this as a kind of challenge. It's all the more important now, because we are facing all the problems and challenges that come with our closer economic integration with China. There is really an urgent need to train [more] scholars.

But so far, Chinese studies in Southeast Asia is still at a gestational stage. It hasn't reached the kind of levels we see in Japan, which has a longer tradition; I look to Japan as an inspiration for the kind of intellectual work that is not limited to any single language, and is capable of works of translation across many different languages.

LANUZA:  What are your views on China's future?

HAU:  I really believe it's only the Chinese in China who can answer that. Only the Chinese in mainland China can answer questions about what they want China to be, and what kind of China they want for themselves and for their neighbors. It's very difficult now; I think China is at a phase in its history where it is basically flexing its muscles and making itself felt, because it has grown as a regional and global power. Like any other country, some still need to be more aware of the implications of their actions—their country's actions —on neighboring countries.

For example, in relation to the South China Sea/West Philippine Sea issue, we need to sit down and talk to each other. It's not just at the state level. I think, that people-to-people interaction might be a more important resource for creating mutual understanding between China and its neighbors, far more than what is being undertaken at the state-to-state level, even though that is also very important.

LANUZA:  Thank you, Professor Hau.

*Florencio Mallare*

**Expert: Florencio Mallare**
**Interviewer: Sining Kotah**
**Interview Date: November 25, 2015**

## Personal background and identity as a China watcher

KOTAH: So your journalism career started your life as a China watcher?

MALLARE: I don't know how. Well, I don't know how to put it myself... I was involved with this. Because as a journalist, I was very curious about my identity. Who am I? How did I come to be here in the Philippines? What is my role now? As a member of the community, all these questions came out during my 8 years, I think, as a journalist.

KOTAH: But just a regular journalist, not specifically left-leaning...

MALLARE: It was left. I was jailed for that. For 2 months, in 1954, I was just 22 years old then, but not because of my job. Well, I was only a few months into my job, but they charged me because of my past activities. During the Japanese occupation, I joined the subversive, left-leaning movement.

KOTAH: It was against the Japanese definitely, and not against the Philippine government.

MALLARE: No, no, no, precisely. That was our defense.

KOTAH: So it all started there. Would you consider yourself a China scholar or a China watcher?

MALLARE: Now, as a journalist, you began to think of your own identity and that of the whole community. Because of that, I am glad I ended up co-authoring a book with Zhuang Guotu from Xiamen University. He and I co-authored *The History of the Chinese in the Philippines*. He was the Director of Xiamen University's Research Institute.

KOTAH: So if you are going to look at this one, you are not only a China watcher. You are a China scholar. You were able to come up with this. You are a scholar.

MALLARE: No, I am a journalist. I am glad I was able to co-author that. It took 4–5 years to finish that.

194    *Florencio Mallare*

KOTAH: But what was it that made you decide that you wanted to focus your study on the Chinese?

MALLARE: In my case, I was charged with subversive activity, and one of the defenses I raised was that I am a Filipino. My citizenship was once questioned as the government was trying to drag me into the subversive issue because of my involvement in the defense of the Chinese Commercial News and the Yuyitungs. And to put up a good defense, I had to defend my citizenship and touch on the pertinent law, the so-called Chinese Exclusion Law. What is the Chinese Exclusion Law all about? How did it come about? What was its effect? All of these are found in this book.

KOTAH: But did you take up journalism in college? Or was it political science?

MALLARE: Political science. I am a lawyer. I finished Pre-Med. But I ended up in Pre-Law, and then I finished my Law degree.

KOTAH: Did you have any formal schooling in or exposure to Chinese Studies?

MALLARE: No. It was all personal.

KOTAH: Personal, practical experience? But if you have some topics to discuss on the Chinese in the Philippines, what do you think will be your subject and your focus?

MALLARE: The important one is the Chinese Exclusion Law. It was a law stating that the Chinese are not allowed and welcome in any territory controlled by the US. I think it was pointed out by Tessy Ang See. Throughout the world, there are only two kinds of this law, one in the US and one in South Africa. Now in the case of US, in the 1890s, the Philippines was invaded by the armed forces of General Otis. Within I think a few months, the Chinese Exclusion Law was extended to the Philippines.

So you can see that this is the reason why of all the countries in the world, the Philippines has the fewest number of Chinese. And the number here cannot (be) compared with those of Malaysia and Indonesia because of the effectiveness of the Chinese Exclusion Law.

KOTAH: So everybody opted not to become a Chinese?

MALLARE: No, Chinese are not allowed; not welcomed.

KOTAH: Yeah, that was before, so that would be your focus?

MALLARE: Yes. You see that I have compiled here a series of laws, including the naturalization law and the Filipinization law. People keep on saying that the first notion of Philippines-ness was established in 1935. But I think I was able to point out that its emergence occurred earlier. We were able to find out that the Filipinization Law was very extensive. Through this law, the Filipino Chinese did not go into industry; they were only limited to retail and commerce; and our citizenship was so limited that it was very difficult to apply to become a Filipino citizen.

Interview Transcripts 195

But prior to that, the Chinese were in danger of being deported. I think in the US, the Chinese were not allowed; they were not even qualified to apply for naturalization because they said that the Chinese were born to be liars. And in our setting, theoretically, you can apply to be naturalized, but you can also be easily de-naturalized.

KOTAH: Yeah ok, but of course, all this was part of your involvement as a journalist at the same time, and eventually, as an attorney.

MALLARE: I am interested in this book; my contribution pertains to the Filipinization Law, followed by the citizenship law, naturalization law, and then the deportation law. This is my area of interest.

KOTAH: Was there any national event or any personal experience that really led you to tell yourself to steadfastly work on this one?

MALLARE: No, people were clamouring to come out with a history of our own; that motivated me. That's why we try to fill that gap. We know the nuances, the feelings, the emotions; and so Xiamen University depends on us; so we succeeded. And my approach is to use this to study the Tydings-McDuffy Law and the Filipinization law to understand the Chinese in the Philippines.

Thoughts and engagements with China studies scholarship

KOTAH: Now, what are your thoughts about Philippine education on China, about Chinese Studies?

MALLARE: Given the lacking mention of negative actions against the Chinese, this can be a supplementary study.

KOTAH: So there were no studies on these negative actions?

MALLARE: There is nothing in the Philippine laws against deportation; schools did not emphasize it. We didn't know what "deportation" was until after graduation.

That is a part of history. You are from PCC? PCC's SyEng, do you know him? During his time, SyEng's position was quite high. He was the chair of the Chinese Chamber of Commerce, as well as the chair of the education association. So why did he agree to become the chairman of PCC? It was because the image of PCC as a left-leaning institution. He wished that he could satisfy, neutralize, or save the PCC. But did he? No, because Pao Ki Tung and Tiu Kiak Kun were deported.

KOTAH: Were they the leftists banished to Taiwan? These people you mentioned now, Pao Ki Tung and Tiu Kiak Kun...Were they deported to Taiwan?

MALLARE: Yes... Jailed! He couldn't find a way to satisfy the clamour of the rightist Kuomintang.

KOTAH: Why were these rightists saying that PCC was too leftist? Was this the case?

MALLARE: That was the image.

KOTAH: Image only, but were they really doing something against the government?

MALLARE: None. Just like what the Chinese say, "reign of terror..."

196   *Florencio Mallare*

KOTAH: When was that? It was roughly in the 1960s? The reign of terror was in the 1960s?

MALLARE: 1950s and 1960s. Up to this point, after seeing several commemorative journals of PCC, I've not seen any mention of the deportations of the likes of Pao Ki Tung and Tiu Kiak kun. When Chung Tiong Tay became the chairman of PCC, he made a very big contribution. What was it? He corrected the image of the PCC, changing its reputation from a leftist to the neutralist organization. How specifically? He asked Chua Bun Kiok to become a board member.

The PCC is like that; so is the Tsinoy community.

KOTAH: Why do you think it's like that, Mr. Mallare?

MALLARE: Rightist...

KOTAH: Until now?

MALLARE: Yes. A lot of people in the Tsinoy community don't know. What are we actually doing? What is the Tsinoy community doing? About the deportation.

KOTAH: Well then, why weren't these things discussed? Would it be because the integration has been too deep that those things are considered as history, as a distant past, which have not been given importance?

MALLARE: Which is wrong.

KOTAH: Ok... now you feel that, for example, schools would teach about Chinese culture and matters pertaining to the Chinese. They have to include this part of history to let young people know. What is your view on that?

MALLARE: It has to be taught, but no need for it to be too detailed. America did it well. Why were negative events discussed in such a way? Take the Chinese Exclusion Law. America apologized for it.

You should take a look at it, to know how important it is, to know what we are doing. I am Florencio Mallare, how did that come to be? I put up a defense, I am a Filipino, and why am I called Florencio Mallare? These things...they all have a reason behind them. Historically, it could be traced to the Chinese Exclusion Law.

KOTAH: But you were a natural born (Filipino) right from the start, isn't it? Or were you a naturalized Filipino? Meaning to say, were you pure Filipino?

MALLARE: At that time, because of the Chinese Exclusion Law, all of those were fake. Those (papers) were bought.

KOTAH: If you were to do Chinese studies, what do you think will be the best method? Like you said, it's all over the place... So if we really would like to say "ok, we're going to do it" ...

Right now, I suggest....China lacks people here in the Philippines. The Chinese are not familiar with our country. Right now, when they write something, they give it to me to take a look whether it's appropriate or not. It's like that. But I'm old now. Xiamen University has a lot of funds, but where do they find the people to do research on the

*Interview Transcripts* 197

Philippines? That's why you should go and join them. They have this big mistaken notion that Marcos was close to China; therefore there was no Filipinization law during his term. That's not true! I found out that's not true. They were very thankful. I said, "Wrong, it wasn't like that." We can play that role of correcting their impressions and perceptions.

KOTAH: Ok, now since you have a lot of interest on this topic, have you ever tried organizing a kind of forum for debate?

MALLARE: At that time, we had an association headed by (Theresa) Cariño. Have you heard of it?

KOTAH: Is it PACS?

MALLARE: PACS, Yes.

KOTAH: But when you joined those activities, did you also present papers?

MALLARE: Yes, yes. I presented papers; it takes time, you know; it's very tedious.

KOTAH: Yes, you would have to do a lot of research. The next question is, how do you describe your relationship with other Chinese studies scholars? Who are those Philippine Chinese studies scholars? Theresa Cariño? Bernardita Churchill, Tessy Ang, Go Bon Juan, they are too, right?

MALLARE: Theresa Cariño is for politics. Tessy is a bit more on the Chinese, not China, like the others.

KOTAH: But you are all focusing on different things. Yours is more on the laws on how, you know, those laws affected.

MALLARE: No, no, no. Law is only as an instrument, for me. Through these laws then you... I do not write legal stuff...

KOTAH: So your relationship with them in terms of doing Chinese studies is ok? Just that you have different focus points?

MALLARE: Who are you referring to?

KOTAH: With Dr. Churchill and others.

MALLARE: Not the same. Mine is more similar to Tessy's.

KOTAH: More similar to Tessy's and who else?

MALLARE: Go Bon Juan. Bon Juan used to work here.

KOTAH: So these are the ethnic Chinese; people who really feel they are still Chinese? Because, for example, Dr. Cariño is Singaporean?

MALLARE: You ask them, they are not. That's my advantage; they did not do it through laws to understand Chinese. Or maybe because I'm a lawyer. I went to U.P. Law Center. I was looking through the laws. So that was how it came about.

KOTAH: Now, do you think you have involved yourself in the policy-making, in consultation, or in risk analysis of anything about the Chinese in the Philippine?

MALLARE: No, I haven't. I'm not, up to this point, I'm not a scholar. If it comes my way and is interesting, I do not lose interest.

KOTAH: So you can say it's a personal interest.

198  *Florencio Mallare*

MALLARE: Personal interest, yes. And then now, we have this relationship with Xiamen University, which is completely up and running to this day.

KOTAH: So up to now, you maintain this kind of cooperative relationship?

MALLARE: Yes, yes!

KOTAH: And I suppose that beyond this project, you wish to embark on other things?

MALLARE: I am doing it. I'm waiting for him (Xiamen University) to approach me; if he wants me to submit something for review, then I will do that. For instance, we gave it to Bon Juan to take a look, and asked him for comments.

KOTAH: If you had an ally who could help you in broaching ideas or putting ideas or suggestions together, is there such a person in the Philippines to help you do so?

MALLARE: It's ad hoc.

Views on China's future and relationship with the Philippines

KOTAH: At least you thought about it. I think that was a turning point because you thought of knowing more about it; that was why you dug into the past, into history. So now that you feel China has placed such importance on the field, what do you think is China's future?

MALLARE: I am very partial; China will overtake.

KOTAH: It will?

MALLARE: Last century, it was England who practically ruled the world for 200 years; then it was America for a century. I think it's about time China will take over.

KOTAH: So do you foresee the weakening of American influence? Will there be a decline? Will China's influence become bigger? Because everyone is a bit afraid of China. I don't know, but it seems like that those who are not Chinese-Filipinos perceive that China will come and take over.

MALLARE: Bully!

KOTAH: Yeah, bully.... They would rather be bullied or controlled by America rather than, you know, be controlled by China.

MALLARE: Lately, the selling point of the West is democracy, freedom, and rule of law. China said we would agree to that. We will agree that democracy is universally acceptable, but we will try to improve the contents of its concept; there is nothing wrong with that. Would you know where is China weak at?

KOTAH: They don't know how to do advertisement. I feel that it is too quiet.

MALLARE: Yes, it does not know how to advertise.

KOTAH: Maybe because, you know, the Chinese value humility? Does it have an effect? China says there is no need to brag about these things. I don't really know.

MALLARE: Talking about the China Sea, you know, in international law, we have that so-called sphere of influence which is accepted, that is, when your country is strong, you can claim adjacent areas as your sphere of

*Interview Transcripts*   199

influence, which nobody should invade. This concept was the basis of the Monroe Doctrine, the U.S. claim that Central America and South America are part of its sphere of influence. That was accepted, but why is it that China cannot claim the same now? An even deeper issue is, do you know about the Air Defense Identification Zone?

That's not a Chinese invention. A long, long time ago, Europe and the US used this concept to claim airspace. Why was it correct back then, but now that China is doing the same, it becomes wrong? Why? That has been practiced. China is just copying from the US and the Europe. Then when you did that, it was not wrong. Now China is doing it, it is wrong?

KOTAH: I think that's because they are forestalling China. Because they know that if not for its corruption, China was also a very strong power before.

MALLARE: So, these are also poisoned by propaganda. China is very weak; its claim on the South China Sea is wrong, and the Philippines' claim is valid. What is the basis for the Philippines to claim?

KOTAH: It was based on a recent international law pertaining to 200 nautical miles. That looks like the Philippines' basis for claiming it.

MALLARE: It's still an issue for China that it does not know how to do public relations. The focus should be "What is the basis of the Philippines in claiming it?" That should be the focus. There was none at all; not from the Treaty of Paris, not in the 1898 constitution, and not in the 1932 constitution. There was none. There is no basis. There is also one thing wrong there. Afterwards, the Philippines was saying it had a claim on Freedom Land; China at that time tactically didn't know how to handle it. "Is that what you claim? Freedom Land?" Now the Philippines is not claiming Freedom Land. Instead, it wants to claim the Scarborough Shoal because they found out that Freedom Land has no resources.

KOTAH: It is just an island.

MALLARE: And that's where China is weak at; it loses to other parties.

KOTAH: But at that time, maybe it was because China was undergoing a period of consolidation and did not put much attention to claiming that it was theirs, so they missed the opportunity. And now, the Philippines is vocally claiming it. During APEC, it insisted on bringing up the issue.

MALLARE: China wanted to look good, so President Xi came. If you look at China from the Japanese occupation until today, you should be proud of it. After so many thousands of years, this is the only time that it is on its own.

KOTAH: I feel that perhaps during the time of Mao Zedong, China wanted to prove that it was not the aggressor, so there were things that it was not able to deal with.

MALLARE: Like in the case of the Philippines, how do you say that it is right? China says, "Okay, you say it's yours, I say it's mine. Let's sit down and talk." The Philippines did not want it. The Philippines would say, "You are big and I am small." And then it had to form a group with others to become bigger and to control China. You want to be bigger to have an advantage. So you go back to the position of China.

Right now, China's problem is that they have a unit called the External Affairs Office. They have this understanding; we are in a position here in World News. We cannot antagonize the Filipinos, which is even more wrong. We are Filipinos, but I love China so much. So you have to allow me to be neutral.

# Charlson Ong

**Expert: Charlson Ong**
**Interviewer: Yvan Ysmael Yonaha**
**Interview Date: January 18, 2016**

YONAHA: Let's [talk about] one of your works, *Men of the East*. What are your motivations in writing it? Are you promoting a political idea?

ONG: Not really. I've always liked to write. I started writing in the 1980s. There weren't many publications then. So there was a lot of playwriting and I tried to write plays. But then there was a problem of language when I decided on the characters I'd work with. So writing in fiction English became the more feasible way. I thought this was the material that I knew. You have to write what you know.

YONAHA: What do you mean when you say the problem of language?

ONG: Because if I used Filipino, which is the primary language of Philippine theatre, I would have to use a lot of pidgin Tagalog for authenticity since most migrant Chinese spoke Tagalog that way. But it could be very controversial. I wasn't ready to do that. Maybe now I might.

YONAHA: I see. So the choice of medium is a form of sensitivity for the reader?

ONG: Partly, yes, and also because I thought I handled English better than [I do] Filipino. Also, of course, [there were] personal influences because I read in English. I read Asian-American writing.

YONAHA: Let's talk about *Embarassment of Riches*. One reader thought that it was a kind of meta-history.

ONG: *An Embarrassment of Riches* is more consciously political because it was for the PH centennial. Although I started writing the book before the centennial contest was launched. I wanted to come up with a book with a feel of a hundred years after 1898, to locate the imagined community in Southeast Asia, because I thought a lot of our literature especially in English from Nick Joaquin down paints us as Latin, Hispanic. Catholic. I wanted to write a Philippine novel where the imaginary is located in Southeast Asia because we've never done that. I think it's practical, or even more appropriate because our economy is really Southeast Asian. I wanted to write as well about the Chinese in Southeast Asia.

202 *Charlson Ong*

YONAHA: Do you have a particular motive that made you tackle these things or you wrote it because it is available in our collective memory?

ONG: I think it's partly that. It's where I'm coming from and the work of fiction or literature is also towards defining that sense of identity. At some point, the personal and your sense of community merge.

YONAHA: So if, for example, a hundred years from now, somebody dug up this book, read it, and then said that Charlson Ong tried to situate the Chinese within Philippine history so that it's no longer just the Chinese but interspersed with Philippine history, would you say that it is a fair assessment of what you've done?

ONG: Yeah. In fact, I think the most concise reading of the book was made by Caroline Hau. In her book *The Chinese Question*, there is a chapter on *Embarrassment of Riches.*

YONAHA: Aside from the theme of nationalism and ethnicity, another term is about the *lannang* and *huanna*? Can you elaborate on this tension, for example? As I understand it, there's tension from within the group to not go out, and then there's tension from the outside.

ONG: Like in any minority. *Lannang* means "our people" so it's an "ingroup." So it's an ethnic identity. *Lannang* literally means "us" or tayo in Filipino. Everyone who is not *lannang* is *huanna*. So if you are not *lannang*, you are an outsider.

YONAHA: In a lot of times this is greeted with a sense of shame, especially when a relationship blooms between the *huanna* and the *lannang*. But at the same time, it happens a lot.

ONG: It happens a lot. In the past up to the early part of the 20th century, there was an exclusion of women from China. They could not come to the Philippines with their husbands. So it was very much a bachelor society and men usually took on common law wives here. There were much fewer Chinese women than men in the Philippines then. So if you didn't have money, you could not marry a Chinese woman. And of course, if they had some status, they wouldn't suffer being second wives. So the convenient thing was to have a second wife who was local. And since most of the migrants were blue collar—they were not well-heeled or educated—the women they had contact with were usually their laborers, laundry women, and the like. So if you marry local, the assumption for some *lannang* was that you were marrying "down," so there was discrimination. But there was also discrimination of locals against the Chinese.

YONAHA: I see. It explains the hostility such as the father of *Ah Beng*[1]? When *Ah Beng* arrived with his mother and sister, he was very hostile.

ONG: Yes, because the family wasn't asked to come. In other words, many of the migrant males had both families here and families in China. If you weren't asked to come, don't come, right? At some point, the patriarch might ask the children, the sons, to come and help. But otherwise, they wanted their first family to stay in China so they could remarry here.

*Interview Transcripts* 203

YONAHA: [and] this is interspersed, for example, with [story of] the girl that Ah Beng's mother got deported[2]?

ONG: Ah, the one sent away by the mother.

YONAHA: Yes.

ONG: I based those characters on a bit of family lore. My grandfather supposedly brought my grandmother back to his natal home when she was pregnant. He wanted her to stay there with his family so he could be single again in Manila. But my grandmother was headstrong, so after giving birth she came back here on her own with her her young sons. My grandfather didn't like that and they became estranged.

YONAHA: Let me ask you a more methodical question. How do you imagine different personas, creating stories for each of them, and somehow all of them tie down together in the end?

ONG: I don't know. In *Banyaga*, I did not have any outline. It started out as a screenplay. Someone asked me to do a screenplay on the Chinese. I refused because I had a previous negative experience with screenwriting and unless there's already financing I don't give more than a synopsis or a sequence treatment. Anyway, he was insistent so I ended up writing an entire detailed screenplay. It didn't sell. Then Mano Po[3] came out [and] I decided I would novelize my script. I would rewrite it into a book. At that time, the National Commission for Culture and the Arts had a contest for a novel in English.

I submitted the whole bunch and I didn't get the grant. And then I got a job in Davao in 2004. I didn't know many people there and didn't socialize much so I used the time to finish the book. Of course, I did have a structure to work with because of the screenplay. There were also developed characters, although when I novelized it, of course some aspects changed.

YONAHA: I noticed something while reading through your work. In our previous conversation you mentioned that you worked as an editor abroad, right? And then one of the characters works as an editor abroad[4].

ONG: That's a story I wrote because I went to Taipei. It's called "Another Country."

YONAHA: But that's not you?

ONG: Of course it's very close to my experience because I went there after [the] EDSA [People Power Revolt]. I was jobless. They recruited me here and I went there. Then I stayed for around 7, 8 months. And then I wrote a story—*Another Country*, which is included in the book *Men of the East*—my first collection of short fiction.

YONAHA: Okay. So you presented a certain image of the complex nation-building happening in the Philippines. I have questions about how it was received. First, how was it received by the Chinese community here?

ONG: I think it was relatively okay because I think my audience is a younger generation who read in English. Probably my main critic or my main

204   *Charlson Ong*

advocate of sorts has been Caroline Hau. I think she's critiqued every significant work of mine. Shirley Lua as well of La Salle has critiqued some of my work. So I think it's okay. Then there's a student edition of my short stories titled *A Tropical Winter's* Tale published by the UP Press. It's called the Chinese question and it's about Southeast Asia. It will help you because it's concise and it is about the Chinese question in Southeast Asia. So there's a part on the *Embarrassment of Riches*. And then Indonesia and Malaysia are also featured.

YONAHA:  Is there a new story in the pipeline?

ONG:  I've been working on... Actually my new collection 'Of that Other Country we now speak and other stories' published by the U.P. Press has just come out (2016). It's a collection of stories written over the last 20 years. But I don't do a lot of short fiction anymore. I've been working on a novel where one of the main characters is also Chinese. He is Tsinoy but he's a surgeon. He's a heart surgeon. But it has to do also with the Black Nazarene[5], the white lady[6]. So I'm trying to pull them together in a narrative.

YONAHA:  Are you involved in any professional societies, associations that deal with this kind of subject?

ONG:  No. I am friends with those from KAISA (*Kaisa Para sa Kaunlaran* or Unity for Progress). I've known them from the past but I'm not an organization person. So they're my friends. Teresita Ang See is a friend. But I don't work directly with them.

YONAHA:  May I know the reason why? Is this a personal decision?

ONG:  Yeah. I am not an advocate. I mean, I write my stuff but I'm a very solitary person.

YONAHA:  Because Teresita Ang See really pushes Chinese-Filipino integration in the Philippines.

ONG:  They are activists. It's not my style.

YONAHA:  What are the national events in the Philippines or in China that have influenced your writing about China.

ONG:  Well, when I was growing up, the politics between the right, between the Kuomintang loyalists and the left, the Communists, was strong, although the Philippines is basically Kuomintang because it's a merchant community. So the left was a minority. My father was a Kuomintang sympathizer. I think the recognition of the People's Republic was a big deal. And then—well, in the community itself—I think 1954, the year of the retail trade nationalization law, was a big turning point for the community. In fact, I'm writing a book now on the founder of the Makati supermarket and Unimart, Henry Ng. His family is Cantonese. So a lot of the Cantonese came to work for him eventually as they had to give up their own retail businesses. The Cantonese are mainly in the grocery business. So it affected them a lot. I think the retail trade nationalization was a big deal. Because it was mainly against the perceived Chinese domination of

*Interview Transcripts*  205

*sari-sari*[7] stores, but it also had a big effect on agriculture because the Chinese store owners were also the creditors and contract buyers of the farmers.

YONAHA: What is your opinion regarding textbooks or pedagogical materials that portray the Chinese a certain way?

ONG: I don't know if there are any. I think part of my writing maybe stems from that. When I was growing up, there was not a lot of... there was no material. Anyway, when I was growing up, the iconic Chinese in mass media was Akong. He died already. Akong Santosi was a character on TV played by a drummer named Bert Delfino and he looks Chinese. Probably he had some Chinese ancestry. So there was a sitcom before, called *Kuwentong Kutsero* that had an Ilokano lawyer speaking pidgin English and a gay person and a host of other comic characters who would meet in Akong's sari-sari store and Akong was in traditional Chinese costume...he had a cap and I think, a pigtail. So he was not a terribly bad figure. He was the comic relief. Of course he was always trying to make money. Akong is the main stay and then sometimes some extras would appear and speak in Chinese. I remember that my parents or grandparents would not like it because these extras seemed to have no steady livelihood and were exploiting their ethnicity to make money at the expense of the community.

Not much presence [on mass media] until 1975, through *Maynila sa mga Kuko ng Liwanag*. It's based on the book by Edgardo Reyes *Sa Mga Kuko ng Liwanag*, but it became *Maynila sa mga Kuko ng Liwanag*. It's partly shot in Chinatown. The story is that of this guy, Julio, from the province, who comes looking for his girlfriend, Ligaya Paraiso, who became a mistress of a Chinese. She is a kept woman in Ongpin, Chinatown. Julio finds Ligaya and the Chinese and ends up killing him. Maybe it's a very big deal because it's the first time that a Chinese in a local movie is the main villain, and the manner of his killing is quite ghastly. That was a long time ago and then now you have *Mano Po* and all that. So that made me think that there's more to this. Maybe someone should write something else right? Something that is more... that is more of a complete picture. So I think that was part of it.

YONAHA: Has there been a paradigm shift in the way you view the Chinese and consequently the way you have portrayed them?

ONG: Paradigm shift. I wouldn't say so. I mean there has been a widening of it because I've travelled. I've looked into race relations in Malaysia, Singapore, the US. I don't think there has been a paradigm shift because I am a natural born citizen so I didn't experience some of the problems faced by those who were Chinese nationals. Even in UP, many local born Chinese students were considered aliens back in the day. They had to present "alien certificates." And then, I grew up here, and went to Xavier which is a Chinese majority school, so I did not experience personally much outright bigotry, not to my face.

206  *Charlson Ong*

For instance, there is this issue in the use of "instik." In fact, Caroline Hau edited a book [related to this]. Maybe you should read that also. It's a collection of writings by Chinese-Filipinos. It's called *Intsik*. So she used something I wrote as the foreword because I argued for the use of the word, the term, which is historical. It has no pejorative meaning. It means "your uncle." During the Spanish era, the word for local Chinese was "sanglay" or "instik"—Intsik Pawa (the nickname of the Revolutionary General Pawa), right? So it has historical context. It doesn't mean anything derogatory. It should be used and it should be reclaimed, like [the term] "Moro." So Caroline used that as the title of that collection which was also translated to Chinese.

And then Teresita's group, KAISA, came out with *Tsinoy* which I don't mind and it might become the 'successor' term for 'Instik' historically. They coined Tsinoy because to them *intsik* is very sensitive although it has no derogatory meaning. It has all the derogatory, emotional associations, connotations because when they were growing up, it seemed malicious when you were called that. So that's maybe one example.

YONAHA: Are there any other instances that you included yourself in such discourses?

ONG: Well, I've written some but maybe again I can send it to you. They are about representations. But most of the material is already in my creative work. In other words, when I write the novels, it's to create a larger representation and that's my work, in the same way that Muslim writers are now creating more work on Muslim Filipinos. For instance, I think we might soon see a big literary work which will give us a more concise look at the Muslim community in the country. Yeah. It's in the literary work. So there, I don't get involved in these arguments because I think it's already in the work.

YONAHA: Can you tell us some of your trips to China? What did you do there? What's the primary purpose?

ONG: My first trip to China [was when] I went as a translator for a movie delegation from the Cultural Center of the Philippines. There was a co-production between China and the Philippines, *Hari sa Hari* by Eddie Romero (1987) It's a movie about a sultan of Sulu who went to China to seek the support of the Ming Emperor Yongle.

YONAHA: The one who died in China?

ONG: Yes. And he died there. Vic Vargas plays the sultan. So they went to shoot that in China during the Marcos era. Then the EDSA [Revolt] came. So after that, 1987, they were going there because the movie was opening in China [and] they asked me to go as a translator. So I went and then what happened then was that my father suffered a heart attack in 1984—this was 1987. Shortly before we were about to go, he had another attack and I thought I wouldn't be able to go. Then when we were about to leave. He seemed fine. But apparently, he had another one, the

Interview Transcripts  207

third and the week I was in China, he was in and out of the ICU. When I returned there was no one home, so my cousin told me my dad was in the hospital. I went to the hospital and he was gone. It was like he just wanted me to go and see China.

So that was my first trip, 1987, for that. To Xiamen and Beijing. And then after that, years later, there was an exchange between the Yunnan writers and the Philippine Writers' Union. So we went to China again but in Yunnan province. And then again, a few years ago, because China has this entire department that maintains ties with ethnic Chinese across the globe. So every year, they have this gathering of ethnic Chinese worldwide that is hosted by the Chinese government but you have to be maybe under 45 at the time. They invite you over and I was invited. So I went. There was a Philippine delegation, there were Americans, and there were varied peoples. So we went again to Beijing and to the hometown of Confucius in Shandong province.

YONAHA: Very interesting. So as far as the Chinese government is concerned, they still monitor you as an overseas Chinese?

ONG: Maybe "monitor" is saying too much, but they have this whole department or agency that keeps ties with all these people of Chinese descent all over the world. So every year they invite over these people under 45 who have some Chinese ancestry. And then you have this whole gathering... So they're very conscious of maintaining links, I think. They keep these things open.

YONAHA: What do you think is your prime contribution to views and perspectives about China here in the Philippines? I mean whole experience of China here in the country.

ONG: Yeah, the idea is to broaden or to deepen the idea of nation and community. I think that's the main work—to deepen and broaden the idea of community, of nation, of ethnicity, to problematize it, and then to broaden and help people understand it. I think that's the work. As far as China is concerned, I think right now, a lot of the traffic is [happening in] both ways. There are many Filipinos working in China now, so I think it's going the other way. The labor movement is going the other way. Filipinos are working in China.

YONAHA: Do you have comments about this whole academic establishment dedicated to Chinese Studies?

ONG: There are a number of foreign foundations involved in Chinese Studies worldwide and some competition among them. One can never discount the possibility of political influence building in their activities. There is always the matter of "soft power projection." I think they should be transparent. And if we allow them into our universities then they should allow us into their universities as well.

While we should be open to scholarly collaboration with foreign institutions, we should also scrutinize them. Maybe they can fund programs but under a UP institution. We certainly need a lot more research

208 *Charlson Ong*

on China. In fact, I think the Asian Center has to do much more and should take the lead in terms of strategic thinking with regards to our relationship with China that is growing ever more complex.

YONAHA: Is there anything else I've missed that is important about your perspective in China, in Chinese Studies?

ONG: I think we're sort of behind in our Chinese studies. I think we've always been. Part of the work I think [of] *Embarrassment of Riches* is to re-orient our thinking in Asia because even our imaginative thinking is always western. So I think we are kind of delayed in those terms because we have always seen ourselves... as Western.

## Notes

1 Ah Beng is one of the major characters in the novel Banyaga. Upon arriving in the Philipppines and in his father's shop, they were met with disappointment instead of welcome.
2 Ah Beng's father had a concubine whom he visits regularly even after they arrived. His mother decided to report her to the authorities and this resulted to the concubine's deportation.
3 *Mano Po* is a mainstream Filipino movie about Chinese-Filipinos.
4 See Men of the East.
5 The Black Nazarene is the center of a popular devotion in the Philippines. Thousands of people flock to the church to participate in the procession of the image of Jesus the Nazarene.
6 A haunting female ghost wearing white.
7 Small stores in the Philippines selling assorted goods. Sari-sari = Assorted

*Ellen Palanca*

**Expert: Ellen Palanca**
**Interviewer: Dorcas Juliette Ramos-Caraig**
**Interview Date: January 27, 2016**

## Professional experience

RAMOS-CARAIG: How did you begin as a Chinese scholar?

PALANCA: I am an ethnic Chinese and I attended Chinese schools but after college, I did not dwell on my Chinese heritage. Perhaps it was because of the anti-Chinese sentiment at that time. During and after college, I never thought of studying about China. At that time, China was a closed country. The impressions of China we knew then was very negative—from the anti-Communist slogans we chanted in grade school as well as high school. There was little real news on China. Newspapers were mostly owned and managed by the KMT, and what were in the newspapers on China were very negative portrayals. Starting in 1972, here in the Philippines, was the Martial Law period. Hence, during all those years, all newspapers, including Chinese newspapers, were closed down. Hence, news materials in Chinese or about China were not readily available. I did not dwell on my Chinese identity, wanting to be integrated into the mainstream.

When did I start to study about China? In the eighties, there was a lot of news about China opening up. Foreign press such as Time and Asiaweek was full of this surprising announcement. I became very intrigued, wondering how it would happen.

One day, in 1984, a Chinese professor from Shanghai came to visit the Ateneo. He was in his sixties and was teaching at the University of Finance and Economics (SHUFE). Prof. Xie Shu Shen was quite western-oriented. Before the war, he was educated in St. John's College in Shanghai and went to Columbia University where he met Ambassador Alfonso Yuchengco. They continued to keep in touch. He was invited to visit the Philippines then by his friend Alfonso Yuchengco. Mr. Yuchengco arranged for him to visit universities. I met him when

210　*Ellen Palanca*

he visited the Ateneo de Manila University where, together with some school officials and faculty members, we had a meeting. After that meeting, the professor approached me and asked if I would like to teach a course on Western Economics at SHUFE. Well, that started my journey as a China watcher.

Because I was very intrigued about China opening up to the world, I didn't want to lose that opportunity to see first hand China's transformation to a market economy. I was already married then and had an 11-year-old son, but I didn't want to lose the opportunity. My husband was very understanding and supported my decision.

Hence I left for China in 1985. It was my first time to step on Chinese soil. At that time China was still very conservative. One could see many elements of the old society and planned economy. Many men still were Maosuit. Women wore only drab color clothes. Although it had been 5 years since it started to move toward a market economy, many still used coupons (instead of money) to buy things. Most universities hired foreign teachers to teach. They were mostly caucasians who were there to teach English. However with China opening up, SHUFE saw the importance of market economics. That year for the first time they invited foreigners to teach Western Economics. I taught Microeconomics, Macroeconmics, and International Economics. There were three of us teaching Western Economics. Our students were graduate students–all very bright and eager to learn. The other two economics professors were both from the North America—one from the U.S. and one from Canada. The three of us joined the other foreign teachers and were part of the university's Foreign Language Department. But we were in touch with Prof. Xie of its Economics Department.

RAMOS-CARAIG:  And after that, what happened?

PALANCA:  After one school year, I came back to the Philippines. I went back to teach at the Economics Department of Ateneo. And I was appointed to be the chair of the department in 1987. In that year, the University set up the Chinese Studies Program, which was a special program under the Office of the President. (It was much later before the program was integrated with the School of Arts and Sciences.) I was not involved there as I was full time with the Economics Department. However, I became more involved in the Philippine Association for Chinese Studies (PACS).

RAMOS-CARAIG:  Can you tell me a bit more about PACS under your leadership?

PALANCA:  I was the president for nine years, from 1993 to 2002. We held a few conferences and a few books came out from those conferences. A very interesting conference was a rare occasion when representatives of both China and Taiwan were present at the forum. The conference proceedings—China, Taiwan and the Ethnic Chinese in the Philippine Economy—came out in 1995. There is also the book on *China in the Pacific Century* published by PACS in 1997. The book consists of papers by the three well-known Filipino media people in Beijing—Chito Sta.

Romana, Jaime FlorCruz, Eric Baculinao. The papers were from talks given in forums organized by PACS. When the three Filipino journalists were able to travel after the EDSA revolution in 1986, PACS, with the help of World News, organized forums and conferences for them to speak. In 1996, two notable symposia were held – one at the Philippine Cultural High School at the Ateneo de Manila University.

From 1998 to 2000 the Philippine Institute for Development Studies (PIDS) and the Philippine APEC Study Center Network (PASCN) organized a research project on China's economic growth and the ASEAN. I was asked to be the director of a research project and I invited many China experts who were PACS members to join. It was the first group research project on China undertaken in the Philippines. Several conferences were held on the to disseminate the research outputs. I made sure PACS was made a sponsor, together with PIDS and PASCN. I am happy to have had the chance to work on this project and edited the book on it, which came out in 2001. The book, however, is a PIDS/PASCN publication, and not a PACS publication. My article there is entitled China's Trade with the ASEAN: Changing Patterns and Implications for the Philippines. Other scholars who were in the team were Aileen Baviera, Benito Lim, Raul Fabella, Rosalina Tan, and Joseph Lim.

When Joseph Estrada was president and he made a trip to China in 2000. We only had rough drafts of the book at that time. I heard that those were his inputs for that trip. Studies on China are sorely lacking in the Philippines. We don't have a good China policy because there is no solid research on China. Other Southeast Asian countries more effort on doing such research on China. I was told by a colleague in Malaysia that the University of Malaya established the Institute of China Studies because their Prime Minister wanted research on China to be done for policy-making.

RAMOS-CARAIG: You were also the director of the Chinese Studies Program at Ateneo. Can you share your experience on that?

PALANCA: In 1996, I was asked to head the Chinese Studies Program. I felt more the need to do research on China and Chinese Studies. I combined my two research interests—economics and China—and focused on the Chinese economy. Since then I have been doing research on Chinese economics. I also developed a course on Chinese Economy for undergraduate students. Another area I study is the growth of ethnic Chinese businesses here in the Philippines.

RAMOS-CARAIG: Can you tell us about the curriculum of the Chinese Studies Program at that time?

PALANCA: The Program was established with support from the alumni of Xiamen University. An exchange program between Ateneo de Manila University and Xiamen University was set up. The Chinese Studies Program was quite tentative and so was just placed under the Office of the Academic Vice President. Young ethnic Chinese faculty were sent to Xiamen University to study Putonghua, the Pinyin system and

212  *Ellen Palanca*

simplified characters used were not common yet among schools in the Philippines. Hence initially, the main thing the Ateneo Chinese Studies Program did was teaching the language, Mandarin or Putonghua as used by people in China. When I took over the directorship, the Program has become part of the University's mainstream academics. I felt that the Program was ready to be more integrated into the college and so I started to set up social sciences and humanities courses that have to do with China—courses such as Chinese literature, Chinese Philosophy, Chinese History, Chinese Economy, Chinese Politics, Traditional Chinese Medicine, etc. We cross-listed the courses with other disciplines and departments to ensure we have enrollees. Teachers were not difficult to develop for these courses. I sent faculty members to Xiamen University for TCM (a medical doctor who had some training in acupuncture), Chinese literature, Chinese history. For Chinese politics and China's foreign policies we had Prof. Benito Lim to teach these courses for many years. When I learned that he retired from UP, I invited him to teach those courses in our Program.

RAMOS-CARAIG:  You have been the director of the Confucius Institute here since it started a decade ago. Can you tell us about how the institute began?

PALANCA:  I heard about it and decided to apply to Hanban. (Hanban is the Chinese acronym for the Office of Chinese Language Council International. In 2004 it started to establish Confucius Institutes around the world for the promotion of Chinese language and culture.) It was 2006 when we applied. I was still the director of the Chinese Studies Program. Hanban officials came to our university to check and they saw that we were quite established in doing the Chinese Studies program. Although having done work in Chinese studies is not a requirement as there were a lot of universities that established Confucius Institutes that didn't have background in Chinese studies at all. They can start with no background at all and build it up. For example, countries in Africa or Middle East do not have many ethnic Chinese which means that Chinese language is not popular at all. It will be harder for them, but as the saying goes, "a journey of a thousand miles begins with a single step." Hanban is willing to support in different ways, not just through funding, but also by sending teachers.

RAMOS-CARAIG:  Were there a lot of students initially?

PALANCA:  Ateneo de Manila University already offers Chinese language classes (by the Chinese Studies Program) to its own students. Hence the classes offered by the Ateneo Confucius Institute have to find its own market. We cater these classes to people outside of the university. Mostly professionals. We also created extra-curricular classes for Ateneo High School students. Hence it's much more difficult for us to get students. We had to advertise in newspapers, print flyers, and in the case of Ateneo High School, approach school officials. In other words, we do

Interview Transcripts   213

not have a captive market. There were not many students initially. Ateneo was not known for being a Chinese language institution. Moreover, at that time, 10 years ago, Chinese was not deemed an essential language to learn. There were not many job offerings wherein knowing the language is an advantage. However, professionals tend to attach quality with the Ateneo brand, and so those who need to learn the language do come to us, rather than to private language institutes. It is more the ethnic Chinese that doubt the quality of Ateneo in teaching Chinese.

RAMOS-CARAIG: So what do you think has changed over the years?

PALANCA: People have become aware of China and now feel the need to understand it. With its phenomenal growth, China is a force one cannot ignore. I think, for individuals, the awareness arose because of the gradual increase in personal involvement with regard to China and the Chinese. One example is the job and business opportunities related to China that can get people interested in China and learning Chinese. Definitely there is more interest now. Now, there really is a demand for language classes. Our language classes have grown a lot since we started. We only offered basic levels (just levels 1 and 2) then. Now we offer Basic 1 to Basic 6, Intermediate 1 to Intermediate 6, Advance Chinese, and Special Topics language courses.

RAMOS-CARAIG: Apart from language, what other courses does the institute provide?

PALANCA: We have painting and Guzheng [Chinese zither], and also tai-chi classes. We also offer Special Topic courses taught in English. We have had several courses on Chinese history (ancient, modern, three kingdoms), Chinese literature, Chinese philosophy, etc.

## Reflections on research

RAMOS-CARAIG: How did your interest in economics shift to China studies?

PALANCA: My background is economics. I did not shift, I just combined economics and China studies. To be relevant to the Philippines my research studies Philippines-China economic relations. I look into Philippines-China trade, ASEAN-China trade, Chinese investments and ODAs in the Philippines, etc. I also do research on Chinese migration to the Philippines as well as the new migrants. Another area of my research is on the ethnic Chinese, in particular, the business of the taipans.

RAMOS-CARAIG: What can you say about the research funding available here in the Philippines? Do you think there is enough funding to do projects related to China?

PALANCA: Funding for research on China is very limited. I have been involved in three major projects on China. I think I mentioned the project China's Economic Growth and the ASEAN. I think it is the one and only project by the government think tank Philippine Institute

## 214 *Ellen Palanca*

for Development Studies (PIDS) about China. The project was undertaken with funding from PASCN. PIDS talks about doing another project on China. It seems that people do feel that there is a need to study about China, but they never get it prioritized. Another problem is that there are not many scholars interested in doing research on China. The second project on Chinese economy I was part of was a project a few of us faculty at the Ateneo Economics Department/Chinese Studies Program proposed to the Ateneo Institute of Philippine Culture in 2008. These were some of people who work on the PIDS project. The paper outputs from this project was published in The Rise of China: Three Essays on China's Economy and 'Soft' Power. Aside from my essay, the other essays were those of Joseph Anthony Lim and Benito Lim[1].

RAMOS-CARAIG: Do you also get research funding from organizations and agencies outside the Philippines?

PALANCA: Oh yes. Right now, I am involved in a project on Chinese Capitalism in Southeast Asia. This is the third major project on China that I have been involved in. The project is funded by the Thailand Research Fund. The participants are basically 10 scholars, each preparing two papers on a Southeast Asian country. I take care of working on Chinese capitalism in the Philippines.

Relations with China scholars, professionals, government and other connections

RAMOS-CARAIG: Have you ever been involved in policy and consultation with the public and private sectors?

PALANCA: Not directly but through the PIDS. Our research papers were turned into policy papers.

RAMOS-CARAIG: How about transnational research projects on China and Chinese Studies? Have you ever participated in such projects?

PALANCA: Yes. I have done several. I am also one of the authors in the book Southeast Asian's Chinese Businesses in An Era of Globalization: Coping with the Rise of China, which was edited by Leo Suryadinata and was funded by the Institute of Southeast Asian Studies in Singapore.

I have an article on Chinese Education in Malaysia and the Philippines: A Comparative Study in the Journal of Malaysian Chinese Studies. I am surprised that it has been very much read and quoted by researchers and scholars. This research was funded by SEASREP.

As the director of the Confucius Institute, I have been able to get the Institute to published a couple of books. We had published a coffee table book, Chinese Painting in the Philippines, and also the proceedings of an international conference on Chinese Language Teaching and Education in a Globalizing Southeast Asia (organized by the Ateneo Confucius Institute). Talking about coffee table book, my first one was on Chinese Filipinos which I did as the director of the Ateneo Chinese Studies Program. My son was the writer while I did general editing.

*Interview Transcripts* 215

## Self-perceived contribution to views and theories on China or Chinese studies

RAMOS-CARAIG: What do you perceive as your contributions to views and theories about China or to Chinese Studies?

PALANCA: Since the 90s, I've been advocating that we explore China for trade and investments. Such a view is based on my research on China's trade with the ASEAN countries, particularly with the Philippines. This view was also based on my many visits to China when I gotnto observe the many needs of the Chinese which we could fill. At that time, our investments and trade relations with China were very low compared to our Southeast Asian neighbors. I actually have been telling people— not just the ethnic Chinese here, but all businessmen here—to engage China economically.

From my research, I saw that there were industrial niches that we could fill. China offers a lot of opportunities for us in many areas. But we never really took advantage of them. For example, Malaysia and Thailand, produce basically the same agricultural products (fruits and seafood). We have a same kind of comparative advantage profile. But Malaysia and Thailand have been able to export processed food and foodstuffs to China these last couple of decades. We seem to stay at the level of exporting unprocessed fruits (bananas and mangoes) and raw minerals, and not look for export niches which have more value-added.

Now China has reached another development level. Wages are high and they are more focused in high-tech manufactures. Perhaps there are still opportunities for us.

I consider my research work recognized when after the China-ASEAN project, I was delegated by the Department of Trade and Industry to represent the Philippines in the Joint Research Team to study the feasibility of the proposed ASEAN-China Free Trade Area in 2001.

## Evaluation of future prospects of China Studies in the Philippines

RAMOS-CARAIG: So from your perspective, what do you think will be the future of Chinese Studies in the Philippines?

PALANCA: Well, it should be bright because more people are realizing the importance of studying about China. Moreover, there is now support from the Confucius Institutes and Hanban. Aside from teaching Mandarin, the Confucius Institute Headquarters launched the New Sinology Program, which will accept graduate scholars and young faculty to do research work there in China.

Also, there are plans for the Ateneo Confucius Institute to offer a master's degree in education, major in teaching Chinese as a foreign language. And because of these, I believe that there is much potential for Chinese studies to develop here in the Philippines.

216 *Ellen Palanca*

RAMOS-CARAIG: I've read your work comparing Chinese schools among Southeast Asian countries, specifically one that compares those in the Philippines with those in Malaysia.

PALANCA: Chinese schools here and in Malaysia are very different. In public schools in Malaysia, the government allows schools to teach using the students' mother tongue (Malay, or Chinese). But only up to grade school. There are however some Chinese who insist on their children having education using Chinese as a medium of instruction. There is a group of such Chinese to set up in Malaysia private schools that use Chinese as a medium of instruction. However, the Malaysian government does not give support and does not recognize the graduates from those schools. The graduates of these so-called "Independent schools" cannot go to universities in Malaysia. However, ironically, universities in other countries do recognize them and allow them to study in their universities. Hence many of the students from these Chinese schools go to the United States, Hong Kong, Taiwan, for their college education.

Another thing is that Malaysia has this affirmative action program. Because of the New Economic Policy, Malays were accorded majority of the slots in universities. So even if the Chinese wanted to enroll, it was difficult to get into Malaysian universities.

Things have improved quite a lot in the past decades. There is now a university, the Tunku Abdu Raman University, which is set up by the local Chinese there. The university offers a couple of courses on Chinese Studies which are taught in Chinese. There are two Confucius Institutes there now. There was resistance initially as the Confucius Institute name suggests an ideology which they feared might be in conflict with Islam. Indonesia also had the same problem, but now already has six Confucius Institutes. Meanwhile, Thailand has sixteen Confucius Institutes and eighteen Confucius Classrooms. Chulalongkorn University has a very extensive Chinese Studies Department.

In the 1950–1960s, there was no Chinese school in both Thailand and Indonesia, but there were China-related courses offered in universities. And they have Chinese staff and experts to teach these courses. Students majoring in Chinese studies can speak Chinese fluently even if they did not go to a Chinese school. In the Philippines, we did not have universities offering Chinese studies courses until recently. Ateneo now has China Studies majors, although the enrollment is not high. There is not much interest in studying China and the Chinese language among the students.

## Note

1 This endeavor was supported by a grant they received from the Merit Research Awards (MRA) Program of the Institute of Philippine Culture.

# *Jose Santiago "Chito" Santa Romana*

**Expert: Jose Santiago "Chito" Santa Romana (or Sta. Romana)**
**Interviewer: Lucio Pitlo III**
**Interview Date: April 14, 2016**

PITLO: China has gone through a lot before attaining its present status. The country suffered from many socioeconomic and political policies, as well as programs, which led to failures, like the Great Leap Forward and the Cultural Revolution. Do you think the Filipinos would have the strength to try different approaches and be willing to pay the price like the Chinese?

SANTA ROMANA: Yes. That is the problem in the Philippines. Look at 1986 EDSA Revolution. Its price was not that great, so there was really no meaningful and enduring transformation. Now the Marcos family is back in positions of political power. They are still around. In China, they could have been sent to jail or another set of leaders had taken over. Our price was Martial Law, but looking back, it was not. But that was our version of a price or sacrifice.

In a sense, the leadership transition in EDSA was less violent. Marcos was an authoritarian leader who grew corrupt and was overthrown. But US involvement mitigated a potentially violent outcome of the leadership change. If Americans had not intervened (i.e. rescued Marcos), the resolution to the crisis could have been more drastic and possibly bloody. When a crisis is peacefully resolved, people tend to disregard and cherish the outcomes. That is unfortunate.

I hope there won't be such a high price or sacrifice, but either way, we will have to go through it again. Just as a restoration took place after the French Revolution, so did the same happen in the Philippines after 1986. The oligarchs and political dynasties returned to power. It's a cycle. Direct experience teaches people but after a generation, the lessons sometimes get lost. In our experience, when we activist youths talked with our parents, they would always tell us that we never experienced, what it was like to live during the Japanese war period. Now, it's our turn as former young activists to tell our children and grandchildren

218 *Jose Santiago "Chito" Santa Romana*

that they never experienced what Martial Law was like. We basically sound like our parents. Anyway, people have to experience a crisis. Hopefully with wisdom. What is important is that we institutionalize change and deliver its gains. And this I think is the lesson of China and Communist Party rule. They were almost on the verge of collapse; what Deng did was to produce rapid economic growth, which became the new source of the Party's legitimacy; they delivered the goods again, so to speak. Now that is the problem confronting the Party – it has to sustain these gains and continue delivering.

PITLO: Would you say that your interest in Chinese Studies developed as a consequence of your experience in China? How did your experience help you in your media work covering China?

SANTA ROMANA: Yes. My experience in China contributed a lot to my work as a foreign journalist. What was particularly helpful was that I was able to work with a Western/international news organization while watching and observing China. Although I lived there, and my livelihood depended in a sense on my being in China, I was also an outsider. This gave me a more detached view. Even so, it helped that I was able to view the country from the inside, having lived and worked there, since I got to know people's sentiments and talked to them. For instance, do you know that during the Cultural Revolution, especially during its radical phase, you could already feel their frustration and hear their complaints over its excesses, especially against the Gang of Four's and Mao's harsh policies? In the same vein, when Deng was rehabilitated and began undertaking reforms, you could hear people talking that what he was doing was good for China. At the same time, mass media was heating up with articles against the Gang of Four. It's like being close to the railway tracks and you can hear the train coming. Anyway, because I had an insider's view of the country, I knew that there were forces which one could not read about in the media, ones that you had to read between the lines, so to speak, in order to detect. So my China experience really helped a lot in that respect.

PITLO: What did your China experience teach you in terms of understanding and forecasting goings-on in China?

SANTA ROMANA: It taught me to be a little skeptical. That you should never accept what's on the surface. You may know about it, but it is almost like the art of reading tea leaves. It is never easy. That is why China watching actually became part of my life. First is because I lived and worked there, and then I worked as a foreign journalist who had to explain what was going on in China to an international audience.

PITLO: So not everything is as it seems?

SANTA ROMANA: Yes. That was lesson 101. Bu qingchu (not clear) compared to bu zhidao (not knowing). It's like something is out there but it is not clear. Remember the Lin Biao incident I told you about? When they are going through an internal struggle, they will never admit it. But when they are done and ready, they will acknowledge it. It has to be resolved first. It is the same thing when you go through ancient or contemporary

*Interview Transcripts* 219

Chinese history. My China experience really helped me a lot in terms of trying to figure out China.

But even the Chinese people can be skeptical about their government. For instance, while I was studying Chinese language in school, Zhou Enlai made his famous speech in 1975 where he outlined "The Four Modernizations." I studied that speech together with my Chinese dorm mates; we discussed it while eating in the canteen. It was interesting that they were very skeptical about it. On the one hand, they wanted the goals to be achieved; they wanted China to be a modernized country. On the other hand, they were very skeptical about whether they could achieve this. Some of them did not believe it was achievable because of their experience during the Great Leap Forward and the Cultural Revolution. I think it is accomplishing and being able to pursue the reforms that convinced a lot that there is hope for better times.

PITLO: In Mao's time, China positioned itself as – and was seen by many as well – as a model for agrarian countries that wished to pursue socialism and to oppose revisionism and Western imperialism. But later, China would have a rapprochement with US. How was this explained to you by your Chinese hosts and what was your take on it?

SANTA ROMANA: China was a model for developing countries and for revolutionary movements worldwide. At that point, Mao was also trying to sound a call to oppose revisionism and to argue that he was a true Marxist; that China's track was the revolutionary way; and that the egalitarian model produced by the Cultural Revolution attested to this authenticity.

On the Sino-U.S. rapprochement, I remember we kept asking our hosts about it, about why China was doing this. They gave very interesting answers. It had something to do with their interest in international politics. Again, they quoted Mao. They were studying an article of his written during the Anti-Japanese War, "On Policy." I became familiar with it. Mao's method of analysis focuses on contradiction: what the principal contradiction was and who the principal enemy was. Before the Japanese invasion, the principal enemy was Chiang Kai Shek's Kuomintang. And when the Japanese came, they became the principal enemy. The Communist Party, therefore, sought to unite with the Kuomintang against the principal enemy. That was the whole point of the article. That same analogy was applied to the Sino-US rapprochement. China at that time faced two enemies and had to decide who the principal enemy was and then try to forge a tactical unity with the other. In essence, it was an application of the aphorism, "The enemy of your enemy is your friend." Anyway, it was very clear at that point that the Soviet Union was the principal threat to China and, therefore, U.S. President Nixon was welcomed.

PITLO: Was the rapprochement with the U.S. a recognition that there was something wrong with China's economic model at that time?

SANTA ROMANA: The rapprochement was tactical, and it had to do with China's view of international relations. As far as socialism was concerned,

## 220   *Jose Santiago "Chito" Santa Romana*

realization about its limits would come later, not during the time of Mao, but of Deng's. In Mao's time, there was semblance of such a realization since China was already importing Western technologies. But it did become more pronounced during the Deng period when the idea of a socialist market economy was adopted. Under Mao, it was a pure socialist-planned economy.

A good lesson in China Watching concerns the transition from Mao to Deng, particularly its position in relation to Mao's legacy and the fall of the Gang of Four. I do not know if you have ever heard of Hua Guofeng, who came into power after Mao died. The Gang of Four was arrested, tried, and punished. At that point, it was very interesting because the Chinese were celebrating; they were out in the streets and presenting Hua Guofeng as the new leader. But there was also lot of discussion on who possessed the correct path, the Gang of Four or the new group? For a long time, the propaganda was that the Cultural Revolution was good, but eventually the Chinese changed their position about it. At any rate, the Cultural Revolution became a basis for evaluating Mao. During that time, there was a lot of questioning. It was difficult to situate yourself. It took a while before you could make sense of what was going on because debates were happening, some of it openly in newspapers. That was where the Chinese method of debating disclosed itself. The distinction between the early Mao and the late Mao emerged as a basis for analysis and for assessing his contributions. Mao's early philosophical works on the importance of practice was used as the criterion to determine truth: how do you know who is right? The answer was practice, which became the sole criterion of truth.

PITLO:  Seek truth from facts?

SANTA ROMANA:  Yes. This approach came about during this time. Actually, it was Mao who originally used the expression "seek truth through facts," which Deng used to criticize the Cultural Revolution and its mistakes. This was the period of confusion when it was not clear who was right and wrong.

PITLO:  So bu qingchu?

SANTA ROMANA:  At that point, yes. But the point is that basically, by gauging the sentiments of the people, you could see who was popular. You see, what happened was that Mao offended the workers, as their salaries remained constant for a very long time. Thus, when it was raised even by a little, it was big news. It was not in the papers, but people were talking about it: that their pay increased under Deng. At one point, when Mao was still alive, that economic incentive was attacked. At that time, you could tell that, in a sense, there was a philosophical debate on who was right in terms of how to mobilize people. The problem with Mao is that he became a little more abstract and utopian. Mao really believed you could transform people through political incentives alone, while Deng emphasized economic incentives, though his

*Interview Transcripts* 221

is actually somewhere between the two positions. Even so, the contrast was so stark.

Under Mao, things were so extreme that peasants were neither allowed to own their own plot of land nor to grow their own crops. His vision was different. Mao thought that having private plots of land would engender capitalism. It affects food security if you cannot even cultivate subsistence crops for your family. You had to rely on the state, and for a while that was the conventional wisdom, until it was reversed and you no longer had to produce everything for the state and you could plant crops according to your needs. Even within Marxist-Leninist-Maoist theory, interpretation had always triggered big debates. Basically, you had Mao, who, while conducting the revolution against the Japanese and the Kuomintang, was pragmatic. He did not follow Lenin whose idea was revolution in the cities, and instead went to the countryside because that was where most Chinese lived and because China was, then at least, largely an agrarian country. This shows that Mao adjusts. But as he got older, he went back to the books and became more dogmatic. I guess he got stuck in his old age, unable to travel anymore to really see the situation on the ground. He became more detached.

For Deng Xiaoping, he had different ideas about the Great Leap Forward, whose implications he saw when he was sent to the countryside after his fall during the Cultural Revolution. He was working in a factory and lived in Jiangxi, together with other purged officials. So when they came back to power, you had a core group who shared the same ideas, which were a critique of Mao's economic policies and represented the desire to achieve economic development. That helped strengthen their political will to institute economic reforms.

PITLO: So China watching became a habit?

SANTA ROMANA: It became my life because all my adult years were spent understanding China, which has been a challenge.

PITLO: But nothing is as it seems?

SANTA ROMANA: Yes. You cannot judge from the surface. Instead, you have to view it in the context of their history. The Chinese people have a very strong culture heavily influenced by Confucianism. And there is a Marxist veneer, as well as Maoist and Dengist veneers too. You have to see the situation from there; and the bottom line is that you have to understand that human beings are influenced by all these cultural and historical forces. We are the same but yet we are different. We have our own culture and our own history. It is just that I do not expect it to be easy to understand China. I mean you could experience it yourself. If you live in China, there are certain things you have to get used to, which is not so easy. Basically, we have to find our own way of understanding and navigating in China, but also need to consider their experiences.

My point now is that I view myself more as someone trying to understand China better. I do not want to focus on whether we can use

222  *Jose Santiago "Chito" Santa Romana*

the Chinese model. No. In that sense, I could say that I have matured. Rather, I want to see what we could learn from China; there are lessons that can be looked into, but you cannot take them as a whole. But looking back in time, I would not call myself a Maoist. I was interested to learn. And I lived, learned and experienced China, particularly during the Cultural Revolution.

PITLO: Did you realize the inapplicability of China's experience and model for the Philippines? I mean it takes a certain type of culture and tenacity for sacrifices to make that happen.

SANTA ROMANA: Yes. But at that point, I was more interested in the how. I thought there were lessons that could be drawn from the way they fought the Japanese or the Kuomintang. But even that is different. They are a mainland or continental country, while we are an archipelago, so even the strategies will be different. Though general principles may be applicable. It is about how you apply and practice them, and you adjust as you go along based on the results. You really have to "cross the river by feeling the stones." And feeling the stones is always interesting.

PITLO: So to that extent, the Chinese leadership was really not that dogmatic and blindly accepting established Marxist tenets?

SANTA ROMANA: No, this was Deng. Mao was really loyal to the Marxist classics. As he grew older, the interpretation and vision he had was very purist. There was an aspect in his judgment, which maintained that the people's will would achieve huge things like the Great Leap Forward and Cultural Revolution. If one mobilized the people, then you could achieve such objectives. But of course, this is where you also become a little manipulative. You may have achieved desired results for certain goals, but you cannot sustain that zeal unless you have a material foundation.

SANTA ROMANA: Yes. He played that. He really showed that if used for certain goals, the human spirit can achieve even seemingly impossible goals, but sustaining it over a long period of time is the question.

PITLO: Would you say that from then until today, the foundations for analyzing China remain the same so much so that recent developments do not surprise you anymore?

SANTA ROMANA: No. I am still surprised at how the pendulum is swinging back. I understand it would swing, but this story or joke of President Xi Jinping as the second coming of Mao does seem to be the way he is going. It is really serious. And it is interesting to know the counter-reaction to that. How long can this go on? And where will it end? And then you go to the disputes – why can they not see that what they are doing is actually producing a different effect?

PITLO: You mean the backlash against what China is doing in the disputed waters?

SANTA ROMANA: Yes. It becomes more complicated because of President Xi Jinping's need to cater to nationalist sentiments internally, obtain the support of the military, consolidate his own power, and address the

*Interview Transcripts* 223

economic problems that China now faces, and how all these will affect China's behavior. In some respect, it is surprising because he seems to be turning out differently from Deng and some of the things that Deng did.

PITLO: You mean policy reversals?

SANTA ROMANA: Yes. It seems that some of the old approaches are coming back to life, but we are not there yet. An example is the move from collective leadership to a strongman or strongman politics. That is one change it seems. Xi seems to be rewriting the rules of Chinese politics by sidelining collective leadership along with the rest of the Standing Committee.

PITLO: You must have heard about the alleged letter going around calling for Xi's resignation. What is your take on it?

SANTA ROMANA: Yes. If you read that, you could see the counterargument, a critique of Xi Jinping's policies. So you could see the intense, ongoing factional struggles.

PITLO: But we can only see this because of the extent of the letter's getting leaked in public. Most of the dynamics of inner-Party struggle escapes public eye.

SANTA ROMANA: Yes. Most of it won't appear until they are ready. But while the struggle is happening, you will only hear a lot of stories. The problem now is how to sift for what is right and accurate because sometimes rumors dominate.

PITLO: That was very Chinese? So then or now are the same?

SANTA ROMANA: Yes. The same way that the Lin Biao affair was covered. There were many rumors or stories about what really happened; it was hard to know the truth. Up to now actually, questions have been raised as to why he did not succeed in assassinating Mao. Was it true that the daughter spilled the beans?

PITLO: But at that time, what really happened to the plane allegedly carrying Lin Biao?'

SANTA ROMANA: I think it was confirmed that the skull recovered from the remains of the plane were his. The question of most people at that time was why he had to flee to the Soviet Union. Because if he was able to flee there, it would have been really big news. But you could see he was desperate because the original plan was to go to Guangzhou. But where would he go there? There might have been some kind of civil war, but it was hard to imagine how he could win against Mao. So eventually, when his plan came to light, you could see his desperation. And of course that incident reveals that Lin Biao was not in favor of rapprochement with the U.S. He was not yet convinced that the Soviet Union was the main enemy. But he was already the number-two man behind Mao.

PITLO: So he was really very close to the top position.

SANTA ROMANA: Yes. But that has been Chinese politics. Hu Yaobang, Deng Xiaoping, and Zhao Ziyang were all partners and they really liked each other, and yet the two were not able to read Deng's mind – that Deng

## 224 *Jose Santiago "Chito" Santa Romana*

was only after economic freedom and not political liberties. For their part, they went all the way, but Deng stuck just to economic freedoms. Lin Biao and Mao were close, but I think there was an aspect of the two having different assessments of the situation then. And there may also have been a power play aspect. To a certain extent, Mao also used Lin Biao to be able to get back in power during the Cultural Revolution and then he saw Lin Biao's weakness. And Lin Biao too wanted power. He was supposed to succeed based on the Constitution, yet he would still not get the top post. So the only way to do so was for Mao to die, especially since Mao would have changed the constitution again. I mean this was the problem of not having an institutionalized set-up, so Deng tried to institutionalize leadership succession when he took the reins of power.

Now, with Xi, I think China is treading on some dangerous ground. It seems his leadership is becoming personalistic again. That is what makes it interesting. The drama continues and it's intriguing to see how long will the Communist Party survive. The Soviets fell and the Communist Party of China almost went to the brink of collapse. And I think it is critical that the Chinese leadership address the economic challenges. If they cannot deliver the economic goods, then they could commit the same mistake of the Soviet Union. China may engage in the arms race, which they cannot sustain, and could eventually lead to collapse. Or there are also internal challenges that may lead to the country's downfall. But it is still an open question and only time will tell.

PITLO: That is why you think the One Belt, One Road (OBOR) initiative will become existentially crucial for the Chinese leadership?

SANTA ROMANA: It is a key. But it remains uncertain if it can be a way out, which Xi is looking for. That is why one analysis posits that the main beneficiaries of OBOR will be state-owned enterprises, and exporters like companies engaged in railway, construction, and steel manufacture which are all suffering from domestic overcapacity. That is why it is important that the OBOR succeeds. But another explanation is that OBOR is the answer to how China can break away from encirclement (China's perception is that US, along with its allies, are encircling or containing China's rise). But there are many challenges along the way, and you can see that Xi is trying to cope with the situation. He is not ready for an outright confrontation with the US, but he has problems now: how to come up with a new development model. Deng's model no longer works (China's manufacturing-based export-led development model seemed to have served its time and the country had already developed industrial overcapacity resulting to limited growth, hence the country has to find a new development model). The economic boom is over but he needs it to sustain political legitimacy. So as far as he sees it, he needs to tighten social and political control, especially on civil society, but in doing so, he is swinging back. And whether he can continue this strategy remains to be seen. It is no longer the same China. There are now other forces at work. So the joy of China watching continues.

# Index

activism 31, 58, 63, 118, 121
activists 2, 41, 76, 86
actors 5, 110, 113–14
advocacies 5, 14, 58, 60, 63, 68
AFP *see* Armed Forces of the Philippines (AFP)
agents 25, 29–30, 36, 45, 86, 89
aliens 58, 82, 84–5; illegal 101; registration fee 12, 89
amnesty 101
Ang See, Teresita 131–8
anthropologists 29, 69–70, 114
anthropology 3, 21, 29, 61, 69
Aquino, Benigno 33
Aquino, Corazon 30
Aquino, Cory 1, 18, 30, 33–6, 68
archipelago 57, 81, 89, 100, 119
archives 63, 71
Armed Forces of the Philippines (AFP) 31–3
ASEAN *see* Association of Southeast Asian Nations (ASEAN)
Asian Center (UP) 88, 99
Association of Southeast Asian Nations (ASEAN), 16; scholars 17
authoritarianism 28, 46, 48, 119
authorities 7, 124
autonomy 46–7
auxiliary theory 25

Baculinao, Eric 139–44
Baviera, Aileen 145–52
bans 49, 82, 93
Beijing Consensus 26–7
Beijing intersection 18, 44
Beijing Olympics 43
biases 13
bicultural families 70
bombings 42
Bush, George 34

capital 76, 81
capitalism 20
career 23–4, 69, 91, 117, 119–21
Cariño, Theresa; interview 153–60
catapulted economic liberalism 27
Catholicism 69, 81
Catholics 69–70, 99
CEGP *see* College Editors Guild of the Philippines (CEGP)
censorship 40, 44, 55
CFR *see* Council of Foreign Relations (CFR)
children 59, 70–1, 75, 85, 89, 98
China; bureaucracy 49, 122; Catholic Church 69; MODEL 14, 27, 55, 119; watchers 7, 10–12, 23–25, 52, 107–11, 113, 115, 117, 119
Chinese; Civil War 113, 123; community 62–3, 65, 68, 124; culture 91, 100, 103, 112, 120; descent 84, 92–5, 97–8, 100, 102–3; diaspora 8, 12, 72–3; government; 41, 45, 84, 9; history; 53, 72, 120; mestizos 70–1, 82; nationalisms; 71, 82–4; nationals 85, 88, 93, 101; overseas 5, 72, 84; schools 85, 90, 100
Chinese Communist Party 39, 54; National Conference on Propaganda Work 55
Chinese Exclusion Act 73, 82–3, 124
Chinese Exclusion Law 57, 83
Chinese Filipinos/Chinese-Filipino matters 5, 13, 18, 58, 63, 68, 74, 76, 90, 100, 102, 108
Chineseness 2–3, 5, 13, 76, 107–13, 115–18
Chu, Richard; diasporic studies.59–60, 68–76; interview.161–8
citizens 45, 47–8, 51, 58, 66, 114
citizenship 65, 84, 89, 100, 110, 115; law 83, 195; rights 89, 100

## 226  *Index*

CNN 45, 47, 51
Cold War 34, 56, 91, 122
collaboration 9, 19, 102
collectivism 7, 25
College Editors Guild of the Philippines (CEGP) 31
colonials 73, 101, 115
colony 72, 81–2
commerce 59, 94
Communist(s) 59, 75, 92
Communist Party of China 13, 39–40, 43, 54
Communist Revolution 92
Communist Party of the Philippines (CPP), 23, 32
community 2, 4–5, 7, 9–10, 19–20, 22, 56–7, 63–8, 74–6, 87–9; imagined 71, 99; indigenous 108, 113, 124
conferences 10, 36, 61, 72–4, 88, 101
conflicts 25, 50, 92, 122
Confucianism 29, 112, 115
consumers 4, 16
corruption 19, 31, 85
Council of Foreign Relations (CFR).45–6
CPP *see* Communist Party of the Philippines (CPP)
curriculum 85, 117

Deng, Xiaoping 26–8, 69 *see also* opendoor policy
dictatorship 30–1, 34–6, 63
diplomacy 3, 18, 39; diplomatic relations 8, 18, 41, 58, 60–1, 91, 94
disputes 8, 45, 51–2, 54
dissertation 71–2

economic growth 19, 34
economics 4, 61, 82; economy 14, 17, 33, 43–4, 50, 64, 82, 99
EDSA *see* Epifanio Delos Santos Avenue (EDSA)
education 58–60, 85–6, 89–90, 95, 117, 121
Epifanio Delos Santos Avenue (EDSA) 30, 33, 92
ethnic Chinese 61–2, 67, 70, 75, 93, 95
ethnicity 6, 70, 86, 89, 98, 101, 124–5
evolution 4, 7, 14, 20, 23–5, 39, 46, 115–16
exchanges 17, 41, 47, 63, 117
exile 16, 41

family 11–12, 58–9, 70–1, 89, 91–2, 97

Federation of Filipino-Chinese Chambers of Commerce and Industry, Inc. (FFCCCII) 65–6
Filipinization of Chinese schools 85, 100
Filipinization Law 58
Filipino-ness *vs.* Chinese-ness; A Priori Codes 86–7; counter-narratives 96–102; cultural resources 90–3; forms of nationalism 83–6; networks and institutions; 87–9; power relations 89–90; public encounters 93–5; Spanish occupation, impact on 81–2
Filipinos 13–15, 67–8, 70–1, 82–4, 89, 93–5, 100–1, 103, 122–5; and Chinese 89, 117; citizen 61, 83, 101; mainstream society 68, 95
First Quarter Storm (FQS) 30–1
FlorCruz, Jaime 169–76
foreigners 43, 49, 60
foreign; media 44, 46–7, 49–54, 56; policy 8, 16, 36, 39, 45–6, 53–5, 119
FQS *see* First Quarter Storm (FQS)
freedom 41, 63

genealogy 71, 164
generation 4, 7, 18, 20, 60, 75, 84, 115; elder 67, 75; new 74–6; younger 63, 76, 93
Go, Bon Juan; interview 177–83; Tsinoy studies.58–68
Golden Shield project.48
government 18, 24, 32, 40–1, 45, 48, 81, 85, 90; agencies 18, 46, 52
grants 35, 87–8, 124
Great Leap Forward 40

Hau, Caroline; interview 185–92
heritage 90–1, 96–7, 102–3
high school 15, 60, 85
historian 3, 62, 69–70
historical institutionalism (HI) 29–30
history 7–8, 28–30, 62–3, 69–71, 74–5

identification 72, 74, 100
identity 8, 10–11, 60–1, 70–1, 76, 83–5, 87, 89–93, 97, 103, 113–15; collective 40, 112, 125; ethnic 10, 70
ideology 10, 14, 40, 55, 83, 117, 119
immigration 57, 75, 85; bill 84; patterns 168
incentives 81, 87–8
individualism 25, 29
individuals 20, 28–29, 111
in-group 110–12, 115–16
institutionalism 24, 29, 36

## Index    227

institutions 26, 28–30, 41, 86–7, 92, 99, 102
international relations 8, 29, 98, 117–18
International Society for the Study of Chinese Overseas (ISSCO) 72–3, 76

Japanese Occupation 57, 62
Jesuit 60, 69
Jesuit Volunteers of the Philippines (JVP) 68–9
journalism 8, 24, 34, 40, 45, 48, 51, 53
journalists 2, 10, 14–16, 18, 23, 41, 44–6, 48–9, 53, 120
JVP *see* Jesuit Volunteers of the Philippines (JVP)

*Kabataang Makabayan* (Nationalist Youth) 32
*Kaisa Para sa Kaunlaran* (Kaisa) 9–10, 63, 65, 67, 74–6, 96–7, 101, 103, 119, 121
kidnappings 94–5, 101
Kuomintang 13, 65, 92, 118

labor unrest 49–50
land reform 41, 49
laws 8, 29, 32, 60
leaders 9, 28, 39, 41, 43, 45–7, 49, 51, 53, 55, 66–7
leadership 26, 66, 103
Lee, Kuan Yew 27
local Chinese 14, 61–2, 65–8, 70, 85, 100

Mallare, Florencio; interview 193–200
Mao, Zedong 27–8, 36, 40–1, 43, 55; mass media during and post-era 42–5
market 7, 49, 56
martial law 30–3, 35, 42, 58, 65
Marxist ideology 40; veneer 29
Marxist–Leninist–Maoist teaching 32
mass media 39–40, 43–6, 48, 53–4; contemporary Chinese 45–8; during and post-era of Mao 42–5; production of narratives 49–53
media 2, 4, 8, 16, 39–40, 42–5, 47–9, 51, 53, 55–6, 64, 98
membership 7, 110, 112, 149, 159
mestizos 70–1, 73, 75, 83, 89, 94, 98
migrants 67, 75, 109, 112, 114
migration 2, 70, 85, 107–8
military 30–1, 33–5
minority 13, 103
modern China 8, 70, 107, 117
motivations 10–11, 120

nation 91, 96, 100–1, 123
National Commission for Culture and the Arts (NCCA) 88
national interests 45, 52, 61, 115, 122–3
nationalism 48, 52, 70–1, 74, 84, 123
National Summit on Peace and Order 58
National Taiwan University 20–2, 54
National Union of Students of the Philippines (NUSP) 23, 31
nation-states 71, 90–1
naturalization 58, 83–5
NBC news 47, 51
NCCA *see* National Commission for Culture and the Arts (NCCA)
neoliberalism 26, 29, 36
New People's Army (NPA) 32
newspapers 40, 68
non-governmental organizations (NGOs) 4, 41, 101
NPA *see* New People's Army (NPA)
NUSP *see* National Union of Students of the Philippines (NUSP)

Ong, Charlson 201–8
open door policy 43
Orientalism 107

PACS *see* Philippine Association for Chinese Studies (PACS)
Palanca, Ellen 209–16
*Partido ng Komunista ng Pilipinas* or Party of Philippine Communists (PKP) 32
PDRC *see* Philippines-China Development Resource Center (PDRC)
People's Republic of China (PRC) 56–7, 60–1, 85, 90, 94, 107–8, 114–15, 117
PET *see* Presidential Electoral Tribunal (PET)
Philippine(s) 8, 10–20, 29–32, 34–6, 57–86, 88–94, 97–105, 115–27; government 66, 84, 91, 95, 100; society 12–14, 28, 33, 58–9, 62, 67, 74–5, 101
Philippine Association for Chinese Studies (PACS), 6–7, 9–10, 18, 86, 101–2, 119, 121
Philippine-China Development Resource Center (PDRC) 10, 121
Philippines-China relations 4, 18, 46, 54; analytical approaches and perspectives 4–5; historical timeline 57–8; knowledge communities 7; mavericks communities 5–6; personal bonds 7–10; thinkers' inception 10–20
Philippine Cultural College 95–6
Philippine Revolution 57

228 *Index*

PKP *see Partido ng Komunista ng Pilipinas* or Party of Philippine Communists
police 49–50, 65
politics 14, 17, 108, 115, 119; political economy 8, 19, 27, 36
Polytechnic University of the Philippines (PUP) 41
population 52, 81–2, 86, 102, 109, 115, 117; indigenous 108, 112–14
post-Chineseness; altercasting 108–12; culture and ethnicity 123–5; in-group and out-group moves 117–23; theoretical propositions 112–16
poverty 16, 68
power 29, 31, 33, 40, 47–8, 51, 53, 55, 94, 124
PRC *see* People's Republic of China (PRC)
Presidential Electoral Tribunal (PET) 31
priests 60, 120–1
propositions 74, 115–18, 121, 167; auxiliary 115; plausible 115; Proposition II 116, 120; Proposition III 116, 123; third-order 116
PUP *see* Polytechnic University of the Philippines (PUP)

Qing Dynasty 69

race 82, 92, 110
racism 86, 94, 117
Reagan, Ronald 34
Red Flag 33, 43
Red Guards 28, 33–4
religion 8, 32, 68

Santa Romana studies; de-Marcosification 30–6; developmental exceptionalism 26–8; epistemic orientation 23–4; political history and culture 28–30; situated learning theory 24–5; social evolution paradigm 24–5
Santa Romana, Jose Santiago "Chito"; interview 217–24

schools 60, 75
SEASIA *see* Southeast Asian Studies in Asia (SEASIA)
security 4, 16
self-identities 70, 109–10, 112–13, 116
SEP *see* social evolution paradigm (SEP)
Singapore Model 27
Sison, Jose 32
situated learning theory 24–5
slogan 18, 44
social change 24, 29, 36, 82
social evolution paradigm (SEP) 24–5
social identity theory 112
socialization 25, 95
social sciences 25–6, 29, 61
sociology 21, 29, 61
soft power 39, 47–8, 55, 99
SONA *see* State of the Nation Address (SONA)
Southeast Asian Studies in Asia (SEASIA) 88
sovereignty 35, 50, 118
Spanish–American War 57
Spanish colonial period 70, 73, 94, 98
State of the Nation Address (SONA) 30
stereotypes 71, 102
students 31–3, 36, 41–2, 44, 60, 69, 73–4; leaders 23, 31, 41, 45

teachers 44, 60, 95
technology 59, 76; surveillance 48, 56
Tsinoy (Chinese-Filipino) studies; Chu, Richard's research 59–60, 68–76; Go Bon Juan's research 58–68; historical timeline 57–8
trust 7, 20, 51, 53, 117

US Embassy 35

victims 53, 66
Vietnam War 35, 41

War(s) 15, 54, 63, 88, 91, 93, 97
World War II (WWII) 75, 113, 123

Yong Hap (Integration) 14

Printed in the United States
By Bookmasters